SHARM E
Travel G

Exploring the Magic Beneath the Waves and the Spirit of Egypt's Desert with Helpful Tips and Itinerary Suggestions

Susan Gibson

Copyright © 2025 by (Susan Gibson)

All rights reserved. No part of this book may be reproduced, distributed, or transmitted in any form or by any means, including photocopying, recording, or other electronic or mechanical methods, without the prior written permission of the publisher, except in the case of brief quotations embodied in critical reviews and specific other noncommercial uses permitted by copyright law

TABLE OF CONTENTS

INTRODUCTION..6

CHAPTER 1:
WELCOME TO SHARM EL-SHEIKH......................8
  A Brief Journey Through Time............................9
  Why Sharm Isn't Just Another Red Sea Resort.......12
  Best Time to Visit..15
  Culture and Etiquette in Sharm..........................17
  Insider Tips for First-Time Visitors.......................21

CHAPTER 2:
PLANNING YOUR TRIP....................................26
  Visa and Entry Requirements............................27
  Currency and Budgeting for Sharm.....................31
  Getting There...36
  Getting Around...40
  Helpful Platforms to Book Your Trip....................46

CHAPTER 3:
ACCOMMODATION OPTIONS............................51
  Neighborhood Breakdown.................................52
  Top Resorts, Boutique Hotels,
  and Budget Options...57
  Staying by the Sea..62
  Desert Retreats..65
  Family-Friendly, Couples' Hideouts,
  and Solo Gems...68

CHAPTER 4:
MUST-SEE ATTRACTIONS................................73
  Ras Mohammed National Park...........................74
  The Old Market...78

    Al Sahaba Mosque..81
    Naama Bay..84
    SOHO Square..88
    Daybreak at Mount Sinai....................................92

CHAPTER 5:
FUN OUTDOOR ACTIVITIES..................................95
    Diving Deep..96
    Snorkeling Spots You Can Swim to From Shore....101
    Desert Safaris and Dune Bashing.......................105
    Camel Treks and Bedouin Sunset Dinners..........109
    Kitesurfing, Paddleboarding, and Jet Skiing.........113
    Stargazing Nights..118

CHAPTER 6:
FOOD AND DRINKS...122
    Must-Try Dishes..123
    Best Local Restaurants.....................................126
    Street Food Finds...129
    Luxurious Dining by the Sea.............................132
    Alcohol, Coffee, and Shisha Culture in Sharm......135
    Vegan, Halal, and Gluten-Free...........................139

CHAPTER 7:
CULTURAL EXPERIENCES..................................143
    Meet the Bedouins..144
    Art, Music, and Handicrafts...............................146
    Museums and Galleries....................................149
    Festivals and National Holidays in Sharm............152
    Unique Finds and Best Souvenirs......................156

CHAPTER 8:
DAY TRIPS AND HIDDEN GEMS..........................161
    The Colored Canyon...162

Dahab for the Day…………………………………….164
  Saint Catherine's Monastery……………………167
  Nabq Protected Area……………………………….170
  Quiet Beaches Locals Keep to Themselves………173
  Spice Shops, Local Farms, and
  Other Unexpected Stops…………………………177

CHAPTER 9:
NIGHTLIFE IN SHARM……………………...………..180
  Beach Clubs and Lounges…………………….181
  Live Music and Cultural Shows Under the Stars…184
  SOHO Square After Dark……………………….186
  Best Spots for Sunset Cocktails and Chill Vibes….189
  Night Markets, Hookah Cafes, and
  Open-Air Cinemas……………………..………..193

CHAPTER 10:
PRACTICAL INFO AND TAILORED ITINERARIES…196
  Health, Safety, and Emergency Contacts…………197
  Avoiding Common Tourist Scams…………………200
  Packing Essentials……………………….…………204
  Info for Seniors and Disabled Travelers……………208
  Sustainable Tourism Practices………………..……211
  Common Arabic Phrases You Need……………….214
  Useful Apps and Websites…………………………218
  3-Day and 5-Day Itinerary Options…………………220
  Tailored Itineraries by Travel Style……...…………223
CONCLUSION……………………………..………..228

INTRODUCTION

Before you unpack your bags, before the sun hits your skin or the salt stings your lips—pause. Stand still. Listen.

Because Sharm el-Sheikh doesn't welcome you with grand monuments or roaring boulevards. It begins in silence. Not empty silence—but the kind that's full of waiting. The kind that makes your heartbeat feel louder than usual. The kind that only happens where desert and sea have been watching each other for centuries.

Here, the land is ancient, but it doesn't flaunt its age. It whispers it through the wind brushing across jagged mountains, and in the rhythm of Bedouin drums heard from somewhere you can't quite find. Beneath your feet: sand that's seen prophets, pharaohs, and wanderers with no names. In front of you: the Red Sea, clear as liquid glass, holding secrets in technicolor—shipwrecks, coral cities, entire worlds you won't see until you dive in and surrender.

Sharm el-Sheikh is not a destination. It's a shift.
It rearranges your senses. Time moves differently here—days stretch out beneath a harsh sun, while evenings are gentle, warm, and perfumed with

cardamom and tobacco. You'll eat food cooked with memory, meet strangers who feel vaguely familiar, and learn that "doing nothing" often reveals everything.

You might arrive thinking this is a beach escape. But stay long enough, and you'll notice something deeper. This is a place where stillness pulses. Where the luxury isn't in marble floors or chilled towels, but in the untouched. The raw. The real. A place that asks nothing from you—except that you notice.

So don't rush. Let the place reveal itself slowly. Talk less. Taste more. Watch how the light changes the same rock face every hour. Swim until your thoughts go quiet. And if you're lucky, you'll leave Sharm not only with a souvenir—but with something you didn't realize you were missing.

Welcome to a place that doesn't just offer beauty.
It dares you to feel it.

CHAPTER 1:
WELCOME TO SHARM EL-SHEIKH

Sharm el-Sheikh isn't just a coastal city—it's a living paradox, where untamed desert cliffs lean toward tranquil coral bays, and where ancient silence coexists with the murmur of global travelers. This chapter sets the tone for everything to come. We begin by peeling back the surface to explore the deep roots of this land—how it evolved from an overlooked fishing village into one of the Middle East's most magnetic and misunderstood destinations.

We'll then step into the spirit of Sharm today—its rhythm, its edges, and what makes it so different from anywhere else along the Red Sea. You'll understand why it's more than a resort town. Why the air feels different. From weather patterns that sculpt the experience to the unspoken social norms that shape every interaction, this chapter is a guide to being here—not just arriving.

Lastly, you'll get grounded advice no one tells you at the airport—like how to navigate first-time culture shocks, how to connect without offending, and how to step lightly in a place that rewards sensitivity.

A Brief Journey Through Time

Before Sharm el-Sheikh became a place of five-star hotels and underwater weddings, it was little more than a silence between two extremes—where the Sinai Mountains dropped into the Red Sea, and nothing much moved except the wind and the occasional Bedouin caravan. There were no neon signs, no dive schools, no fusion restaurants. Just a small fishing settlement surrounded by water too wild to tame and a desert too vast to chart. But even then, Sharm held something—an invisible gravity that drew people in, even if only to pass through.

This stretch of coastline didn't make much noise in ancient texts, but it has always been a crossroads. The Sinai Peninsula itself—rugged, spiritual, defiant—has been walked by prophets and warriors. It is the land of Exodus, which serves as the backdrop for revelation. Mount Sinai rises just a few hours inland, casting a long shadow over the region's identity. Even if Sharm wasn't named directly, its land remembers. And so do the people. The Bedouins, whose families have lived in the desert for centuries without needing permanent walls, carry an oral history far older than anything carved in stone.

In the modern era, Sharm's name finally entered global consciousness not through tourism—but through conflict. The Suez Crisis of 1956, as well as the Arab-Israeli wars of 1967 and 1973, thrust this small outpost into the centre of worldwide power dynamics. Israel invaded Sharm el-Sheikh in 1967, recognising its strategic location at the mouth of the Gulf of Aqaba. For over a decade, the area was slowly modernized with military intent—roads, airstrips, ports—until Egypt regained sovereignty in 1982 through diplomatic negotiation rather than force. That peaceful handover gave Sharm its nickname: "The City of Peace."

But its rebirth wasn't just political. Something shifted in the collective imagination. Travelers began arriving not to conquer, but to exhale. The water here is so clear it feels sacred. The reefs, which are among the most biodiverse on Earth, have become a pilgrimage place for divers. Word spread fast: Sharm el-Sheikh was a paradise hiding in plain sight, offering spiritual stillness, luxury comfort, and raw adventure all in one breath.

By the early 2000s, tourism boomed. Direct flights arrived from Moscow, Rome, London. Multinational resorts rose along the coast like castles on sand. Nightclubs, marinas, luxury malls—it all came fast. But Sharm, at its core, didn't try to be something else. Unlike other resort towns that feel manufactured, Sharm always seemed to already be. The land shaped the city—not the other way around.

And beneath the surface of modernity, the old rhythms never left. Fishermen still cast nets at sunrise. Bedouin guides still read the stars more fluently than maps. And the mountains still turn crimson every evening, exactly as they did before anyone came here looking for a poolside cocktail.

To know Sharm el-Sheikh is to understand that its story didn't begin with the first tourist, nor will it end when the flights go quiet. It has always belonged to the land, the sea, and the silence between them.

Why Sharm Isn't Just Another Red Sea Resort

From a distance, Sharm el-Sheikh might seem like just another Red Sea getaway—sunny weather, beachfront hotels, snorkeling tours, and the usual parade of souvenirs. But the truth is, Sharm doesn't behave like a typical resort town. It's quieter in its confidence. More layered. Less about what it offers on paper, and more about what it stirs up inside you once you're here. Here's why Sharm stands apart—and always will.

1. It's Rooted in the Sacred, Not Just the Scenic

Unlike other beach towns built for leisure alone, Sharm lives in the spiritual shadow of Mount Sinai, a mountain that echoes across three Abrahamic faiths. You can feel it in the air. There's an unseen thread tying the coral reefs below to the stars above. This isn't just a vacation spot—it's sacred geography. And this affects how the land holds you.

2. The Sea Here Doesn't Entertain—It Transforms

The Red Sea in Sharm isn't just beautiful. It's surreal. Unlike other coastal regions where the sea is a backdrop, here it leads. The reefs at Ras Mohammed, Tiran Island, and even off simple hotel piers are world-class ecosystems, bursting with life in colors that don't seem possible above ground. You don't just swim—you surrender. And when you resurface, you often feel… altered.

3. It's International, But Not Imitative

Sharm speaks many languages—Arabic, Russian, English, Italian, Ukrainian. Its visitors come from every corner of the globe. But it doesn't bend to them. It holds its own shape. While many resort towns lose their local flavor trying to appeal to everyone, Sharm manages to absorb the world without losing its Egyptian heart. You'll still hear the call to prayer echoing across the bay at dusk. You'll still eat bread baked by hand. You are in Egypt, and you will not forget it.

4. The Desert Is Always Watching

Drive ten minutes out of town, and the mood changes. The sea disappears, and the desert steps in—wild, vast, and so quiet it hums. You can sleep under the stars in a Bedouin camp, ride a camel through canyons, or watch the sunrise cast shadows on a land that hasn't changed in centuries. Sharm isn't hemmed in by city blocks. It stretches. And that space invites stillness.

5. Peace Isn't a Marketing Slogan Here—It's History

Sharm's title as the "City of Peace" isn't a tourism tagline—it's a real-world recognition of the role it played in diplomacy between Egypt and Israel. This is a place that has known conflict and chosen peace. The result is a strangely powerful calm that you can't quite put your finger on, but you feel it—in the way people talk to each other, in the gentle patience of the locals, and in the unspoken agreement that life here moves a little slower, a little softer.

6. It's a Mirror—Not a Stage

Perhaps most surprisingly, Sharm doesn't try to impress you. It doesn't perform. It reflects. However you arrive—stressed, elated, curious, closed off—Sharm will hold up a mirror. The mountains, the reef, the silence... they show you who you are when no one's looking. That's the difference. You don't leave Sharm with just photos. You leave with something quieter, deeper, and—if you're paying attention—something lasting.

Sharm el-Sheikh defies expectations. It isn't simply a place to relax by the water—it's where sacred ground, living coral, and ancient silence converge. This isn't a stage built for tourists; it's a destination that quietly invites reflection, depth, and awe.

Best Time to Visit

Sharm el-Sheikh is a year-round destination in theory—but not all seasons are created equal here. The city never quite sleeps, but it definitely shifts. The wind changes. The sea breathes differently. And depending on when you arrive, you'll either be basking in perfection or blinking through heatwaves that test even the locals.

Let's be honest: the greatest time to visit Sharm el-Sheikh is from late October to early April. These are the golden months—when the sun warms without scalding, and the sea invites you in without hesitation. Daytime temperatures hover between 22°C and 28°C (72–82°F), perfect for diving, desert trekking, and simply being outside. Nights are cool enough to sleep without blasting the AC, and the wind carries a softness that's rare in the Sinai.

If you're dreaming of diving, November and March are your sweet spots. The water is still warm, visibility is exceptional, and the dive sites are far less crowded. You'll share Ras Mohammed's reefs with fish—not flocks of fins and GoPros. For land adventures, like hiking Mount Sinai or camping in the desert, December and January offer crisp mornings and evenings that invite fire circles and star-watching without the threat of heatstroke.

That said, May through September isn't off-limits—but you'll need to embrace the sun on its most intense terms. Daytime temperatures can climb past 38°C (100°F), and shaded areas become essential, not optional. Prices drop, and crowds thin, but unless you're staying strictly poolside or deep underwater, you'll need to pace yourself. Even locals avoid midday activities during peak summer. Still, for budget travelers or heat lovers, it's doable—with planning.

Avoid visiting during Eid holidays and New Year's Eve if you're not a fan of packed hotels and inflated prices. Sharm becomes a magnet for both local and international crowds during these times. If you're after solitude, choose the quiet windows—like the first two weeks of December or mid-February, when the weather is perfect but the beaches are blissfully half-empty.

While Sharm el-Sheikh is technically a year-round escape, it truly shines between late October and early April. This is when the weather is kind, the sea is calm, and every outdoor moment feels like a gift. Visit in winter to hike and explore, or in early spring and late fall for world-class diving and warm beach days without the burn. Choose your season, and Sharm will meet you there—but pick the right one, and it will feel like the city was waiting just for you.

Culture and Etiquette in Sharm

Sharm el-Sheikh is warm in more ways than one. Visitors often describe the locals as hospitable, easygoing, and gracious—but like anywhere with deep cultural roots, there are unspoken rules that shape the experience. Sharm is more relaxed than many parts of Egypt, thanks to its global visitor base, but understanding its cultural rhythm helps you blend in rather than stand out—and shows a level of respect that's always appreciated. Here are the key things to know:

1. Modesty Is Respected—Even by the Sea

While Sharm is liberal compared to cities like Cairo or Alexandria, it's still part of a Muslim-majority country. Swimwear is fine on the beach or at the pool, but covering up when you leave those spaces is expected. That means no walking through hotel lobbies or markets in bikinis or shirtless. Lightweight clothing that covers shoulders and knees is best for town visits, especially in Old Sharm or local mosques.

2. Greetings Matter More Than You Think

In Egypt, greetings are a form of social respect. A simple "Salam Alaikum" (peace be upon you) goes a long way—even if you don't speak Arabic. A smile and a respectful tone often mean more than perfect pronunciation. For men, a firm handshake is standard. For women, wait for the other person to initiate. In Bedouin settings especially, take your cues from your host before making physical contact.

3. Tipping Is the Norm—Not a Bonus

In Egypt, tipping — often called "baksheesh" — isn't just appreciated, it's woven into everyday life. It's not just a reward for great service—it's often expected. Tip porters, drivers, cleaners, and guides, even if just a few Egyptian pounds. It shows gratitude, supports low-wage workers, and prevents awkwardness. Don't worry—small amounts are fine. It's the gesture that counts.

4. Public Displays of Affection? Keep It Subtle

Holding hands is generally okay, but kissing or hugging in public (especially between couples) is frowned upon. Sharm is more tolerant than other areas, but it's still polite to keep romantic gestures private. What's normal back home can be seen as disrespectful here—especially in markets, local restaurants, or when surrounded by families.

5. Shoes Off Means Respect On

When entering a mosque or a private home, always remove your shoes. You may not find yourself in either often—but if you do, this simple gesture speaks volumes. In Bedouin tents, the same rule frequently applies. Look for signs or ask your host. If you're unsure—just follow what others do.

6. Photos: Ask Before You Click

Always ask before taking someone's photo, especially Bedouin people, women, or children. Some may decline politely, and that's okay. It's not just about privacy—it's about dignity. Even in local markets, snapping without permission can come off as invasive. When in doubt, smile and gesture first. Respect is universal.

7. Time Moves Differently—And That's Not a Flaw

Punctuality is flexible in Egypt. "Now" may mean five minutes… or thirty. Tours may start a bit late. Dinner might arrive slowly. Do not interpret that as rudeness; it is a cultural rhythm. Things unfold at their own pace here. Relax into it. The more you resist, the more frustrated you'll feel. The more you embrace it, the more local you'll become.

8. Religion Isn't for Debate

Islam is deeply woven into Egyptian life—even in a relaxed town like Sharm. Avoid making jokes or criticisms about religion, especially during Ramadan or prayer times. If you hear the call to prayer echoing across the bay, pause for a moment. You don't have to participate—but honoring the moment is a quiet sign of respect.

9. Hospitality Is Real—Accept It Graciously

Egyptians are famous for their hospitality. If someone offers you tea or a seat in their shop, it may just be kindness, not a sales tactic. You're never obliged to buy—but never rush hospitality either. Sit. Sip. Ask questions. Sometimes, the best travel memories begin with "Would you like some tea?"

Sharm may feel international, but its heart beats with Egyptian and Bedouin traditions. Visitors who understand its unwritten codes—modesty, patience, gratitude, and genuine curiosity—often leave with richer, warmer stories than those who rush through on autopilot. This isn't about restriction. It's about rhythm. Move with it, and Sharm will open up to you in ways no guidebook can promise.

Insider Tips for First-Time Visitors

Most travel guides will tell you where to go. This section tells you how to be there. Sharm el-Sheikh may welcome millions of tourists, but it rewards travelers who pay attention. The kind of person who notices how the mountains shift at sunset, or how a shopkeeper's smile softens when you greet him in Arabic. These aren't just tips—they're quiet keys. Unlock them, and Sharm reveals a version of itself most people never see.

1. Your Hotel Isn't the Main Character—Don't Get Stuck in It

Many visitors come to Sharm and never leave their resort. And why would they? There's food, music, a private beach, and a swim-up bar. But if that's all you see, you didn't visit Sharm—you visited a bubble. The soul of this place lives outside the gates. Take one afternoon to wander Old Market, sip mint tea in a Bedouin tent, or speak with someone who grew up here. That one detour might end up being the most human, beautiful part of your trip.

2. Don't Judge the Desert by Daylight—Wait for the Night

During the day, the desert looks like a silent furnace. Impressive, sure—but unforgiving. But at night, it becomes a cathedral. The stars appear in layers. The silence becomes music. Take a stargazing trip or stay overnight in a Bedouin camp. Bring no expectations. Let the land show you who it becomes when no one's looking.

3. Haggling Is Theater—Play It Kindly

In local markets, prices are rarely fixed. But haggling isn't a battle. It's a dance, a social ritual. Don't scowl. Don't storm off. Smile, laugh, enjoy it. Begin at half the offered price and move up from there. The shopkeepers aren't trying to rob you—they're just doing their part in a tradition. If you buy something after a friendly back-and-forth, everyone wins. Especially you.

4. Want the Best Seafood? Eat Where the Taxi Drivers Do

Forget the waterfront tourist traps with identical menus and inflated prices. If you want grilled snapper or fried calamari that tastes like home-cooked magic, ask a local cab driver where they eat. Most will point you to family-run places tucked away behind gas stations or dusty alleys. No Instagram filters—just pure flavor and fair prices.

5. Bring Cash—and Small Bills

Yes, cards are accepted in many places. But in taxis, local cafés, markets, and for tips? Cash is king. And not just any cash—small denominations matter. 5s, 10s, 20s in Egyptian pounds (EGP) will make tipping and quick transactions much easier. Change is often "not available," and rounding up can become frustrating if you're not prepared.

6. "InshAllah" Is a Real Answer—Learn to Hear What It Means

You'll hear this phrase a lot. It means "God willing," but in practical terms, it can mean yes, no, or maybe—depending on tone, smile, and eye contact. A cheerful "InshAllah!" often means "Yes, just be patient." A slow, vague one might mean "Don't count on it." You'll learn to read it. And when you do, you'll be one step closer to understanding the Egyptian rhythm of communication.

7. Dive Shops Are Not All Equal—Ask About the Crew, Not the Boats

Don't just pick a dive center based on flashy signs or TripAdvisor stars. Instead, ask about the dive masters. Who's leading the trips? How long have they worked here? The boat doesn't matter as much as the people guiding you underwater. The best instructors know the reefs like old friends—and can turn a normal dive into a spiritual experience.

8. Silence Is Not Emptiness—It's the Point

First-timers often feel uncomfortable with how quiet Sharm can get once you step off the main strip. No honking traffic. No blaring music. Don't rush to fill the silence. Sit in it. Walk with it. You'll find it speaks volumes once you stop expecting noise.

9. Fridays Feel Different—Here's Why

Friday is the sacred day in Islam, like Sunday in the Christian world. Expect late openings, quieter streets, and more people in mosques—especially at noon. It's not a bad day to plan a beach afternoon or dive trip, but be aware that certain shops and government offices may be closed. Use the rhythm, don't fight it.

10. Be Curious, Not Just Polite

Locals here are used to tourists who nod, smile, and disappear. But if you show real curiosity—ask a waiter about a dish's ingredients, or talk to your driver about where he's from—you'll unlock a different level of connection. Egyptians are storytellers by nature. If you listen, they'll tell you things that don't fit on maps.

11. Stay in an All-Inclusive Resort—But Use It Strategically

All-inclusive resorts in Sharm can feel like worlds of their own: buffets that never close, pools that never empty, and staff who remember your name by Day Two. If you're looking for comfort, value, and ease—this is the move. But here's the real trick: don't let the convenience cage you in. Use the resort as your launchpad, not your boundary. Book an independent dive trip. Talk to people who aren't paid to serve you. The all-inclusive bubble is safe and smooth, but the magic of Sharm lives just beyond the lobby doors.

The difference between visiting Sharm el-Sheikh and experiencing it lies in the small things most guides never mention. From choosing a dive shop based on people, not equipment, to understanding the quiet power of Friday afternoons—these insider tips help you see Sharm with wiser eyes. And yes, staying at an all-inclusive resort can offer comfort and ease—but the real magic begins when you step outside that comfort zone. Be curious. Be aware. Travel deeper. Sharm always has more to show you—but only if you know how to look.

CHAPTER 2:
PLANNING YOUR TRIP

Sharm el-Sheikh might feel like a world apart, but getting there—and getting it right—starts long before your feet touch the sand. This chapter is your compass. It's about preparing with intention, so that when you do arrive, you're not stumbling through confusion or frustration. Whether it's entry requirements, cash flow, or booking hacks, this section is where calm confidence begins.

We'll also cover the real costs—what you should expect to spend, what you can save on, and where it's worth splurging. And because we're not here to play it safe—we'll show you the best platforms and tricks to book flights, stays, and local experiences that feel personal, not pre-packaged.

The truth is, most people over-plan the wrong things and under-prepare for what actually matters. This chapter will help you reverse that. We'll handle the technical stuff with clarity and the soft stuff with experience—so you can arrive in Sharm ready, grounded, and already ahead of the crowd.

Visa and Entry Requirements

Before the beach towels hit the sand or your dive gear touches water, there's paperwork—small, but essential. Getting into Sharm el-Sheikh is generally simple, especially compared to other destinations in the region. But the simplicity can be deceptive. The rules vary depending on your nationality, how long you're staying, and where in Egypt you plan to go. This section breaks it all down clearly, so your arrival feels like a breeze, not a bureaucratic blur.

Short Visits to Sharm? You May Not Need a Visa

If you're flying directly into Sharm el-Sheikh International Airport and planning to stay in the South Sinai region only—including Sharm, Dahab, Nuweiba, and Taba—for 15 days or less, you can enter visa-free. At immigration, you'll receive a free entry stamp in your passport. This exemption covers most passport holders from the EU, the UK, the US, Canada, Australia, and several Gulf nations. No forms, no online applications, no lines at the visa desk—just walk through.

But beware: this visa-free stamp is only valid within the Sinai Peninsula. If you decide mid-trip to visit Cairo, Luxor, or any other part of Egypt, you'll need a full tourist visa—and you won't be able to get it in Sharm. You'd have to leave and re-enter with the right one.

Want to Explore Beyond Sinai or Stay Longer? Get a Tourist Visa

For stays longer than 15 days or if you plan to visit other parts of Egypt, you'll need a standard tourist visa, which gives you 30 days of access throughout the country. There are two main ways to get one:

1. Visa on Arrival (VOA)

- Available at Egyptian airports for citizens of over 70 countries, including the US, UK, EU nations, Canada, and Australia.
- Cost: $25 USD, cash only (have it ready when you land).
- Valid for 30 days, single entry.
- Pick it up from the visa kiosk before immigration control—do not proceed to passport control without it.

2. E-Visa

- Apply online via the official Egypt e-Visa Portal.
- Ideal if you prefer to skip the airport lines or want peace of mind.

- Apply at least 7 days before travel.
- Expect to pay roughly $25 USD for a single-entry visa, or about $60 USD if you plan to leave and re-enter.
- Once approved, print out your e-visa and tuck it securely alongside your passport — digital copies alone may not cut it at the border.

Passport Rules You Need to Know

- Make sure your passport won't expire within six months of your arrival — that's non-negotiable.
- At least one empty page is required for your entry stamp.
- For peace of mind, store a digital or paper copy somewhere safe, just in case your original goes missing.

Crossing from Israel? There's a Loophole

If you're entering Egypt by land from Israel via the Taba Border Crossing, you'll also be granted a free 14-day visa on arrival—but again, it's only valid within South Sinai. Going beyond Sinai still requires a full tourist visa, which you must arrange before arrival. Border crossings into Egypt can also take time, especially during peak travel days.

Don't Overstay—Here's Why

Egypt doesn't take visa overstays lightly. Even a few extra days can result in hefty fines, travel delays, or being flagged for future entries. If you think you may extend your stay, do it through the Mugamma (government office) in Cairo or consult your hotel about options before your visa expires.

For most travelers, entry into Sharm is surprisingly smooth—but small oversights can become major headaches. If you're sticking to South Sinai and staying under 15 days, you'll likely qualify for the free entry stamp. If your plans stretch beyond that, get a tourist visa in advance or at the airport. Know your limits, keep cash handy, and don't assume you can "figure it out later"—in Egypt, planning ahead pays off.

Currency and Budgeting for Sharm

Sharm el-Sheikh can be as budget-friendly or as luxurious as you want it to be. It's all about understanding where your money is going and how to make it work for you. Whether you're splurging on fine dining or simply soaking in the view with a falafel in hand, understanding local prices and currency will help you make the most of your experience. This section will give you the tools to plan your expenses wisely and save you from surprises on your bill.

Currency Basics: The Egyptian Pound (EGP)

The official currency in Egypt is the Egyptian Pound. The symbol for Egyptian Pounds is usually "LE" or "EGP" (you'll see both used interchangeably).

Exchange Rate: As of mid-2025, the exchange rate is roughly 1 USD = 48 EGP, but this can fluctuate, so it's always worth checking current rates before exchanging your money.

ATMs & Banks: ATMs are widely available in Sharm el-Sheikh, and most accept international cards. However, be aware of potential withdrawal fees from your home bank. You'll find ATMs at the airport, shopping centers, and hotel lobbies. Banks like HSBC and CIB are common and offer exchange services.

When you exchange cash at a currency exchange, it's often better to do so before arriving in Egypt for better rates, but rates are still reasonable at airports and hotel exchanges. Avoid exchanging cash with street vendors unless you're prepared for marked-up rates.

What Things Actually Cost (on average):

Local Meal (street food): Expect to spend around 30–50 EGP for a delicious falafel, shawarma, or koshari from a local vendor.

Mid-range Restaurant Meal: For a fresh seafood platter or local Egyptian dishes, expect to pay between 100–250 EGP per person in a mid-range restaurant.

Coffee (local café): A simple cup of coffee at a local café will cost you around 20–40 EGP, making it a great option to sip and watch the world go by.

Bottle of Water (500ml): Staying hydrated is key, and a small bottle of water will cost around 5–10 EGP.

Taxi (per ride within Sharm): A typical taxi ride around Sharm ranges between 50–150 EGP depending on the distance, though make sure to agree on a price before setting off.

Sharm Museum Entry: If you're keen on history, expect an entry fee of about 60–100 EGP to visit one of Sharm's smaller but interesting museums.

Beach Resort Day Pass: For a luxurious day by the pool or beach, expect to pay anywhere from 200–400 EGP for access to some of Sharm's best beach clubs or resorts.

Budgeting: What You'll Spend & How to Save

Sharm has a diverse selection of experiences, from luxury resorts to small street food booths. Here's how to break down your budget by experience:

1. Budget Travelers (Under 500 EGP/day)

- Focus on street food, local restaurants, and public transport.
- Stay in guesthouses or budget hotels (250–350 EGP per night for a decent room).
- Skip the fancy excursions and opt for simple experiences like visiting local markets, walking the beaches, or a day trip to nearby Nabq Bay.

2. Mid-Range Travelers (500–1,500 EGP/day)

- Stay in 3- or 4-star hotels (600–1,000 EGP per night).
- Experience a combination of street food and mid-range dining.
- Explore dive sites, go on a desert safari, or have a spa day (usually 200–500 EGP).
- Budget for taxis or use the Sharm shuttle service.

3. Luxury Travelers (1,500–3,000+ EGP/day)

- Stay at 5-star resorts or luxury all-inclusive hotels (1,000–2,500 EGP per night).
- Dine at upscale restaurants and enjoy seafood platters (300–500 EGP per person).
- Explore private diving tours, private boats, or exclusive day trips.
- Shop for high-end souvenirs and luxury goods at resorts or upscale malls.

Money-Saving Tips:

1. Book Local Tours in Advance: Some of the best tours (like Ras Mohammed National Park or Mount Sinai) can be cheaper when booked locally, either directly through your hotel or at one of Sharm's reputable travel agencies.

2. Water & Snacks: Stock up on water, snacks, and fruit from supermarkets instead of buying them at resort shops or convenience stores, where prices can be marked up.

3. Avoid Airport Exchanges: While it's tempting to change money right after arrival, the exchange rates at airports are usually poorer. Instead, wait until you're in town or use ATMs for better rates.

4. Public Transport: While taxis are convenient, using public minibus services can save a lot of money if you're comfortable with local transport. They're quick, frequent, and will get you around Sharm for a fraction of the price.

Sharm el-Sheikh can be a destination for every type of budget, from the backpacker to the luxury seeker. By understanding local currency, anticipating costs, and using a few simple tricks to save on dining and transport, you'll experience all the magic Sharm has to offer without breaking the bank.

Getting There

Your journey to Sharm el-Sheikh begins long before the first glimpse of the Red Sea. Understanding how to get there, how to navigate the airport, and how to get to your resort or hotel will ensure your arrival is smooth and stress-free. This section will guide you through flights, transfers, and all the essential details so you can begin your Sharm adventure the moment you step off the plane.

Flights to Sharm el-Sheikh

Sharm el-Sheikh International Airport (SSH) is the primary entry point for international visitors coming to the Sinai Peninsula. The airport is small but efficient, handling both domestic and international flights, mainly from Europe, the Middle East, and occasionally North America. It's a major hub for tourists heading to Sharm and nearby areas like Dahab and Nuweiba, with a steady flow of flights, particularly during peak season.

Where to Fly From:

From Europe: There are regular direct flights from major cities such as London, Moscow, Rome, Berlin, and Paris. Many flights are seasonal and tend to increase in frequency during the winter months

(October to April). These flights are typically charter flights, with carriers like easyJet, Ryanair, and Wizz Air offering budget options.

From the Middle East: Frequent flights come in from cities like Dubai, Abu Dhabi, and Doha, catering to travelers from the Gulf region. These routes are typically short-haul flights that offer excellent access to the region.

From North America: While direct flights are rare, you can easily connect via Cairo or Dubai, with a layover at a major airport before arriving in Sharm.

Booking Tips:

1. Airfares to Sharm el-Sheikh can fluctuate depending on the time of year. Book at least 2-3 months in advance to get the best deals, especially during peak seasons such as Christmas, New Year's, and Eid.
2. Flights from Europe typically range from 4 to 6 hours. From the Middle East, expect a shorter flight time—around 1.5 to 3 hours.

Getting from the Airport to Your Hotel

Upon arrival at Sharm el-Sheikh International Airport, you'll find getting to your accommodation to be relatively straightforward. The airport is conveniently located near major tourist areas like Naama Bay and SOHO Square, so your transfer will be quick and easy.

1. Pre-arranged Hotel Transfers

Many hotels and resorts offer airport transfer services that can be booked in advance. This is often the easiest way to ensure a smooth and stress-free arrival. Whether you're coming in at midnight or midday, having a driver waiting for you at the airport means you can skip the taxi lines.

Tip: When booking your accommodation, inquire about transfer options. Some hotels offer private transfers, while others provide shared shuttle services. Prices will vary according to the type of transfer and the distance to your hotel.

2. Taxis & Ride-Hailing Services

Taxis are readily available at the airport. Look for the official taxi stand just outside the arrivals hall. Fares from the airport to popular areas like Naama Bay or Sharm Old Market typically range from 100–150 EGP, depending on your destination and traffic.

Sharm el-Sheikh also has ride-hailing apps like Careem and Uber. While not as widely used as taxis, these apps offer a more predictable fare and allow you to avoid negotiating prices. Rates are often slightly cheaper than standard taxis.

Tip: Always agree on the fare upfront if you take a taxi, especially for trips outside the main tourist zones.

3. Airport Shuttles

Shuttle buses can be a more economical option for those traveling solo or in groups. These are shared transport services that drop passengers off at multiple locations within Sharm. Fares are usually about 50 EGP per person for a one-way trip.

While this is a more affordable option, it's less convenient if you're on a tight schedule, as it involves longer wait times and multiple stops.

Getting to Sharm el-Sheikh is a straightforward process from any major destination. The airport is well-connected, and multiple transport options are available to take you from the runway to your hotel. You can choose a pre-arranged hotel transfer for convenience, a taxi for a direct route, or a shuttle for a more budget-friendly option. Your journey to this Red Sea paradise will be easy and efficient, allowing you to start your adventure without hassle.

Getting Around

Once you're settled in Sharm el-Sheikh, you'll quickly find that getting around is easier than it might seem—if you know the right options to use. The city is compact, and most popular destinations are just a short ride away. Whether you're hopping between beaches, heading to a restaurant, or exploring a nearby market, Sharm offers a variety of transportation options that can suit any budget or preference. Here's how to get from Point A to Point B without any hassles:

1. Taxis: The Most Convenient (But Not Always the Cheapest)

Taxis in Sharm el-Sheikh are readily available and are often the most convenient way to get around. They're particularly useful if you're in a rush or need to get from one end of town to the other without the hassle of waiting. However, there are a few things you need to know to ensure you're not overcharged.

Haggle for a Fair Fare: Most taxis don't use meters, so you'll need to agree on a price before you get in. For short trips within popular tourist areas like Naama Bay or Sharm Old Market, expect to pay between 50–100 EGP. Longer trips, like to Ras

Mohammed National Park or remote beaches, can cost upwards of 150–200 EGP.

Taxi Stands vs. Hailing on the Street: You'll find taxis waiting at designated stands at popular spots like hotels, resorts, and shopping areas. Hailing one on the street is also possible, but it's often more expensive—especially if the driver thinks you're a tourist unfamiliar with local rates.

Tip: Always confirm the price before entering the taxi and try to have small bills handy for both the fare and any tips.

2. Ride-Hailing Apps: Convenient and Transparent

For a more modern and predictable experience, consider using ride-hailing apps like Uber or Careem, which are available in Sharm el-Sheikh. These apps can provide a clear, upfront fare, eliminating the need for negotiations.

Prices: Ride-hailing services tend to be slightly cheaper than traditional taxis for shorter rides, and you can often see the fare estimate before you book.

App Availability: While Uber and Careem are available, coverage can vary, especially in more remote areas. You may have to wait a few minutes for a ride to be assigned, but the pickup location is clearly communicated, and you'll know exactly where to meet your driver.

Tip: If you're headed to a popular tourist spot, like SOHO Square or Naama Bay, ride-hailing apps are often your best bet. But if you plan on going to the desert or a more offbeat destination, taxis may be easier to find.

3. Minibuses: The Budget-Friendly Option

Minibuses are the local transportation choice for many residents, and they can be an affordable, if somewhat chaotic, way to get around Sharm. These are shared vehicles that run specific routes and are typically packed with locals heading to their destinations. You'll often see them running between Naama Bay and the Old Market, or to nearby hotels and beaches.

Cost: The fare is usually around 5–10 EGP per person for short trips. It's extremely budget-friendly, but expect crowded conditions, no air conditioning, and no set schedules.

How to Use Them: You can catch a minibus from the main roads or from bus stops around the city. Most drivers will yell out the names of their destinations, so listen carefully and hop in when you hear yours.

Tip: While minibuses are an excellent option for budget travelers looking to stretch their money, they can be uncomfortable and crowded. If you're not in a rush, they're a fun way to experience local life and travel cheaply.

4. Car Rentals: For the Adventurous Explorer

If you're planning on exploring more of the Sinai Peninsula beyond Sharm el-Sheikh, renting a car might be a good idea. It gives you the flexibility to go off the beaten path and visit places like Dahab, St. Catherine's Monastery, or the Colored Canyon at your own pace.

Rental Costs: Expect to pay between 300–600 EGP per day for a small car, depending on the season and rental company. Prices may go higher for larger vehicles or luxury rentals.

Local Driving Tips: While driving in Sharm is relatively safe, the roads outside the city can be more challenging to navigate. Signage may not be as clear in remote areas, and driving styles can be aggressive, so always drive with caution.

Tip: If you're not familiar with local road rules, consider hiring a local driver for day trips or excursions. This way, you can relax and enjoy the ride without the stress of navigating unfamiliar roads.

5. Walking & Bicycles: Simple, But Effective

If you're staying in areas like Naama Bay or SOHO Square, walking is often the easiest and most pleasant way to get around. These areas are pedestrian-friendly, with scenic strolls along the beach, bustling shops, and plenty of open spaces to wander.

Cycling: For those who enjoy being a bit more active, renting a bicycle is a great option. Many hotels offer bike rentals, or you can find local shops with rates of around 50–100 EGP per day. Cycling around Sharm gives you the chance to explore at your own pace without relying on public transport.

Tip: If you're just exploring within the tourist zones, walking or cycling is often the best way to go. It's free, it's healthy, and you'll see much more of the local color and charm.

Getting around Sharm el-Sheikh is about choice. You can opt for the convenience and reliability of taxis, the simplicity of ride-hailing apps, the affordability

of minibuses, or the freedom of renting a car. If you're looking for a more relaxed pace, walking or cycling can offer a unique way to explore. Knowing your options will help you navigate the city at your own speed and budget, ensuring you make the most of your time in this beautiful coastal town.

Helpful Platforms to Book Your Trip

Booking a trip to Sharm el-Sheikh isn't just about choosing flights and hotels. It's about using the right tools to make smarter decisions, avoid overpriced tourist traps, and access experiences that feel personal—not mass-produced. With so many platforms promising the best deals, this section cuts through the noise to share what actually works.

Flights: Where to Start and When to Book

If you're flying into Sharm el-Sheikh, you're likely booking either a direct international flight or a connecting one through Cairo. Timing and platform choice can affect your entire budget.

Skyscanner – A top pick for finding flexible dates and comparing hundreds of airlines at once. Use the "Whole Month" feature to spot cheap fares across several days.

Google Flights – Best for visual tracking and smart filters. It shows fare trends and tells you when prices are expected to rise.

Momondo – Often digs up lesser-known routes and charter flight options, especially from Europe.

Tip: Book flights at least 6–8 weeks in advance during peak seasons (Dec–Feb, and Easter holidays). Prices rise sharply the closer you get.

Accommodation: Find More Than Just a Bed

Sharm's hotels range from ultra-luxury to inexpensive guesthouses. But the platform you choose can affect more than the price—it affects the vibe.

Booking.com – Great for both big-name resorts and small local stays. Reviews are generally reliable and cancellation policies flexible.

Airbnb – If you're staying longer than a week or traveling as a group, an apartment or villa may be more cost-effective. Some options include private beach access or local hosts.

Agoda – Often features exclusive deals in Egypt, particularly for Asian or Middle Eastern travelers.

Tip: Avoid just booking the "cheapest option." Check location carefully—some budget places are far from central Sharm, requiring extra transport.

Tours and Activities: Book Smart, Not Generic

You can find countless day trips, desert safaris, and diving excursions in Sharm—but quality varies wildly. Booking through trusted platforms helps avoid disappointment.

GetYourGuide – Offers vetted tours with user ratings. Ideal for structured excursions like Mount Sinai climbs, snorkeling trips, and Bedouin dinners.

Viator – Curates both standard tours and private experiences. Excellent for travelers who want more control or personalization.

Local Tour Desks – Once you arrive, compare prices and ask questions at physical tour desks in Naama Bay or Old Market. You'll often find better deals by going direct—just make sure the operator is licensed.

Tip: Never book excursions from random beach sellers. Some are legit, but many offer poor service or unsafe equipment.

Transportation and Transfers

SharmTaxiService.com – A local gem that most tourists overlook. This app is built specifically for getting around Sharm, offering 24/7 service with upfront booking, airport pickups, and a choice of vehicle types—from simple rides to private vans. It's not flashy, but it works—and when you land at midnight or need a quiet ride out to the desert edge, it's the kind of tool you'll be glad you downloaded.

Careem – Available in Sharm as a ride-hailing app. It's reliable for local trips but also offers scheduled rides, which is helpful for early-morning airport returns.

Tip: If your hotel offers a free or low-cost airport transfer, always take it. Taxis at the airport can be overpriced unless negotiated ahead of time.

Travel Insurance & Trip Protection

While Egypt is generally safe for travelers, insurance is a must—especially for diving, hiking, or camel safaris.

SafetyWing – Affordable and tailored for short-term international travel. Covers health, accidents, and trip delays.

World Nomads – Ideal for adventure travelers who plan to dive, hike, or do water sports. Coverage includes gear loss and emergency evacuation.

Book the essentials—flights, accommodation, one or two tours—and leave the rest open. Sharm is a place that rewards spontaneity. The best moments often come from local discoveries: a café you didn't plan for, a beach that isn't on any map, a conversation that shifts your entire mood. Use platforms to prepare, but let the experience surprise you.

Smart planning isn't about over-scheduling—it's about using the right platforms to set a solid foundation. From booking your flight and resort to choosing safe tours and trusted transfer services, the tools listed here take the guesswork out of trip planning. Once you've got the essentials covered, Sharm will take care of the rest.

CHAPTER 3: ACCOMMODATION OPTIONS

In Sharm el-Sheikh, where you stay isn't just about beds and breakfasts—it shapes how you experience the city. A beachfront suite in Naama Bay comes with a pulse, a rhythm of music and movement. A cliffside villa near Hadaba wraps you in silence and starlight. This chapter is here to help you choose more than a room—it helps you choose your mood, your pace, your version of Sharm.

Accommodation in Sharm isn't limited to luxury resorts—though there are plenty of those. You'll find boutique hotels with rooftop views, family-run guesthouses where the owner brings tea to your door, and remote retreats in the desert that feel like a dream you forgot you had. There's no one-size-fits-all here. The key is matching you with where you'll feel most at ease.

This chapter walks you through the city's neighborhoods, types of stays, and what each offers depending on your travel style—be it family bonding, solo recharging, romantic escape, or group adventure. The goal isn't just to help you find a place to sleep. It's to help you wake up in a place that feels right.

Neighborhood Breakdown

Sharm el-Sheikh isn't one city. It's a collection of contrasting moods stitched together by the sea and the desert. The neighborhood you choose will shape your days, your nights, and the kind of stories you go home with. You might wake up to coral-blue silence or to the beat of café life just outside your window. Here's a guide to the most distinctive areas in Sharm—and how each one sings a different note.

Naama Bay – The Beating Heart

If Sharm has a downtown, this is it. Naama Bay is bright, walkable, and constantly bustling. Restaurants spill out onto the sidewalks, shops glow late into the night, and beach clubs pulse with life. This is where the energy lives—ideal for first-timers, nightlife lovers, and travelers who want everything within reach. You'll find a mix of international hotels, mid-range resorts, and casual beachfront stays.

- What it offers: Central location, walkable seafront promenade, easy beach access, nightlife, shops.
- Vibe: Social, energetic, full of movement.
- Best for: First-time visitors, groups of friends, solo travelers wanting company.

Hadaba – The Laidback Local's Choice

Perched above the coast with wide views and quiet corners, Hadaba is where you go when you want to slow things down. It has fewer crowds, more space, and a strong local presence. Think rooftop cafés, hidden bakeries, and calm residential vibes. It's home to the beautiful Ras Um Sid reef—one of the best snorkeling spots in Sharm—plus several good-value hotels and boutique stays that don't scream for attention.

- What it offers: Authenticity, quiet beaches, coral-rich snorkeling, affordable accommodation.
- Vibe: Calm, residential, lived-in.
- Best for: Couples, long-stay travelers, photographers, divers.

SOHO Square – Polished, Modern, and Family-Friendly

A manicured slice of Sharm that feels almost surreal. SOHO Square is known for its neon-lit fountains, upscale restaurants, and family attractions like an ice skating rink and bowling alley. It's not where culture hides—but it's convenient, clean, and structured. Luxury hotels nearby often cater to international guests who want comfort without surprises.

- What it offers: High-end dining, modern shops, entertainment for kids, close proximity to the airport.
- Vibe: Polished, curated, international.
- Best for: Families, travelers with young kids, couples who prefer structure over spontaneity.

Shark's Bay – Quiet Luxury with a View

Tucked between Naama Bay and the airport, Shark's Bay is more discreet. The beaches here are often private, the water is calm and clear, and the coral is alive just meters from the shore. This area leans toward quiet, upper-tier resorts and villas—the kind of place where honeymooners sip cocktails at sunset, or digital nomads wake up to the sound of nothing but waves.

- What it offers: Clear waters, exclusive resorts, privacy, strong coral reefs.
- Vibe: Quiet luxury, understated.
- Best for: Honeymooners, couples, travelers craving peace and sea views.

Nabq Bay – Expansive, Breezy, and Growing Fast

Further up the coast, Nabq Bay is a newer, more spacious part of Sharm. Here, wide streets lead to massive resort complexes, and the desert feels closer than ever. It's less walkable but great for families and travelers who don't plan to leave the resort much. The natural beauty is strong here too—Nabq Protected Area offers rare mangrove forests and a rugged, untouched coastline.

- What it offers: Wide beaches, newer resorts, protected nature areas, more space.
- Vibe: Open, breezy, still developing.
- Best for: Families, nature lovers, travelers seeking space and calm.

Old Market (Sharm al-Maya) – The Soul Beneath the Surface

This is where Sharm remembers its roots. Sharm Old Market, also known as Sharm al-Maya, is full of character: winding alleys, scent-laced spice shops, the Al Sahaba Mosque, and basic cafés that cater to residents and the few tourists who dare to venture beyond the shore. It's not fancy—but it's real. Accommodations here are simpler and cheaper, and the atmosphere is grounded, honest, and intimate.

- What it offers: Local culture, great prices, traditional dining, walking access to the marina.
- Vibe: Gritty, flavorful, authentic.

- Best for: Curious travelers, market lovers, budget-conscious adventurers.

Each neighborhood in Sharm tells a different story. Naama Bay dances, Hadaba breathes, Shark's Bay whispers, and the Old Market remembers. Choosing where to stay isn't just a logistical decision—it's an emotional one. Let your priorities guide you: Do you want peace? Proximity? Culture? Comfort? In Sharm, there's a place that matches your rhythm. You just have to listen for it.

Top Resorts, Boutique Hotels, and Budget Options

Sharm el-Sheikh isn't short on places to stay—but the real question isn't just where to sleep, it's what kind of stay fits your rhythm. Whether you're drawn to luxury, charm, or value, this section breaks down some of the best resort, boutique, and budget options to help you land somewhere that feels right, not just available.

Here's a curated mix—not sponsored, not paid—just genuinely worthwhile places that have earned their reputation.

Top Resorts – All the Comfort, None of the Compromise

These are the crowd-pleasers with polish. Think panoramic pools, beach access, fine dining, and seamless service. They're for travelers who want to unwind completely, without worrying about logistics or surprises.

1. Meraki Resort Sharm (Adults Only 16+)

Location: Hadaba
One of Sharm's top-rated adults-only escapes. Sleek design, a private beach, lively pools, and superb

dining make it a go-to for couples or solo travelers seeking both peace and polish.

Bonus: Known for top-tier cleanliness, aesthetic flair, and staff who genuinely care.

2. Four Seasons Resort Sharm el-Sheikh

Location: Between Shark's Bay and SOHO Square
Understated luxury, exceptional privacy, and serious attention to detail. Service here is personal, not performative.

Bonus: Sunset dinners on a cliffside terrace with one of the best views in Sinai.

3. Royal Savoy Sharm El Sheikh

Location: SOHO Square
Elegant and adults-focused, this luxury property pairs quiet sophistication with a central location. Known for spotless private pools, personal touches, and a smooth guest experience from check-in to farewell.

Bonus: Perfect for travelers who want access to nightlife without sacrificing serenity.

Boutique Hotels – Small, Character-Filled, and Personal

If you prefer atmosphere over scale, these smaller properties offer charm, warmth, and a deeper connection to place. You'll find friendly staff, creative design, and a slower pace that lets you breathe.

1. Dive Inn Resort

Location: Hadaba
Quiet, cozy, and away from the tourist buzz. Known for good service, a leafy courtyard, and dive-shop partnerships.

Bonus: Great value for divers or long-stay travelers who want peace and depth.

2. Oonas Dive Club Hotel

Location: Naama Bay (but tucked away)
Feels like an old friend's beach house—with easy sea access and a relaxed, informal vibe.

Bonus: Walk down barefoot for a morning snorkel, then grab a cold drink on your balcony.

4. Aida 2 Hotel Naama Bay

Location: Near Naama Bay's quieter side
Family-run, friendly, and super accessible. Not flashy, but solid, especially if you're not planning to stay indoors much.

Bonus: Surprisingly good food for a small hotel—and a rooftop with heart.

Budget Options – Smart Stays Without the Frills

If you'd rather save money for diving, dining, or day trips, Sharm has plenty of affordable, functional, and traveler-friendly stays that don't sacrifice safety or cleanliness.

1. Amar Sina Egyptian Village

Location: Hadaba
Budget-friendly with a unique, pharaonic-themed design. It's quirky, but sincere.

Bonus: A small on-site dive center and a community vibe.

2. Sharm Dreams Vacation Club

Location: Naama Bay

Apartment-style setups are great for longer stays or group travelers. Clean, simple, and centrally located.

Bonus: Kitchenettes give you a break from dining out.

3. Desert View Hotel

Location: Edge of Nabq
Basic and off-grid, but friendly and safe. A favorite for backpackers or travelers passing through for a night.

Bonus: The rooftop view is unexpectedly stunning—especially at sunrise.

Sharm's accommodation landscape is wide, but not overwhelming—if you know what to look for. Top resorts give you ease and indulgence. Boutique hotels offer personality and intimacy. Budget options let you stretch your stay without sacrificing comfort. The right choice depends less on stars and more on what kind of traveler you are—and what kind of memories you want to make while you're here.

Staying by the Sea

There are hotel rooms—and then there are rooms that open to the sea. In Sharm el-Sheikh, staying by the water isn't just about a good view. It's about feeling the breeze first thing in the morning, walking barefoot from your room to the reef, and falling asleep to the sound of waves brushing the shore. These handpicked beachfront stays don't just put you close to the Red Sea—they immerse you in it.

1. White Hills Resort – For Families Who Want It All

Location: Ras Nasrani
Set directly on a tranquil stretch of beach, this family-friendly resort offers direct water access, spacious rooms, and a calm vibe even in high season.

Bonus: Some rooms have wraparound views of both sunrise and moonlight over the water.

2. Reef Oasis Blue Bay Resort

Location: Hadaba
Positioned right above one of Sharm's richest house reefs, this resort is a snorkeler's dream. The reef begins only a few fin-kicks from the coast.

Bonus: A dedicated floating dock makes sea access smooth, even when the waves pick up.

3. Mövenpick Resort Sharm el Sheikh

Location: Naama Bay hillside
Built into a gentle slope, Mövenpick gives you panoramic Red Sea views from nearly every angle. The beach is down a short path, but totally private and wonderfully uncrowded.

Bonus: Ideal for early risers—the sun rising over the water from here is unforgettable.

4. Stella Di Mare Beach Hotel & Spa

Location: Naama Bay
Despite being near to town, Stella Di Mare feels like a world apart. With sea-view balconies, a lush poolside garden, and direct beach access, it's a refined, quiet option for those wanting beachfront luxury close to city buzz.

Bonus: Excellent on-site diving and a private bay that keeps the sea calm year-round.

5. Sunrise Arabian Beach Resort

Location: Sharks Bay

This resort blends opulent design with beach simplicity, offering tiered pools, direct sea access, and a subtle, elegant take on beachfront living.

Bonus: Incredible coral formations right offshore—and a long promenade perfect for seaside strolls at sunset.

6. Rixos Premium Seagate

Location: Nabq Bay
This sprawling all-inclusive gives you immediate access to its own protected reef, plus a private beach where space never feels tight. Ideal for travelers who want sea + service.

Bonus: Private pier access means reef visits are easy, even for beginners.

In Sharm el-Sheikh, the sea is more than scenery—it's a presence. These beachfront picks don't just give you a view—they give you direct access to salt air, coral wonderlands, and quiet mornings by the water. Whether you're here to dive, sunbathe, or simply let the sound of waves set the tone for your day, these stays bring you as close to the Red Sea as you can get—without getting wet.

Desert Retreats

There's something quietly profound about waking up in the desert. Far from the rhythms of the beach bars and busy bays, Sharm's outer edges offer stays that trade crowds for clarity. Here, you're surrounded by wide skies, whispering dunes, and mountain silhouettes that change color with every hour. These desert stays aren't for everyone—and that's exactly their charm.

1. Bedouin Moon Camp

Location: Near the outskirts of Ras Mohammed
Run by a local Bedouin family, this small desert lodge is rustic, heartfelt, and built for connection. You'll sleep in traditional huts, sip tea by a firepit, and hear the desert breathe at night.

Bonus: Night skies that look like planetariums—no filters, no light pollution.

2. Domina Coral Bay Prestige – Between Desert and Sea

Location: On a vast desert-facing bluff above the Red Sea
While not entirely off-grid, this resort blends high-end comfort with desert surroundings. It's

where luxury meets tranquility—imagine spa treatments with mountain views.

Bonus: Wide terraces and glass-walled lounges that frame the desert like art.

3. Sinai Old Spices B&B – A Hidden Gem in Hadaba's Quiet Backstreets

Location: Hadaba, facing inland
Small, fragrant, and full of personality, this boutique B&B is inspired by the spice trade and desert life. Each room is themed, and the garden feels like a sanctuary.

Bonus: From the rooftop, the line between town and wild Sinai blurs at sunset.

4. Desert Fox Eco-Lodge – True Escape, Off the Grid

Location: Remote desert area between Sharm and Dahab
No Wi-Fi, no crowds—just sustainable architecture, solar lighting, and absolute quiet. If you want disconnection in the purest sense, this is it.

Bonus: Guided sunrise walks into the dunes and nights warmed by fire and stories.

5. Dahab Guesthouse (Side Trip Option) – Laid-Back Desert by the Sea

Location: Dahab, two hours from Sharm
While technically coastal, Dahab's dry, rocky backdrop and bohemian stillness feel more desert than resort. It's a good add-on for travelers seeking Sharm's opposite mood.

Bonus: Yoga on the roof as camels wander the dust tracks below.

Desert retreats near Sharm el-Sheikh offer something no ocean view can—space for stillness, reflection, and awe. These offbeat spots won't give you club beats or buffet lines. What they offer instead is sand underfoot, silence overhead, and stars you can hear. It's not everyone's kind of beauty—but for some, it becomes the most unforgettable part of their trip.

Family-Friendly, Couples' Hideouts, and Solo Gems

Not every traveler in Sharm is looking for the same thing. Some come with little ones and need space to sprawl. Others are here to reconnect in peace, away from noisy crowds. And some just want solitude, a quiet base to return to after long days underwater or in the dunes. This section curates a list of stays that suit families, romantic getaways, and solo adventurers—with intention.

Family-Friendly: Built for Play, Rest, and Comfort

These stays are designed to make traveling with kids easier—and actually enjoyable.

1. Sunrise Diamond Beach Resort

Location: Ras Um Sid
Water slides, a kids' club, and family-sized rooms make this a stress-free pick for those with young travelers.

Bonus: Separate pools for adults and children mean everyone gets what they need.

2. Jaz Fanara Resort

Location: Hadaba
A reef-rich shoreline perfect for safe snorkeling lessons, plus evening entertainment for all ages.

Bonus: Family suites with balconies and a play area built into the design.

3. White Hills Resort

Location: Ras Nasrani
Spacious grounds, multiple dining options, and stroller-friendly paths make this one of Sharm's best new picks for families.

Bonus: Lifeguard-monitored pools and a calm beach entry.

Couples' Hideouts: Where Romance Isn't Forced, It Just Happens

These places wrap you in a kind of peace that lets you reconnect—without distraction.

1. Royal Savoy Sharm El Sheikh

Location: SOHO Square

A haven for adults, with perfect private pools and polished service that lets you disappear from the world together.

Bonus: Sunset cocktails and quiet breakfasts by the sea.

2. Iberotel Palace

Location: Sharm Old Market (Sharm al-Maya)
Elegant and low-key, with a romantic private beach and little need to ever leave the property.

Bonus: Candlelit dining under lantern-lit trees in the garden.

3. Meraki Resort (Adults Only 16+)

Location: Hadaba
Vibrant, stylish, and deeply romantic, with design-forward rooms and nightly music that feels more magic than noise.

Bonus: The beach cabanas are private enough to lose track of time.

4. Cleopatra Luxury Resort Sharm

Location: Nabq Bay

A modern oasis for adults, this resort blends luxury with laid-back energy. You'll find multiple swimming pools, diverse restaurants, a full gym, and daily entertainment—from live music to beach games.

Bonus: Perfect for couples who want a mix of downtime and fun without the kid-club energy.

Solo Gems: Stays That Give You Space Without Isolation

Perfect for independent travelers, divers, digital nomads, or anyone seeking self-paced adventure.

1. Oonas Dive Club Hotel

Location: Naama Bay
A welcoming, low-pressure vibe. No one's rushing you, and the beach is steps away.

Bonus: Easy to meet people—if you want to.

2. Sinai Old Spices B&B

Location: Hadaba
Quiet, quirky, and filled with character. Ideal for writers, dreamers, or anyone craving quiet without loneliness.

Bonus: Rooftop journaling spots with a view of the city's edge.

3. Dive Inn Resort

Location: Hadaba
Affordable, clean, and convenient to dive schools and markets. A good base for individuals who spend their days exploring rather than lazing.

Bonus: Late check-outs and staff who don't hover.

In Sharm el-Sheikh, where you stay matters just as much as what you do. Families need freedom and ease. Couples want privacy and warmth. Solo travelers thrive on quiet independence with the option to connect. The best stays reflect your travel style—and become more than a bed.

CHAPTER 4:
MUST-SEE ATTRACTIONS

Sharm el-Sheikh isn't just a destination—it's a stage where nature, history, and culture put on a show every day. The city invites you to swim through coral kingdoms in the morning, wander through ancient markets by sunset, and stand in the stillness of sacred mountains before dawn. These aren't just attractions—they're invitations. Each one reveals a different side of Sharm's personality, from the quiet mystic to the loud, glowing modernist.

This chapter doesn't aim to list everything—but instead focuses on the essential places that shape the spirit of the city. These are the landmarks that locals still admire and travelers return to in memory. Some are iconic, like Ras Mohammed or Mount Sinai. Others are surprising—modern, electric, or hidden behind mosque doors or café smoke. All are worth your time, not just for photos, but for what they make you feel.

Whether you're the kind of traveler who hops from sight to sight or one who sits in a single place and listens, there's something here for you.

Ras Mohammed National Park

Stand at the southern tip of the Sinai Peninsula, and the desert falls away into water so clear, so deep, it's almost spiritual. This is Ras Mohammed National Park—but don't let the word "park" fool you. It's no ordinary preserve. It's a place where the desert kisses the sea in quiet reverence, and every rock, reef, and ripple seems to hum with life.

The moment you enter, the silence feels purposeful. There's no music here, no crowds shouting. Just wind, waves, and the flutter of something wild moving beneath the surface. This is Egypt's first national park, protected since 1983, and it still feels untouched—like the kind of place you find in dreams or old myths. Divers call it sacred. Scientists call it rare. You'll call it unforgettable.

Ras Mohammed isn't just beautiful—it's geologically dramatic and ecologically profound. Here, sheer coral walls plunge into the deep blue. There are over 1,000 fish species, 150 coral types, sea turtles, enormous clams, and reef sharks. The terrain above water is equally surreal: fossilized coral cliffs, shifting sands, and hidden mangrove groves that thrive in salt water.

This is one of the few places on earth where you can snorkel a reef at sunrise, hike a wind-cut canyon by noon, and watch the sun melt behind Jordan's mountains at dusk—all without leaving the same park.

What to Do (and What Not to Miss)

Snorkeling at Yolanda and Shark Reef

You don't need to dive to experience the magic. The current carries you effortlessly through blooming coral gardens filled with angelfish, barracuda, and—if you're lucky—green turtles. It's like drifting through a submerged forest with the sunlight breaking in like stained glass.

Visit the Earthquake Crack

A dramatic fissure that opened in the earth during an ancient quake. Stand above it and feel small—in the best way. There's a legend that says the earth cracked here out of envy for the beauty below.

The Salt Lake ("Magic Lake")

Locals say swimming in this still, glowing body of water cleanses more than just the skin. It's shallow, calm, and warm like a bath drawn by the sun. On certain mornings, it reflects the sky so perfectly, you forget which way is up.

Mangrove Channel

These salt-defying trees are a miracle in their own right. Watch them grow in still water, with ghost crabs skimming the surface and birds nesting silently overhead. Bring binoculars and a moment of silence.

Desert Lookout Point

Few people make the short hike to the top ridge—but those who do are rewarded with a panoramic view of two continents and three seas. It's wind-swept, empty, and entirely humbling.

Need-to-Know Tips

1. Timing is everything. The best light is just after sunrise or just before sunset. The reefs shimmer differently then, and the park takes on a golden hush.
2. Bring your own gear if possible. Rental gear can be inconsistent, and this place deserves better than foggy masks or leaky snorkels.
3. No vendors, no cafes, no trash bins. And that's the point. Bring water, snacks, and your respect.

4. You need a ticket. Entry costs around 200 EGP per person (cash only), and you'll pay it at the small gate checkpoint. Some tours include the fee—double-check.

5. No drones allowed. The silence here is sacred, and Ras Mohammed protects its peace fiercely.

Ras Mohammed isn't a tourist stop. It's a reminder—of what the earth can look like when left alone. It offers no theme park thrills, no filtered cafés or manicured boardwalks. Just reef and desert, sky and silence. And in that quiet, something timeless waits. If you go to Sharm and miss Ras Mohammed, you haven't really met her soul.

The Old Market

The first thing you'll notice is the smell—cardamom and cumin, maybe clove or grilled corn, mixed with warm air that holds onto scent like it has a secret. Welcome to Sharm el-Maya, home of the Old Market, the city's most enduring pocket of tradition. Come here at sunset, and you won't just see a market—you'll feel like you've stumbled into a living postcard wrapped in string lights and spice smoke.

Unlike the polished resorts or modern SOHO Square, the Old Market is where Sharm exhales its past. Stalls spill into the walkways, their tables crowded with copper lamps, hand-woven shawls, and spices in pyramid-shaped piles. Shopkeepers sit cross-legged, sipping tea and smiling with a knowing patience, ready to tell you stories or sell you a silver pendant—your choice. Cats lounge as if they own the space, and it sometimes feels like they do.

This market isn't about hurrying or ticking off a list. It's about wandering slowly—letting your eyes catch on the curve of a lamp, the fold of a robe, the call of an oud drifting from somewhere you can't see. Every corner is layered. One turn leads to leather slippers, another to a man making flatbread over open flame, and beyond that, a carved wooden doorway that leads into prayer.

The architecture is older, the lanterns are real, and haggling is an art form with more laughter than tension. You'll find mosques nestled between spice vendors and barbers trimming hair under fluorescent bulbs. This isn't themed—it's lived.

Come after sunset, and the atmosphere shifts. Fairy lights switch on, the mosque's minaret lights glow green against the sky, and the whole place hums with a gentle chaos. Kids eat sugar-dusted sweets while parents sip hibiscus tea. If you're lucky, a group of musicians may gather and play, not for tourists, but for the joy of it.

What to Buy (and What to Watch For)

Spices

Avoid the touristy sealed bags. Instead, ask to smell the loose spices—real sumac and saffron don't need labels. Buy by weight and watch them scoop it fresh into paper.

Leather & Embroidered Goods

Local craftsmanship still lives here. You'll find soft sandals, hand-stitched belts, and embroidered jalabiyas that are more wearable art than souvenirs.

Brass, Copper, and Glass

From antique-style lanterns to glass perfume bottles filled with floral oils, these pieces are often hand-made. Don't rush the choice—they're as much about story as shape.

Tips for Visiting

1. Go at night (after 6 PM). That's when it truly comes alive. The crowd is gentle, local, and full of energy without feeling like a tourist circus.
2. Bring small bills. Most vendors prefer cash, and haggling is expected—but done with smiles, not shouting.
3. Cover shoulders and knees modestly. While the area is relaxed, it's also close to mosques and family-run stalls.
4. Talk to the shopkeepers. Ask about their products—they love when you're curious, not just transactional.

The Old Market is where Sharm's soul peeks through the shine of tourism. You won't find loud music or glossy branding here—just light, scent, texture, and time. Walk through it slowly. Let the smells stick to your shirt, the sounds echo in your memory. You'll leave with more than what you bought.

Al Sahaba Mosque

It rises out of the heart of the Old Market like something that shouldn't be real—Al Sahaba Mosque, a sandstone dream etched in minarets and moonlight. During the day, its domes catch the sun like gold. At night, it glows from within, its towers piercing the sky like candle flames. For many, it's the first place in Sharm that stirs something deeper than awe—it stirs reverence, even if you don't speak the language of prayer.

Unlike many mosques in Egypt built centuries ago, Al Sahaba is young—completed in 2017—yet it carries the weight of tradition like an old soul. Two tall minarets, ornate Islamic calligraphy, and Moorish-inspired domes combine to create one of the most stunning works of architecture in Sinai. It stands not just as a place of worship, but as a symbol of coexistence, sitting peacefully at the edge of a market square where voices, music, and bargaining fill the air.

What makes Al Sahaba truly special isn't just its scale, but its detail. Step closer, and you'll see every curve of stonework was carved with care. Inside, chandeliers hang like falling stars. The walls speak in verses of peace. It's not just a religious building—it's an invitation into stillness, into a rhythm of life that moves slower, softer, and with purpose.

Why Visit, Even if You're Not Muslim

Al Sahaba Mosque is more than a religious site—it's a living piece of Egyptian artistry, built by over 800 local craftsmen. Walking around it offers a glimpse into how architecture in Egypt is still a spiritual act, not just a structural one. It's a rare space where tourists and locals pause for the same reason: to look up and feel small in the best possible way.

Non-Muslim visitors are welcome to view the exterior and walk the open courtyard, especially at night when the mosque is lit in golden tones. If you're lucky, you'll hear the evening call to prayer, a melodic echo that seems to soak into the stone around you. It's one of those sounds that roots you to the place you're in—just for a moment, everything else hushes.

How to Visit Respectfully

1. Cover shoulders and knees. A lightweight scarf for women is appreciated even if you don't enter.
2. Visit at night for the lighting, atmosphere, and calmer vibe. Early evening (around 7–9 PM) is ideal.

3. No entry during prayer times, unless you're Muslim and wish to pray. The space is still very much a functioning mosque, not a tourist museum.
4. Photography is allowed outside, but avoid posing or loud behavior. The space deserves gentleness.

After visiting the mosque, take a slow walk back through the Old Market. Many of the best angles for photographing Al Sahaba are from nearby rooftops—some cafés have upper levels with a view. Grab a hibiscus tea, sit up top, and watch the towers light up against the night sky.

Al Sahaba Mosque isn't just a place—it's a moment. A pause. A lesson in how spiritual beauty can be built stone by stone, right in the heart of a bustling market. You don't need to understand the prayers to feel their echo. Just stand quietly, look up, and let it reach you.

Naama Bay

You'll hear it before you see it. The hum of conversation, the splash of a glass being set down, the rustle of palm fronds above an open-air café. Naama Bay is Sharm's pulse point — where travelers from every corner of the world gather, stroll, sip, and surrender to the now. It is hardly calm, but neither is it frantic. It achieves the right combination of intensity and ease.

This is where Sharm first learned how to welcome the world. Once a dusty coastal village with little more than a jetty and a few dive shacks, Naama Bay grew into a vibrant, pedestrian-friendly strip lined with resorts, restaurants, bazaars, and beachfront bars. But don't let the word "touristy" scare you off — it has charm, rhythm, and just the right dose of spontaneity. One moment, you're watching street dancers under fairy lights. The next, you're sipping mint tea beside a man selling handmade leather journals.

Naama Bay isn't trying to be something it's not. It's light-hearted, lived-in, and full of movement. You can spend the whole evening here doing absolutely nothing—just walking, people-watching, and soaking up that sweet, balmy coastal air that feels like vacation distilled into scent and breeze.

Why Naama Bay Matters

Naama Bay is more than just a location—it's a meeting place of cultures and comforts. Egyptians, Italians, Brits, Russians, and solo backpackers all rub shoulders here, often barefoot on the sand. Everyone's here for the same thing: connection, escape, and a good time that doesn't feel forced.

It's also incredibly walkable. Unlike many parts of Sharm, Naama Bay has wide pedestrian promenades. You can move from the beach to a rooftop bar in five minutes, then swing by an ice cream cart or wander into a gallery that looks like it was carved out of coral.

What to Do in Naama Bay

Beach-hop by day

Most major resorts open their beach areas to outside guests for a small fee. Rent a lounger, sip something cold, and just let the Red Sea do its magic.

Walk the strip at night

Lights twinkle from every corner. You'll find live music, hookah lounges, fire-breathers, fortune tellers, and occasional pop-up dance shows.

Try a foot massage on the street

Yes, it's a thing. Surprisingly good, too. Settle into a cushioned bench as someone works the fatigue out of your legs while you sip fresh mango juice.

Take a sunset camel ride on the sand

It may feel cliché, but as the sky turns peach and the call to prayer echoes from nearby mosques, you'll find yourself grinning the whole ride.

Watch the world go by at a café

Sit at Tam Tam, Fares, or any of the dozens of sea-facing cafés and let the night drift around you. Order a mint tea, some basbousa, and just breathe.

Tips for Visiting

1. Go just before sunset — golden hour makes everything softer, and the evening energy builds gradually.
2. Expect friendly vendors, especially along the main strip. Smile, say "la shukran" (no, thank you), and keep walking if you're not shopping.
3. Avoid the midday heat in summer months. The fun starts after 5 PM, when the air cools and the lights begin to glow.

4. No dress code, but lightweight modest wear will help you blend in and feel more comfortable.

Naama Bay is where Sharm lets its hair down. It's lively but never overwhelming, social but not showy, and full of simple pleasures: walking, talking, tasting, and watching the world light up one café at a time. If you only have one night in Sharm to truly feel its pulse, spend it here—doing nothing in particular, and enjoying every minute of it.

SOHO Square

At first glance, it feels like you've wandered out of Egypt and into a scene straight from Dubai or London's West End—LED-lit fountains dance to Arabic ballads and Coldplay hits, British pubs rub shoulders with Lebanese lounges, and neon signs glow in every language imaginable. Welcome to SOHO Square, Sharm's answer to modern nightlife, world cuisine, and family-friendly glitz.

It's clean, polished, and designed for delight. Children giggle as they chase laser lights across the tiled floors. Couples take selfies under a rotating digital globe. And behind every corner, there's something just a little unexpected: an ice bar in the desert, a 6-lane bowling alley, or a high-end spa hidden behind a sushi restaurant.

This isn't Egypt as you know it. But it's Egypt as it adapts—welcoming, experimental, global, and curated for comfort. Some travelers come once and skip it next time. Others return every evening, drawn by the effortless fun of it all. If the Old Market is the city's memory, SOHO Square is its mirrorball.

Why It's Worth a Visit

SOHO Square is one of the few places in Sharm that successfully merges international entertainment with Egyptian hospitality. It's built for variety. You can sip champagne at a piano bar, then walk five minutes and have street-style falafel at a food truck. It's posh yet not pretentious—flashy but still approachable.

Most importantly, it's safe, walkable, and full of options. Families, solo travelers, and couples can all find something to enjoy here. And because it's just minutes from the airport and many major resorts, it's an easy evening out.

Top Things to Experience at SOHO Square

The Dancing Fountain Show

Every night, the main square lights up with a coordinated water and light show. It's oddly hypnotic, surprisingly emotional, and always free.

Ice Bar Sharm

Yes, a real ice bar in the Sinai desert. Rent a heavy coat, step inside, and drink from a frozen glass. It's gimmicky—but it works.

SOHO Bowling Center

Perfect for families or groups looking for a fun, low-key night indoors.

Akuna Matata Food Court

A well-curated international food village offering Egyptian grills, Indian curries, fresh crepes, pizza, and even Korean BBQ. You'll eat well without breaking the bank.

Pangaea Nightclub

A favorite for upscale partygoers—think velvet rope energy, live DJs, and themed nights. Dress sharp if you want in.

Culturama Museum & Art Gallery

Hidden near the side entrances, this mini-gallery features Egyptian contemporary artists and rotating cultural exhibits. It's small, but worth a look.

Tips for Visiting

1. Go between 7–10 PM when the lights are on, the crowds are lively, and most venues are open.
2. Dress smart-casual. It's not a strict code, but flip-flops and beachwear feel out of place.

3. Shuttle buses run from many hotels to SOHO Square (check with your concierge).
4. Don't rush. The magic is in wandering. You'll always find something unexpected.

In SOHO Square, Sharm dresses up, turns on the charm, and throws open the doors to its cosmopolitan side. It's bright, modern, and built for joy—whether you're sipping tea by a fountain, exploring global cuisine, or just walking slowly through light and laughter. Come with no plan, and leave with a dozen small memories you didn't know you were looking for.

Daybreak at Mount Sinai

There are places that feel like destinations—and then there are places that feel like thresholds. Mount Sinai is the latter. Rising 2,285 meters above the desert floor, this isn't just a mountain—it's a story whispered across centuries, where prophets are said to have stood, revelations echoed, and silence still hangs thick in the cold dawn air.

The journey begins at night. Around 1:00 or 2:00 AM, you'll find yourself climbing—guided by Bedouins, headlamps, and the crunch of gravel underfoot. The stars above are unapologetically brilliant, and below, a slow-moving string of hikers glows in the dark like a human constellation. The air is crisp. The mood is hushed. Even those who aren't religious often fall quiet. Because something about this place makes you listen.

Then comes the summit. As the eastern sky begins to blush, you wrap yourself in borrowed blankets, sip sugary tea sold by smiling locals, and wait. And when the sun crests the jagged horizon and washes the rock in gold, it's not just beautiful—it's transformative. Cameras click, but most people just stare, wide-eyed. Some cry. Others pray. No one forgets.

Why It's Worth the Trek

Mount Sinai is more than a bucket list stop. It's a pilgrimage of presence. Whether or not you believe in sacred texts, there's something undeniably moving about watching sunrise from a mountain where thousands have sought meaning. The climb itself is an act of letting go—of noise, of comfort, of everything unnecessary.

The surrounding ranges ripple endlessly into the horizon. No skyscrapers. No traffic. No ads. Just wind, rock, and ancient earth.

What to Expect

The Climb:

The Camel Path (Siket Sayidna Musa) is longer but gentler, culminating in leisurely switchbacks. The Steps of Repentance, built by monks, is a steeper but shorter stairway of over 3,000 stone steps. Most visitors go up via the Camel Path and descend via the steps.

Guides:

Local Bedouin guides accompany you (often required). They're friendly, helpful, and very respectful of the mountain.

Need-to-Know Tips

1. Dress warmly. Even in the warmer months, temperatures at the peak can plummet to near-freezing. Layer up and bring a windproof jacket.
2. Bring cash for tea, snacks, and renting a camel if needed (yes, you can ride part of the way).
3. Start the climb between 1–2 AM to make it in time for sunrise (around 5:30–6:00 AM depending on the season).
4. Respect the silence. This isn't a place for loud music, drones, or casual chatter. The mountain speaks—if you let it.
5. Stay hydrated, but bring your own water—prices go up with altitude.

Daybreak at Mount Sinai is more than just a photo opportunity; it's a holy exchange between sky, stone, and spirit. You don't only see the sunrise. You may feel yourself shifting. In a world that rarely stops moving, this climb provides something few places do anymore: quiet that communicates. If you just do one thing in Sharm that will alter you, make it this.

CHAPTER 5:
FUN OUTDOOR ACTIVITIES

If the Red Sea is Sharm el-Sheikh's heartbeat, then the great outdoors is its soul. This city wasn't made to be observed from a balcony—it's meant to be felt, out in the water, under the stars, and across the golden silence of the desert. Sharm gives you freedom in all directions: dive beneath coral cities, race across sand dunes, glide above the sea breeze, or just float still in a salt-blushed bay.

Here, outdoor adventure doesn't mean exhausting marathons or extreme challenges. It means inviting the elements in—letting the sea toss your hair, letting sand dust your shoes, and letting unfamiliar winds remind you that you're not in your routine anymore. Whether you're a thrill-seeker or a sunset-watcher, this chapter offers ways to play, connect, and breathe.

From world-renowned dive sites to off-grid Bedouin dinners, from paddleboards on turquoise glass to stars blinking over fire-lit camps—every activity here is a memory in the making. This isn't a checklist. It's a menu of moments waiting for your "yes."

Diving Deep

There are few places on Earth where the ocean opens up like a gallery — no glass, no gate, just you and the living artwork below. Sharm el-Sheikh isn't just good for diving. It's legendary. For decades, divers have traveled thousands of miles just to drop into these waters and come face to face with kaleidoscopic coral gardens, ghost-like shipwrecks, and swirls of life so vibrant it feels surreal.

What makes Sharm special isn't just the visibility (though it stretches up to 30 metres on good days) or the marine diversity (over 1,000 species). It's the proximity. You don't need to sail for hours to find something spectacular. In many cases, you can take a 10-minute boat ride—or even just walk off the beach—and end up in a blue world full of shimmering walls, eagle rays, lionfish, and even curious turtles that drift by like slow-moving dreams.

Whether you're taking your very first breath through a regulator or hunting down hammerheads, Sharm has the site for you. Here's where to go — and why.

Top Dive Sites in Sharm: Pick Your Depth

Ras Mohammed National Park (Shark & Yolanda Reef) – For Experienced Divers

Where the Gulf of Aqaba meets the Gulf of Suez, the currents bring nutrients—and life explodes. This is the dive site. Expect sheer drop-offs, schools of barracuda, soft corals in every color imaginable, and an eerie wreck trail of bathroom fixtures (yes, toilets!) from the Yolanda cargo ship. It's bizarre, brilliant, and not to be missed.

Jackson Reef (Tiran Island) – Big Fish, Strong Currents

Located in the Tiran Strait, Jackson is for those chasing thrill and scale. Manta rays. Hammerheads. Tuna slicing through blue. This site is famous for its powerful currents and occasional shark sightings. It's raw, beautiful, and rewards confident divers.

Temple Reef – Perfect for Beginners

Just off the coast from Naama Bay, Temple is a gentle, accessible dive site with columns of coral that look like ancient ruins. It's calm, shallow, and teeming with life—perfect for beginners or those just getting their fins wet.

Thistlegorm Wreck – History Meets Haunting

This WWII British cargo ship was bombed by German forces in 1941 and now lies intact on the seafloor, complete with motorbikes, rifles, and ghostly crates of boots. It's one of the most iconic wreck dives in the world and a must-do for anyone qualified to go deep.

Dive Centers to Trust

1. Camel Dive Club & Hotel (Naama Bay)
PADI 5-star centre with strong safety standards, great instructors, and daily boat trips.

2. Emperor Divers (Multiple locations)
Professional staff, multilingual, and excellent for courses or gear rental.

3. Reef Oasis Dive Club
Offers both beginner sessions and tech diving. Friendly vibes, great for couples or families.

Tip: Always check if your chosen center is PADI or SSI certified, and make sure gear is properly maintained. Don't be afraid to ask questions—your safety matters.

Not a Diver Yet? Here's Your Entry Point

- You don't need to be qualified to experience the wonder.
- Introductory Dives let you go down 5–10 meters with a dive master. No experience needed.
- Discover Scuba Diving (DSD) is a half-day program that lets you taste diving before committing to a full course.
- PADI Open Water Certification can be completed in 3–4 days in Sharm, and there's hardly a better classroom.

Expect to pay $40–60 USD for a try dive, $300–400 USD for a full certification course (all gear included).

Essential Tips Before You Dive

1. Don't dive within 18 hours of flying — plan your dive days early in your trip.
2. Skip the sunscreen before a dive — it's harmful to corals. Use reef-safe options only.
3. Stay hydrated and well-rested — dehydration is a common cause of discomfort underwater.
4. Be honest about your comfort level — good instructors will tailor the dive to your needs.

To dive in Sharm is to step into a world that rewrites your sense of scale, color, and quiet. These waters

hold wrecks, wonders, and creatures that don't flinch when you appear—they just keep moving like you're part of the reef. And once you've breathed beneath these blues, it's hard to forget the silence, the weightlessness, the light rippling like a cathedral window. Dive once, and you'll want to return. Dive twice, and you may never want to leave.

Snorkeling Spots You Can Swim to From Shore

Not everyone wants to strap on a tank and plunge deep. And the beauty is that in Sharm el-Sheikh, you don't have to. Some of the most spectacular underwater scenes here are just a few fin-kicks from the shoreline. With a simple mask and snorkel, you can drift above rainbows of coral, schools of butterflyfish, parrotfish, and even curious sea turtles, all in water so clear it feels like glass.

Sharm is uniquely suited to shoreline snorkeling thanks to its fringing reefs—natural coral walls that run parallel to the coast, teeming with marine life right at the edge. No boats. No long swims. Step in, float out, and look below. The current often helps guide you along, making it feel like you're flying over a living reef.

This section offers the best places where the shore and the sea meet in perfect harmony—and where you can experience the Red Sea's magic with just your breath and a little curiosity.

Top Shore-Access Snorkeling Spots

Ras Um Sid

This is the local favorite. Ras Um Sid, located near the lighthouse, has a stunning drop-off and lush coral gardens that are just steps from the shore. Expect vivid coral formations, glassfish clouds, and the occasional blue-spotted stingray. The reef runs along the cliff edge, so access is best from the jetty or beach stairs.

Sharks Bay

Despite the name, don't panic—no sharks here. Just calm, shallow waters and a rich underwater scene. Perfect for families and beginners, with resorts like Sharks Bay Umbi and Sunshine Divers providing safe, easy access. The seagrass beds here also attract turtles and the odd seahorse if you're patient.

The Gardens (Near Naama Bay)

Near Garden, Middle Garden, and Far Garden are three interconnecting reefs located just a stone's throw from Naama Bay's main promenade. Each one is accessible via specific hotel jetties, with Near Garden being the most convenient. It's peaceful, nearby, and home to soft corals, anemone fish, and moray eels.

Montazah Reef

Less known, more pristine. Located between Sharks Bay and Ras Nasrani, Montazah offers quiet reef access with surprisingly rich biodiversity, especially in the early morning. Less crowded, and ideal for confident snorkelers wanting something peaceful.

Gear, Safety & Local Tips

1. Rent vs. Bring: If you have your own mask and snorkel, bring them — rental gear can be hit-or-miss. Many dive shops rent daily for under $10 USD.
2. Reef shoes: Wear them when walking in shallow water, but never on the reef itself. Coral is delicate and easily damaged.
3. Floatation vests: Highly recommended for beginners or less confident swimmers. Most hotels offer them.
4. Watch for jetties and zones: Don't snorkel in boat lanes, and always follow local signage. Some resorts require use of specific jetty points to protect the reef.
5. Leave no trace: No touching, standing on, or collecting from reefs—your respect keeps them alive.

When to Snorkel

Early hours between 8 and 11 AM offer the clearest views underwater and the liveliest reef action. Waters are calmer and the sun is gentle.

Late afternoon: Also pleasant, but currents may increase. Bring a rash guard to protect from sunburn.

Avoid windy days: Surface choppiness can reduce visibility. Check local flags or ask hotel staff before heading out.

Snorkeling in Sharm el-Sheikh is like drifting across a living canvas painted by nature. You don't need to dive deep to feel wonder—you just need to float. From shallow coral gardens to dramatic underwater cliffs just meters from shore, every breath you take through that snorkel reveals a different shade of the Red Sea's quiet magic. In this part of the world, all you have to do is look down... and let the sea show you something unforgettable.

Desert Safaris and Dune Bashing

You haven't truly felt Sharm el-Sheikh until you've stood in the Sinai Desert — no buildings in sight, no phone signal, just a wide, breathing silence and the hot whisper of wind across the dunes. It's not the emptiness that strikes you. It's how alive the desert is when you finally stop and listen.

Then, just as your mind begins to slow down, comes the adrenaline rush: quad bikes, dune buggies, and 4x4 jeeps launching into the golden nothingness like desert falcons. The ground shakes, sand kicks into the sky, and your whole body wakes up. There's something primal about blasting across this ancient land — an echo of old trade caravans, Bedouin nomads, and unmarked paths that feel both wild and sacred.

But desert safaris here aren't just about speed. They're about contrast — from sand-scorched madness to fire-lit stillness. Many tours end with sunset tea under a woven tent, shared with Bedouins whose families have walked this land for generations. Stories are told. Bread is baked. And the stars? The stars feel impossibly close.

Ways to Experience the Sinai Desert

Quad Biking into the Dunes

Feel the roar under your hands as you power through open trails, past limestone ridges and sand valleys. Quad biking in Sharm is pure fun — no prior experience needed, just goggles, a scarf, and the willingness to get dusty.

4x4 Jeep Safaris

For those who want to go deeper into the desert — think Colored Canyon, Wadi Ghazala, or even Saint Catherine's Monastery — a guided 4x4 safari is the ticket. These rugged rides cut through rock valleys and hidden oases, revealing the Sinai's ancient geological beauty.

Dune Buggy Adventures

Think quad biking, but lower to the ground and twice as bumpy. These open-air buggies are a favorite for small groups wanting something faster and wilder than the standard tour.

More Than Just a Ride

Many safari packages include cultural add-ons:

1. Visit to a Bedouin village, where you'll learn about traditional herbal medicine, desert survival, and storytelling.
2. Enjoy a Sunset dinner cooked underground in the traditional Bedouin zarb method — smoky, tender, unforgettable.
3. Stargazing sessions with telescopes after nightfall, often narrated by a local astronomy guide.

These quiet moments in the desert often leave more impact than the ride itself.

Practical Tips for the Best Desert Adventure

1. Wear closed shoes — sandals will fill with sand and regret.
2. Sunglasses, sunscreen, and water are non-negotiable.
3. Avoid midday safaris in summer — the heat can be dangerous. Opt for early morning or twilight tours.
4. Don't expect signal — embrace the disconnect.
5. Tip your guides — especially Bedouin hosts. Their hospitality is sincere and deeply rooted in tradition.

How to Book

Ask your hotel concierge, or check reputable operators like:

- Sinai Safari Adventures (known for eco-conscious trips)
- Sunrise Tours Sharm (popular for combo desert + stargazing packages)
- Blue Sky Travel Egypt (offers family-friendly options)

Expect to pay around $25–$60 USD per person, depending on the length, vehicle type, and add-ons.

The Sinai Desert doesn't shout. It whispers. And whether you're racing through it in a storm of sand or sipping tea beneath a fire-lit sky, you'll feel it settle inside you. It's not just a place — it's a feeling. One of freedom, wildness, and timelessness. In Sharm el-Sheikh, the desert is not a background. It's the heartbeat of adventure.

Camel Treks and Bedouin Sunset Dinners

There's something timeless about moving through the desert on a camel. The way the saddle creaks, the way the animal sways like a slow ship over sand, and the way the world goes quiet — just wind, distant mountains, and the rhythm of footsteps older than roads. This is not an amusement ride. It's a return to how the desert has always been crossed: patiently, respectfully, one horizon at a time.

Camel treks in Sharm el-Sheikh aren't long expeditions — they're intimate glimpses into Bedouin tradition. You mount your gentle guide at golden hour, ride into the blush of sunset, and arrive at a tucked-away camp where fire glows, tea simmers, and the stars are already beginning to blink into view. There's no rush. No noise. Just you, the desert, and a people who've learned to live with it — not against it.

Then comes dinner. Not just food — an experience. Bedouin men pull hot coals from underground ovens, lifting trays of zarb: tender lamb, chicken, rice, and vegetables slow-cooked to perfection. Flatbread is made fresh before your eyes, tea is poured in glass cups, and stories begin to flow — of stars, survival, and silence. You don't need to understand the language. You'll feel it anyway.

Why Camel Treks Are Worth It

Authenticity: Unlike touristy gimmicks, many camel treks are guided by real Bedouin families who live just beyond the edge of Sharm.

Pace: These rides are short (usually 30–45 minutes), making them perfect for all ages and fitness levels.

Magic hour: Riding at sunset isn't just beautiful—it's immersive. You see the desert soften, the light shift, the earth cool beneath your feet.

You arrive a tourist. You leave a guest.

The Dinner Experience

Most treks end in a traditional desert camp—a circle of cushions and rugs under a low woven canopy. Lanterns flicker. Bread bakes on a metal plate over an open fire. You sit, eat with your hands, and sip on thick, sweet tea brewed with desert herbs like habaq (a kind of wild mint).

Some camps add a touch of show:

- Live oud music

- Bedouin dance performances
- Stargazing sessions with minimal light pollution

Others keep it simple — just the food, the fire, and the stars. Both versions have their magic.

What to Know Before You Go

1. No fancy dress required: Wear long, breathable clothes and a light scarf or jacket for after sunset.
2. Photography is welcomed — but always ask first before taking close-ups of hosts or their families.
3. Tipping is appreciated: The Bedouins offer genuine hospitality and often rely on tourism income.
4. Vegetarian meals available: Just ask in advance when booking.

Booking Options

- Sun 'n Fun Safari and Sharm Wonders offer well-reviewed camel-and-dinner packages starting around $30–$50 USD per person.
- Many hotels partner with local Bedouins — ask at reception for small-group, private experiences.
- For a more rugged vibe, Desert Rose Camp near Wadi Mandar offers overnight stays and

early morning camel rides into the mountains.

Riding a camel into the desert isn't about the photo. It's about the pause—a chance to see the Sinai as the Bedouins do: slowly, simply, reverently. And when the stars rise and the fire crackles, and you're sitting with warm bread in your hand, you'll realize something rare has happened. The desert didn't just show itself to you — it welcomed you in.

Kitesurfing, Paddleboarding, and Jet Skiing

There's something electric about the Red Sea breeze—it doesn't just cool you down; it invites you to rise, glide, and speed across the water. While Sharm el-Sheikh is well-known for its serene coral reefs and underwater silence, its surface thrills are equally spectacular. This coastline isn't just a place to relax. It's a playground — and the wind, waves, and open sea are your toys.

You don't need to be an expert. Whether you're paddling peacefully past the reef or launching into the sky with a kite strapped to your back, these activities are designed for joy — and they bring the Red Sea alive in ways that are both bold and beautiful. The mix of warm water, steady wind, and wide-open bays makes Sharm one of Egypt's top water sports destinations — no exaggeration.

This isn't about showing off. It's about letting go. Letting the wind carry you, the engine roar beneath you, and your body remember what movement feels like when it's paired with laughter. Here's where to ride the wind and water in Sharm.

Kitesurfing: Ride the Wind, Touch the Sky

If kitesurfing is new to you, get ready for a spectacle. Picture a rider harnessed to a soaring kite, skimming across the water with power and grace—occasionally launching into the air for dramatic flips before gliding back down. Thanks to Sharm's steady winds and calm, shallow bays, it's a perfect playground for both first-timers and seasoned thrill-seekers.

Top Spots:

- Nabq Bay – Shallow, wide, and usually less crowded. Perfect for beginners.
- El Fanar – More developed, with deeper oceans and more powerful winds.

Where to Learn:

- Kite Junkies Egypt (Nabq) – One of the most reputable kite schools, offering IKO-certified instructors and full gear rentals.
- Mövenpick Water Sports Center (Naama Bay) – Excellent for intermediate kiters.

Tip: Lessons typically range from $50–$80 per session. A 3-day beginner course will get you standing and sailing safely.

Paddleboarding: Glide at Your Own Pace

Stand-up paddleboarding (SUP) is peaceful, scenic, and surprisingly easy to pick up. Early mornings are best—when the sea is smooth as glass and the sky reflects off the surface like a mirror. You can paddle past reefs, drift into small coves, or just float, breathe, and feel incredibly present.

Rentals:

- Most beach resorts and dive centers offer hourly rentals.
- Expect to pay around $10–$15 USD/hour.

Bonus: Some places now offer SUP yoga sessions at sunrise. Yes, it's as dreamy as it sounds.

Jet Skiing: No Time for Slow

If you want speed, here's your fix. Jet skis are available across Sharm, and many tours offer guided rides through safe open zones where you can truly open the throttle. It's not just a joyride — it's a rush of freedom across blue infinity.

Best Jet Ski Areas:

- Naama Bay – Central and convenient
- Sharks Bay – Less boat traffic, better views

Rental Tip:

Most rentals charge by the quarter-hour. Expect $25–$35 USD for 15 minutes, including basic safety briefing and life jacket.

Note: Jet skiing is often restricted near protected reefs — always follow designated paths and listen to local guides.

Other Options to Consider

- Banana Boat Rides – Enjoyable for both groups and families. Expect laughter, splashes, and the occasional wipeout.
- Parasailing – Soar over the coast when attached to a boat and swept upward. Short but spectacular.

Safety & Tips for All Water Sports

1. Listen to the instructors — the Red Sea is calm, but wind and currents can shift quickly.
2. Wear reef-safe sunscreen — especially on your shoulders and neck.
3. Hydrate — water sports in the sun will wear you out faster than you think.
4. Avoid alcohol before or after — wait until sunset to toast your ride.

The Red Sea is not just a place to plunge beneath. With every kite loop, paddle stroke, or high-speed wave slash, you're not just skimming the surface... you're awakening something in yourself. In Sharm el-Sheikh, thrill and tranquility come in the same package. All you have to do is pick your ride.

Stargazing Nights

Long after the music fades and the waves fall asleep, something ancient stirs above Sharm el-Sheikh. The sky, once a background, becomes the main event. Out here — in the vast open silence of the Sinai — the stars don't just twinkle. They glow, ripple, and speak, if you're quiet enough to listen.

You don't need a telescope. You don't need a degree in astronomy. What you need is distance—from streetlights, screens, and anything that demands your attention during the day. In return, the cosmos offers something we rarely get anymore: perspective. You realize how wide the world really is—and how lucky you are to be standing in this small corner of it, just looking up.

The Sinai Desert, especially just outside Sharm, is one of the best places in Egypt to stargaze. Amazing visibility is produced by the high altitude, dry air, and absence of light pollution. You can often spot the Milky Way streaking across the sky, satellites blinking overhead, and meteor showers tearing through the darkness. And when paired with a crackling fire, a warm cup of Bedouin tea, and the faint beat of a drum somewhere far off? It becomes something more than beautiful. It becomes spiritual.

Best Stargazing Spots in and Around Sharm

Wadi Mandar

Just 20 minutes from the city, this desert valley feels a world away. It's a popular location for evening safaris and Bedouin dinners, but many operators extend the night into full stargazing sessions with minimal setup.

Mount Sinai

If you're up for a midnight hike, the summit of Mount Sinai offers one of the most breathtaking celestial views in the Middle East. The climb starts around 1 AM, reaching the peak in time for sunrise. But the hours before dawn—sitting under a blanket, surrounded by silence—are often the most profound.

Note: Bring layers. It gets very cold up there, even in summer.

Desert Stargazing Camps

Several tour operators offer full-on stargazing packages. You'll travel into the desert, set up camp, and use telescopes while local guides point out constellations, planets, and the stories tied to them from both Arabic mythology and modern science.

Top operators:
- Sharm Stars Safari
- Sinai Sky Tours
- Desert Rose Stargazing Nights

Prices typically range from $30–$60 USD, depending on group size and extras.

What You Might See

- Milky Way Galaxy – Best viewed from April to September.
- Orion's Belt, Scorpio, and Cassiopeia
- Mars, Jupiter, and Saturn, depending on the month
- Shooting stars during peak meteor showers (Perseids in August, Geminids in December)

Tip: Download a stargazing app like Sky Guide or Star Walk 2 to help identify what you're seeing in real time.

No Tour? No Problem. Here's How to Stargaze on Your Own

- Leave the city lights behind. Even the edge of the city near Nabq or Ras Mohammed can be enough.
- Lie flat, facing the sky. Let your eyes adjust for at least 20 minutes before expecting full clarity.

- Keep warm — desert temperatures drop fast at night.
- Bring a friend or journal. Stargazing has a way of stirring thoughts that deserve to be shared or written down.

The Red Sea gives you color, adventure, and sun. But it's the desert sky that gives you awe. In Sharm el-Sheikh, the real magic doesn't always happen underwater or on a mountaintop. Sometimes, it happens in silence — beneath a blanket of stars, with sand under your feet and a thousand constellations keeping you company. You don't have to search for meaning here. Just look up.

CHAPTER 6:
FOOD AND DRINKS

There's a special kind of memory that only taste can unlock. A warm bite of grilled sea bass spiced just right. A street vendor's falafel, crisped at the edges and wrapped in soft baladi bread. A sip of mango juice so sweet it could only have come from Egypt. In Sharm el-Sheikh, food isn't just a necessity — it's a language.

What makes eating in Sharm so unique is its contrast. On one hand, you'll find deeply rooted Egyptian classics passed down through generations — ful Me dames, molokhia, fresh oven-baked aish baladi. On the other, you'll find influences from Italy, Lebanon, Asia, and Europe — thanks to Sharm's role as a global tourist crossroad. One evening you might dine under stars at a Bedouin camp with slow-roasted lamb, and the next, you're swirling pasta with views over Naama Bay.

And it's more than simply what's on your plate. It's where you eat it. Rooftop terraces overlooking the Red Sea. Beach shacks with sand between your toes. Courtyards wrapped in jasmine vines. There's magic in the settings just as much as the meals.

Must-Try Dishes

Some meals fill your stomach. Others tell a story. In Sharm el-Sheikh, the food does both. Here, every bite carries a whisper of Nubian markets, Bedouin tents, Mediterranean coasts, and Red Sea tides. You don't need a reservation at a fancy resort to taste something unforgettable — just curiosity, an open mind, and maybe a napkin in your back pocket.

Sharm's food scene is a collision of Egypt's classic comfort dishes and the region's rich natural offerings — especially seafood. One moment, you're scooping warm ful Me dames with crusty bread; the next, you're cracking into a buttered lobster caught hours earlier from just offshore. And it's not just the ingredients — it's the preparation. Egyptian food is soulful. It's slow-cooked, spice-layered, and proudly unpretentious.

If you only had a few days and one appetite, here's what you should absolutely not leave without tasting:

Ful Me dames

The Egyptian breakfast staple. Fava beans cooked slowly with garlic, lemon, cumin, and olive oil. Served warm with a boiled egg, fresh tomato, and a chunk of aish baladi (local flatbread). Earthy, filling, and ridiculously satisfying.

Taameya (Egyptian Falafel)

Not your average falafel. Egyptian taameya is made with crushed fava beans instead of chickpeas, then spiced with coriander and fried until golden. Crispy outside, green and fluffy inside. Often served in a sandwich with salad and tahini.

Sayadeya (Fisherman's Stew)

A coastal delicacy. This tomato-based seafood stew is seasoned with cinnamon, cardamom, garlic, and bay leaves, and usually includes a mix of local catch — think grouper, sea bream, or calamari — served over rice.

Grilled Red Sea Lobster or Shrimp

Fresh, simple, and the very definition of indulgent. Grilled with butter, garlic, and lemon or baked in foil with herbs and vegetables. No sauces. The sea does the talking here.

Zarb (Bedouin Barbecue)

Traditionally cooked underground in a sand oven, this mix of lamb, chicken, and vegetables comes out smoky, tender, and deeply spiced. Served with rice, fresh bread, and desert tea under the stars — it's more than a dish, it's a memory.

Aish Baladi

No Egyptian meal is complete without it. This whole wheat, pocket-style flatbread is baked in clay ovens and tastes best warm and torn by hand. You can use it as a fork, spoon, or plate.

Basbousa & Konafa

End on a sweet note. Basbousa is a semolina cake drenched in sugar syrup. Konafa is a crisp pastry nest stuffed with cream or nuts and drizzled with honey. One bite and you'll wonder why dessert ever ends.

The must-try dishes in Sharm el-Sheikh aren't just delicious — they're full of personality, history, and heart. Some come from desert fires. Others from boats still dripping with seawater. But each one offers a taste of something ancient and real. Don't rush. Don't hold back. Let the food tell you where you are.

Best Local Restaurants

If you want to understand a place, eat where its people eat. In Sharm el-Sheikh, beyond the polished resort buffets and international fine-dining lounges, there's a second food world — one that's cheaper, livelier, and infinitely more authentic. These are the restaurants where Egyptian families gather on Fridays, where drivers and shopkeepers grab lunch between shifts, and where seasoned travellers whisper, "This is the real stuff."

These spots may not always have English menus or polished interiors. But they'll give you flavour that sticks with you, and a peek into what dining in Egypt truly feels like when no one's trying to impress a tourist. Here's where you'll find tender kofta, bubbling molokhia, fried fish so fresh it still tastes like the sea, and stews that taste like home—if your home had an Egyptian grandmother.

Here are some of the best-loved local favourites in Sharm el-Sheikh:

El Masrien

📍 Old Market, Sharm el-Sheikh
El Masrien is where Egyptian families go to feast. Grilled meats, molokhia, rice-stuffed pigeons,

creamy hummus — it's all here, and always hot and generous. The place is loud, busy, and buzzing with life.

Fares Seafood

📍 Old Market & El Hadaba
Locals come here to pick their fish from the ice trays, then have it grilled or fried on the spot. Simple sides, fast service, and seafood that tastes like the Red Sea itself.

El Tekkia Restaurant

📍 Naama Bay
A humble-looking joint hiding serious flavour. Known for its kofta, kebab, and traditional Egyptian rice dishes. It's not fancy, but it's always full — for a reason.

Gad Restaurant

📍 Naama Bay
Part of a beloved Egyptian fast-food chain — but don't let that fool you. It's Egyptian fast food, which means koshari, taameya, hawawshi, and ful sandwiches made fresh and fast.

El Halaka

📍 Old Market
A hidden gem with no menu. You point at what you want—whole fish, crab, prawns—and they'll cook it their way. The atmosphere is relaxed, the pricing is reasonable, and the food? Pure Red Sea.

Koshary El Tahrir

📍 El Hadaba (newer branch)
One dish. Endless love. Egypt's most iconic street food — koshari — gets the spotlight here. Pasta, lentils, chickpeas, fried onions, and spicy tomato sauce piled into a bowl. It's loud, messy, and unforgettable.

The best local restaurants in Sharm aren't necessarily pretty. But they're real — full of tradition, community, and unapologetic flavour. If you want to know the city beyond the resorts, pull up a plastic chair, tear off a piece of baladi bread, and dig in.

Street Food Finds

Sharm el-Sheikh's street food isn't loud. It doesn't call out with flashing signs or trendy decor. But it smells incredible. Warm cumin. Crispy dough. Roasting meat. Sweet sugarcane juice. If you let your nose lead the way — especially after dark — you'll stumble into one of the city's best kept secrets: the unofficial food tour that begins after sunset.

Street food in Sharm is a world of its own. It's cheap, fast, and full of surprises. One night you're biting into a fresh hawawshi (minced meat-stuffed bread) from a cart near Naama Bay, the next, sipping fresh-squeezed sugarcane juice under neon lights in the Old Market. There's no map for this experience. You just walk, sniff, ask, and taste.

Whether you're looking for a quick bite between activities or want to eat like a local without breaking your budget, these are the street-side legends worth seeking out.

Taameya Sandwiches

These aren't your average falafel wraps. Egyptian taameya — made with fava beans — are greener, fluffier, and spicier than their Levantine cousins.

Fried to order, then wrapped with pickled vegetables, tahini, and fresh tomato.

Hawawshi

This is Egypt's answer to a meat pie. Spiced minced beef put into pita bread and baked or grilled until the edges are crunchy. It's greasy in the best way, with a kick of chili and onion.

Batata (Sweet Potato) Carts

You'll see them — metal carts with big, domed ovens built right in. Inside? Glowing coals and rows of sweet potatoes slowly roasting to caramelized perfection. Grab one, eat with your hands, smile.

Asab (Sugarcane Juice)

Thick, cold, and incredibly sweet, this juice is pressed right in front of you. It's the perfect refresher after a hot day or salty swim. Egyptians drink it like water — and once you taste it, you'll know why.

Egg Sandwiches and Ful Carts

Early in the morning or very late at night, you'll spot small carts serving ful Me dames (stewed fava beans) or fried eggs in buns with salt and black pepper. Cheap, filling, and strangely comforting.

Fresh Fruit Stalls

Watermelon wedges, sliced mango with chilli salt, and chilled guava are all served in plastic cups or paper cones. You eat it as you walk, sticky fingers and all.

Tip: Mango is king here. Don't leave without trying it.

In Sharm, street food is more than just a quick snack. It's a walk through a city's appetite — simple, flavorful, and always close at hand. Forget the white tablecloths and glowing menus. Here, your plate is wrapped in paper, your drink is pressed fresh, and your dining table is the sidewalk. And sometimes, that's exactly what you need.

Luxurious Dining by the Sea

There's something different about a meal when the sea is in front of you, the breeze is gentle, and every course feels like a celebration. In Sharm el-Sheikh, luxury dining isn't just about price — it's about place, atmosphere, and intention.

Whether you're celebrating a honeymoon, closing off your trip with a bang, or just craving something beyond the everyday, these venues deliver more than fine food — they offer culinary theatre under the stars. From fresh seafood brought out whole and grilled table-side, to multi-course Mediterranean journeys with wine pairings and linen napkins — here are the splurge-worthy spots that do it right.

Let's explore the most atmospheric, high-end places in Sharm where your dining experience will be just as memorable as the food.

Reef Grill (Four Seasons Resort)

📍 Sharks Bay
Tucked beside the water, lit by lanterns and the sound of waves, Reef Grill is upscale without being stuffy. The focus here is Mediterranean-inspired seafood — grilled octopus, prawn risotto, sea bass with citrus glaze — all artfully plated and fresh to the

last bite. Try their Lobster tagliatelle, and their signature seafood tower for two.

La Fleur (Royal Savoy Hotel)

📍 SOHO Square

An intimate fine-dining experience, La Fleur offers classic French cuisine with Egyptian warmth. Think filet mignon, duck à l'orange, escargot, and silky crème brûlée — all served in a quiet, romantic setting. Try their Steak au poivre and French onion soup.

Farsha Café (Cliffside Dining)

📍 El Fanar

Set into the cliffs of Ras Umm Sid, it offers low tables, cozy nooks, antique décor, and an open view of the Red Sea at sunset. The food is Middle Eastern fusion, but the real star is the view. Go ahead and try their Lamb tagine, mezze platters, and mint lemonade.

Il Frantoio (Savoy Sharm)

📍 SOHO Square

Step into Italy without leaving Sharm. Under a pergola covered with vines, Il Frantoio serves a sophisticated Tuscan menu that includes handcrafted pastas, slow-cooked meats, and well selected wines. Try their Osso buco, truffle ravioli, tiramisu.

Mahony Seafood

📍 Sharks Bay

A favourite for seafood lovers who want luxury without going overly formal. You pick your fish fresh from the catch of the day, and they prepare it grilled, baked, or fried to your liking — with sauces, salads, and dips that make the Red Sea proud. Their Grilled red snapper with lemon-butter sauce is a must-try.

Sometimes, a great meal is more than just great food — it's the glow of candlelight, the clink of glasses, the scent of salt in the air. These dining experiences offer more than luxury — they offer an atmosphere that lingers. So go ahead. Order the dessert. Watch the waves. Let the night stretch long and soft around you. In Sharm, the sea feeds more than your hunger — it feeds your soul.

Alcohol, Coffee, and Shisha Culture in Sharm

There are three things you'll see almost everywhere in Sharm once the sun dips low: soft coils of shisha smoke rising lazily into the night, the clink of glasses under moonlit patios, and the gentle steam of a strong Arabic coffee poured with care. This chapter isn't about partying or bar-hopping — it's about the quiet rituals and social rhythms that shape how locals and travelers wind down.

In Egypt, coffee is not just a drink, it's a mood. A mini-break. A social connector. A sign that time is slowing down just enough to talk. And while alcohol in Egypt is regulated and handled with discretion, Sharm — thanks to its global tourism culture — offers plenty of relaxed spots to enjoy a cocktail, a glass of wine, or a chilled beer without discomfort or judgement.

And then, there's shisha — known elsewhere as hookah or waterpipe. It's more than smoke. It's about conversation. About ritual. About stretching the night out a little longer with friends or strangers, often with mint tea or hibiscus on the side. Shisha cafes in Sharm come alive after dinner — not flashy or loud, just glowing embers, soft music, and laughter drifting under palm trees.

Coffee Culture: Where Time Slows Down

Egyptian coffee (Ahwa) is strong, small, and served in tiny cups — similar to Turkish style but with a slightly earthier flavour. Ask for it "masboot" (moderate sugar), "sada" (no sugar), or "zeeyada" (extra sweet). You'll also find Nescafé in many places (yes, it's a thing here), alongside espresso and cappuccino in international cafés.

Where to try:
- El Masrien Café in Old Market
- Café Chino at Four Seasons (elevated setting)
- Street kiosks for 10 EGP brews served with a nod

Alcohol in Sharm: What to Know

Egypt is a Muslim-majority country, but in tourist zones like Sharm, alcohol is widely available and accepted. You'll find it in:
- Most hotels and resort bars
- Licensed restaurants
- Duty-free shops (valid within 48 hours of arrival with your passport)

Popular Egyptian beers include Stella and Sakara, while local wines such as Omar Khayyam (red) or Obelisk (white) are passable — not world-class, but decent. Cocktails are generally sweeter and less alcoholic than you might expect elsewhere.

Top places for a drink with a view:
- The Terrace Bar at Movenpick
- Camel Bar Rooftop in Naama Bay
- Sky Lounge at Royal Savoy

Shisha: Slowing Down the Egyptian Way

Smoked through a waterpipe and flavored with everything from apple to mango to cappuccino, shisha is a social staple. Sessions can last an hour or more and often pair with storytelling, laughter, and music. Even if you're not a smoker, trying it once in a scenic café is part of soaking in the culture.

Top Shisha Spots in Sharm:
- Farsha Café (El Fanar) — open-air, cliffside magic
- El Mashrabeya Lounge in Old Market — more local, less touristy
- Café d'Orient in SOHO Square — chic with flavor options galore

Tips
1. Always ask for a fresh head and clean pipe.
2. If it's too strong, request apple-mint — the beginner's favorite.
3. Don't inhale like a cigarette. Sip, don't drag.

From tiny espresso cups clinking on marble tables to the soft gurgle of a shisha pipe under desert stars, Sharm's drink culture is all about rhythm and ritual. It's never rushed. It's about pausing — between dives, after dinner, before dancing — and letting life slow to a conversational simmer. Sipping, smoking, or simply soaking in the mood, you'll find that some of Sharm's richest moments don't come on a plate — they rise in a cup or cloud of smoke.

Vegan, Halal, and Gluten-Free

Sharm el-Sheikh may be a beach destination first, but its dining scene is impressively inclusive. Whether you're vegan by choice, halal by faith, or gluten-free by necessity, you won't have to settle or struggle. What makes it even better? The options here don't feel like compromises. They're colourful, flavourful, and prepared with great care.

Unlike many destinations that offer only one sad salad or a tired veggie burger, Sharm's restaurants — from street-side joints to upscale resorts — have adapted to the global palate of their visitors. Egyptian cuisine itself is naturally generous to plant-based and halal eaters. Think grilled eggplant with tahini, ful Me dames, lentil soup, and crispy taameya — dishes that are accidentally vegan, naturally halal, and absolutely delicious.

And if you need something gluten-free? More chefs here know the term than you'd expect. Many upscale spots have gluten-free pasta, flourless desserts, and even GF bread. Just don't be shy about asking — most waiters are trained to understand dietary terms, especially in hotel and tourist-heavy areas.

Let's break it down by category with specific places and insider tips.

Vegan & Plant-Based Eating

Egyptian food is a dream for vegans. Staples like koshari, lentil soup, and falafel are made without dairy or meat, and full of bold flavors. Many restaurants also offer fresh vegetable tagines, grilled veggie platters, and hummus-heavy mezze spreads.

Best places to try:

- El Masrien (Old Market) – hearty vegan Egyptian classics
- Zigolini Italian Restaurant (Savoy) – offers vegan risotto and grilled artichoke starters
- Vegan Corner at Tam Tam Restaurant (Naama Bay) – a small but thoughtful plant-based section

Local tip: Say "Ana nabaty" (I'm vegetarian) or "Ana nabaty gamed" (I'm vegan). It helps in local joints.

Halal-Friendly Food

Good news: practically all meat served in Sharm is halal by default, because Egypt is a Muslim-majority country. Still, if you want reassurance, most restaurants — especially mid-range to upscale — are happy to confirm it for you.

What's even better is that many resort chefs understand halal-specific nuances (no alcohol in sauces, no cross-contamination with pork). You'll also find alcohol-free zones, mocktail bars, and tea houses that allow for full, flavorful evenings — without compromising your beliefs.

Notable halal-conscious spots:

- El Kababgy (Rixos) – all meat is halal, and dishes are traditional
- Fairouz Lebanese Restaurant – full halal menu with mezze and charcoal-grilled meats
- Sahrawi Grill – a Bedouin experience with halal lamb and chicken stews under the stars

Gluten-Free in Sharm

Gluten-free isn't yet ubiquitous in Egypt, but in Sharm's resorts, upscale restaurants, and some modern cafés — you'll be in safe hands. Items are usually labeled, and staff will alert the chef if you mention celiac or gluten intolerance. Many hotels offer gluten-free bread, rice pasta, or quinoa-based dishes.

Best GF-friendly choices:

- Café Chino (Four Seasons) – offers GF cakes, muffins, and almond flour pancakes

- Sanafir Restaurant – gluten-free grilled fish, rice dishes, and fresh salads
- Viva Bar (SOHO Square) – gluten-free options on request for burgers and wraps

Sharm el-Sheikh may be known for diving and desert sunsets, but its culinary inclusivity deserves applause too. You won't feel like a burden or a picky eater here. With a little awareness and a curious spirit, you'll find that even on the edge of the Sinai, your plate can reflect your needs and your tastes.

CHAPTER 7:
CULTURAL EXPERIENCES

For all its glittering resorts and underwater marvels, Sharm el-Sheikh has roots — deep ones. You may not see them on a glossy brochure or through your snorkel mask, but they're here: woven into the carpets of Bedouin tents, echoing through mosque domes, painted in the hands of local artisans, and carried in the rhythm of old desert songs. To truly know Sharm, you have to pause the sightseeing and let the place speak in its own quiet, soulful language.

This chapter invites you to step beyond the "holiday" version of Sharm and connect with the living culture beneath the surface. It's not about museums with velvet ropes or performances staged for tourists — it's about sipping tea with a Bedouin elder, wandering through street art in the Old Market, hearing stories passed down over charcoal fire, or running your fingers across hand-loomed fabric in a market stall.

You'll discover the places, people, and moments that can't be booked on an app — but stay with you far longer than any excursion. These are the experiences that make your trip feel human, personal, and unexpectedly moving.

Meet the Bedouins

You haven't really felt the Sinai until you've sat with the people who've called it home for centuries. The Bedouins — often romanticized in travel brochures as desert wanderers — are in fact real families, storytellers, camel herders, and craftsmen who have adapted to this arid land with quiet resilience and unmistakable grace.

When you visit a Bedouin camp near Sharm, you're not just going for dinner. You're stepping into a rhythm of life that moves slower, listens deeper, and values conversation over performance. You'll be welcomed not with fanfare but with fresh tea steeped in desert herbs, a simple cushion to sit on, and often, the warmth of a soft-spoken elder who introduces you to their way of life — not as a museum piece, but as something living, shared, and sacred.

Most Bedouin experiences include:

- Traditional tea brewed with desert sage or hibiscus
- Flatbread baked fresh over coals
- Optional camel rides through the dunes
- Music around the fire — not loud, just human: a hand drum, a song, sometimes silence

What makes these nights so powerful is how unforced they feel. You may hear stories about sandstorms and stars. You may eat lentils or lamb cooked beneath the sand. And when you look up at a sky so clear it feels unreal, you begin to understand why the Bedouins have always looked to the stars — for direction, for poetry, for peace.

Where to go:

- Wadi Mandar Desert Camp is a popular site known for its genuineness and kindness.
- Bedouin Dinner Tours through reputable agencies like Sharm Station or Sinai Adventure

Local Tips

1. Bring a jacket — desert nights can be chilly.
2. Respect is everything. Dress modestly, ask before photos, and come to listen more than you speak.

In a place where five-star buffets and poolside cocktails come easy, a quiet night under a canvas of stars with strangers who feel like old friends is something you won't forget. It's one of the few moments where time slows down, phones go away, and you simply exist — eye to eye with someone whose world is different from yours, but no less real.

Art, Music, and Handicrafts

Beneath the polished resort experience and glossy tourist tours, Sharm el-Sheikh hums with creativity — quiet, handmade, and deeply rooted in Sinai identity. You won't find massive galleries or flashy art fairs here. What you'll find instead is something more human: a woven rug dyed with desert herbs, a melody carried by oud strings, a hand-stitched bag made by a grandmother who learned from hers.

While Cairo and Alexandria may lead the way in Egypt's modern art scene, Sharm speaks a different artistic dialect. It's less about trends and more about heritage — the kind passed down, not published. Local artists here don't compete for headlines. They sell their works at market stalls, paint murals in old alleys, or perform live with a drum and a heart full of song.

If you're willing to look beyond the postcards, there's a quiet world of authentic expression waiting for you to notice it.

Handicrafts Worth More Than a Souvenir

In Sharm's Old Market or local artisan stalls, you'll find:

- Beaded jewelry crafted by Bedouin women — not mass-produced, each piece tells a story.
- Woven camel-wool rugs and totes fashioned with traditional Sinai patterns and earthy dyes.
- Copper lamps pierced with constellations are manufactured in workshops hidden behind cafes.

Insider tip: The best souvenirs aren't found in hotel shops. Ask your tour guide where local women sell — or go to El Fanar's hillside bazaars where real artisans showcase their work.

The Music You Didn't Expect to Find

You might stumble into a soft live performance at SOHO Square, or hear oud and tabla rhythms at a Bedouin campfire. But beyond the tourist soundtrack, there are voices worth listening for.

Occasionally, smaller venues and cultural nights will host:

- Traditional Bedouin singers, using poetry and rhythm to tell stories of love, land, and longing.
- Sufi musicians, whose trance-like chanting and slow, sacred drumbeats create a moving atmosphere.

- Young Egyptian fusion artists blending Arabic instruments with jazz, blues, or house beats.

Ask locals at Farsha Café or Camel Bar if any underground shows or folk nights are planned. You might just find yourself sitting cross-legged in a lantern-lit room, listening to a voice you'll never forget.

Now, too many travelers walk away with plastic pyramids and fake papyrus. You can do better. Take time to talk to the artisans. Let them explain the story behind the pattern on that cushion or the prayer hidden in that bracelet's knots. Every item made by hand carries not just material, but memory — of place, of craft, of a human being making beauty in their own way.

In a city best known for coral reefs and cocktails, the soul of Sharm still speaks in handmade patterns and quiet melodies. It doesn't shout, and it doesn't sell itself loudly. But for travelers with open eyes and curious hearts, the art here isn't just local — it's alive.

Museums and Galleries

In Sharm el-Sheikh, history doesn't announce itself with grandeur. It waits — tucked into modest buildings, behind museum doors that most tourists walk past. But if you give it your time, Sharm will show you that its soul runs far deeper than its resorts. These small but significant museums and galleries are windows into the stories, beliefs, and brilliance that shaped Egypt and the Sinai.

Here's where to go when you want to feel connected to the land, its people, and their heritage — beyond the beach towel and snorkel gear.

Sharm el-Sheikh Museum

The city's most important cultural institution. Opened in 2020, this modern museum is home to over 5,000 artifacts from across Egypt's dynastic and Greco-Roman periods. You'll walk through well-lit halls filled with ancient tools, mummified animals, pharaonic jewelry, and displays explaining daily life in early Egypt. Visit for a deeper understanding of Egypt's civilization without leaving Sharm.

King Tut Museum

Located within the Genena City complex, this boutique museum offers a unique opportunity to view high-quality replicas of Tutankhamun's treasures. From his golden mask to his bed, the detail is remarkable and educational — especially if you're not heading to Cairo's Egyptian Museum. Visit for a brilliant introduction to Egypt's most famous boy king.

Fantastic Bombastic Bazar

Part art gallery, part treasure hunt, this quirky space combines handmade crafts with colorful local design. While not officially a museum, it's a gallery of living culture, showcasing Sinai textiles, pottery, metalwork, and beadwork created by regional artisans. Visit for one-of-a-kind items and a glimpse into the local artistic community.

Tip: Ask the staff about the stories behind specific items — many have cultural meaning.

St. Catherine Artisan Shop

A small, quiet gallery connected to the broader cultural legacy of St. Catherine's Monastery. It offers sacred icons, hand-woven rugs, and items inspired by ancient Christian and Bedouin traditions of Sinai.

This is a special area to connect with the Sinai Peninsula's spiritual side.

Tip: Buy directly from monastery-affiliated outlets for authenticity.

Quick Tips

1. Most museums are compact — visits take about 1–2 hours.
2. Entry is affordable, but cash is usually required.
3. English descriptions are limited, so consider using a translation app or short audio guide.
4. Early morning or just after lunch are the best times for quiet visits.

Sharm el-Sheikh may be better known for sun and sea than museums, but don't overlook these cultural gems. They offer something no tour ever can: a slow, thoughtful dive into the heart of Egypt — through relics, rituals, and the hands that still create. Spend a little time with these quiet storytellers, and Sharm will feel even more alive.

Festivals and National Holidays in Sharm

Throughout the year, a collection of festivals and national holidays quietly transform Sharm's streets, skies, and spirit. These are the moments when the city reveals a different side—slower, more reflective, and deeply connected to both Egyptian identity and global celebration.

From spring picnics and jazz under the stars to film festivals and youth summits, these events offer travellers the chance to witness Sharm not as a tourist product—but as a place where people gather, create, honour, and rejoice. If you plan your visit to coincide with any of these dates, you may just leave with more than memories—you'll leave with a story.

Sinai Liberation Day – April 25

Commemorating the final withdrawal of Israeli forces from the Sinai Peninsula in 1982, this day carries deep regional significance. In Sharm, expect Egyptian flags on balconies, school-free streets, and low-key parades, especially around Nabq and the Old Market. It's a good day to visit a museum, sit at a local café, and observe a softer city rhythm.

Sham al-Nessim – Spring Picnic Day

Falling the day after Orthodox Easter, this national holiday celebrates the arrival of spring. Families gather in public gardens and on beaches, bringing food baskets filled with eggs, salted fish, and bread. In Sharm, the atmosphere is light, casual, and joyful—perfect for picnicking by the sea or strolling through local markets where vendors sell seasonal treats.

Red Sea Jazz Festival (Dates Vary)

An open-air music event that brings regional and international jazz musicians to Sharm's breezy coast. Held in venues like SOHO Square or beachside stages, this laid-back festival fills the night with saxophone solos, acoustic sets, and wine-sipping under the stars. It's ideal for travellers looking to unwind with smooth music and coastal air.

Sharm el-Sheikh International Film Festival – Late June to Early July

This growing cultural event showcases films from Egypt, Africa, and around the world. Screenings, talks, and red carpet nights turn Sharm into a surprising hotspot for cinema lovers. Events are often hosted in resort venues, cultural halls, and Genena City, with many open to the public.

Shopping & Tourism Festival – July to August

A high-energy summer festival where retail meets performance. Expect pop-up stalls in Naama Bay, discounts in local shops, folkloric dances, food tastings, and themed nights in resorts. It's a perfect time to grab authentic gifts, enjoy live music, and soak in Sharm's festive spirit after dark.

World Youth Forum – November

Hosted annually in Sharm, this major international event invites youth leaders, entrepreneurs, and change-makers from over 100 countries. While most of the sessions are closed to the public, the city buzzes with cultural exchange, security presence, and side events—concerts, exhibitions, and guest speakers often spill over into the city.

Key Egyptian National Holidays (Observed in Sharm)

Revolution Day (January 25 & July 23) – Streets are decorated with flags; museums may host themed exhibits.

Armed Forces Day (October 6) – Commemorative events, especially near government buildings and public squares.

Eid al-Fitr & Eid al-Adha – These Islamic holidays shift yearly, but mark the end of Ramadan and the feast of sacrifice. Expect large family gatherings, closed shops, and overcrowded mosques.

Islamic New Year & Prophet Muhammad's Birthday – Observed with spiritual music, sermons, and modest public decorations.

You can snorkel through coral gardens and sip cocktails by the sea—but until you've watched Sharm pause for reflection, light up for a jazz night, or hum with youth from every continent, you haven't seen all it has to offer. Time your visit with a festival or national holiday, and you'll experience something deeper: the heartbeat of a city in celebration.

Unique Finds and Best Souvenirs

Let's be honest — no one travels all the way to the Sinai just to return home with a plastic camel or mass-printed "I ♥ Egypt" t-shirt. Sharm el-Sheikh may not have sprawling artisan districts like Cairo, but if you know where to look, you can find souvenirs that carry a real piece of the land, the culture, and the people behind them.

Forget the factory-made fluff. This chapter helps you find items that hold meaning. Think hand-embroidered Bedouin scarves, hand-poured essential oils, rare desert spices, and stones from the very mountains where prophets once walked. Sharm's Old Market, local artisan corners, and even a few hidden shops in SOHO Square offer treasures that tell a story — not just fill a suitcase.

Here are the top unforgettable things to look for when souvenir hunting in Sharm:

1. Bedouin Handicrafts

These aren't just souvenirs — they're time capsules of tradition. Look for:

- Embroidered scarves and shawls in bold, symbolic patterns

- Beaded bracelets and necklaces, often made by Bedouin women cooperatives
- Woven camel bags and fabric wallets stitched with Sinai motifs

Where to find it: Bedouin stands at the Old Market, Wadi Mandar, and desert dinner camps (ask to buy directly from the women).

2. Oils, Perfumes & Incense

Egyptian perfumery has ancient roots. In Sharm, you'll find:

- Pure lotus oil, said to calm the mind
- Jasmine or sandalwood essence, used in traditional relaxation rituals
- Frankincense and myrrh resins—once presented to pharaohs—are now available in small jars

Where to find it: Cleopatra Bazaar (Old Market), SOHO Square shops, or "The House of Oils" near Hadaba.

3. Sinai Spices & Herbal Teas

From hand-ground sumac to dried hibiscus petals used in karkadeh (a popular Egyptian tea), spice shops in Sharm offer an aromatic souvenir for your kitchen back home.

Tip: Look for tea blends used by Bedouins—especially mixes with desert sage, mint, or aniseed.

4. Hand-Blown Glass and Copper Lanterns

These dazzling items aren't just beautiful — they're handcrafted art. You'll find:

- Miniature glass perfume bottles
- Traditional copper lanterns with intricate cut-outs that throw dancing shadows on walls
- Hookah bases in swirled blues and golds (even if you're not a smoker, they make striking décor)

Where to find it: Genena City stalls, some upscale stores in Naama Bay, or boutique artisan pop-ups.

5. Religious Symbols and Stones

Whether you're spiritual or just love sacred artifacts, you'll find:

- Crosses or prayer beads from St. Catherine's Monastery

- Semi-precious stones from the Sinai Mountains (turquoise is the prize)
- Handmade miniature icons or tiny mosaic works crafted by monks

Where to find it: Church-affiliated stores, monastery gift shops, or vendors near Mount Sinai day trips.

6. Desert Photography Prints

Local photographers capture breathtaking desert landscapes — sunrises over Mount Sinai, Bedouin silhouettes against an orange sky, camels crossing rippled dunes. Their prints, sold at select galleries or cafés like Farsha, make for personal, framable keepsakes.

7. Natural Skincare and Wellness Products

Thanks to the region's salt, minerals, and herbs, you'll find:

- Dead Sea mud masks and bath salts
- Sinai clay scrubs
- Olive oil soaps made in nearby Dahab

Where to find it: Organic stalls at Naama Bay or Nabq, wellness shops in resort areas.

Souvenirs should whisper stories — not scream tourist. And in Sharm, you'll find plenty of objects that do just that. Every woven bracelet, grain of spice, or drop of essential oil is a thread connecting you to this place. Take home something made with hands, heart, and heritage — and your memories will last even longer than your tan.

CHAPTER 8:
DAY TRIPS AND HIDDEN GEMS

There's a secret truth about Sharm el-Sheikh: its most unforgettable moments often happen outside the tourist zones. While the beaches and resorts are the city's crown, its soul stretches beyond the coast — into canyons painted by ancient winds, mountain monasteries that echo with silence, and quiet desert paths where Bedouins still live by the stars. This chapter is your invitation to step off the brochure page and discover what most visitors never see.

Day trips from Sharm aren't just about changing scenery — they change your relationship with the land. A morning spent at Mount Sinai doesn't feel like sightseeing; it feels like time travel. A walk through the Colored Canyon isn't just a hike; it's a conversation with the Earth. And then there are the soft surprises: a local spice farm tucked behind palm groves, a beach where no signs point the way, a family-run cafe with the best tea you didn't know you needed.

This isn't about ticking boxes. It's about breathing in a part of Sinai that most people overlook — the wild edges, the quiet corners, the places where you feel more than you see.

The Colored Canyon

Just under two hours from the shimmer of Sharm's coastline lies something you wouldn't expect in Egypt — a sandstone labyrinth carved by time, wind, and silence. The Colored Canyon is not just a geological wonder; it's a moment of awe. Imagine weaving through narrow sandstone walls streaked in hues of rust, gold, rose, and deep amber. No two steps look the same. No camera can quite capture it. It's more than just a site to see; it's a place to experience.

Unlike other canyons around the world, the Colored Canyon doesn't overwhelm with size. It stuns with texture and intimacy. The winding passageways force you to slow down, duck, squeeze, and observe. There's something humbling about walking inside rock that's millions of years old — and yet feels alive with color and quiet. In some sections, the walls close in just wide enough for one person to pass. The silence is total. The temperature drops. And for a moment, you are completely and gloriously elsewhere.

Getting there requires an early start — typically by 4x4 or in a guided tour that includes nearby sites like the Blue Hole or Nuweiba. Most tours depart around 7:00 AM and return by mid-afternoon. The journey itself is part of the experience: dramatic desert roads, herds of camels in the distance, the occasional Bedouin boy waving by the roadside. Tour guides often include a light breakfast or tea in a desert tent before the trek begins. Once on-site, the hike takes about 1.5–2 hours, depending on the route and pace. It's not overly strenuous, but closed shoes, water, and a hat are essentials.

Quick Tips:

1. Best time to go is October to April — avoid summer heat.
2. The journey is easy to moderate (not suitable for those with limited mobility).
3. Bring Water, walking shoes with grip, sunscreen, and a light scarf (for sun or dust).
4. Ask your guide about the folklore behind the canyon's colors — many say it's nature's answer to a forgotten sea.

The Colored Canyon is a reminder that Egypt's magic isn't confined to pyramids or coastlines. It's here, in the rustle of sandstone beneath your boots and the whisper of time between canyon walls. It's the kind of place that stays with you long after you've left — not because of what you saw, but because of what it made you feel.

Dahab for the Day

If Sharm el-Sheikh is Egypt's polished resort gem, then Dahab is its barefoot cousin — slower, softer, and infinitely cooler without even trying. Just a 90-minute drive up the coast, Dahab isn't a day trip. It's a vibe. A little seaside town that draws in divers, yogis, backpackers, and creatives from all over the world — not with glitz, but with soul.

Here, time doesn't race — it strolls. You'll find oceanfront cafés where the waiters might be barefoot and the pillows more inviting than the chairs. You'll hear reggae and Arabic oud music in the same stretch of shoreline. Street dogs nap in the shade next to macrame stands. Shops sell handmade jewelry alongside dive fins and hammocks. There's a sense of freedom here — to wander, to talk to strangers, to sit still. Even the sea in Dahab feels different — calmer, clearer, more generous.

If you're coming just for the day, start early. It's best to leave Sharm by 6:30–7:00 AM, either by private car, hotel-arranged taxi, or minivan tour. The drive is scenic and quiet, trailing the Gulf of Aqaba with the Saudi mountains in the distance. Once in Dahab, make your way to the Lighthouse Reef area — perfect for snorkelling, lunch, and lazy strolling. Grab breakfast at Everyday Café (incredibly chilled with sea views), then wander through the art stalls along the boardwalk. You might lose time sipping a hibiscus tea on the cushions at Ralph's German Bakery, watching kitesurfers skim the water.

If you're up for something active, take a dive or try a freediving taster session — Dahab is one of the world's top freediving spots, especially at the Blue Hole. Don't worry, you don't have to go deep. Even snorkelling here feels like swimming in a postcard. Prefer to keep it dry? Rent a bike and ride among the palm groves, or participate in a brief desert yoga practice under the golden light of sunset.

The town is compact, friendly, and feels safe — even if you're wandering solo. Most locals speak English, and the vibe is always welcoming without being pushy. Leave by sunset to return to Sharm before dark, or stay for dinner and drive back in the evening with a heart full of peace and sand still on your sandals.

Tips

1. Getting there: 1.5–2 hours from Sharm by car. Buses are available but slow and unreliable.
2. Best day to go: Tuesday or Thursday — less crowded, more local.

3. Bring your swimsuit, towel, cash (many spots don't take cards), and flip-flops.

Dahab is not a place you go to "see things." It's a place you go to feel lighter. For a day, you get to forget what time it is, talk to strangers, eat with your hands, and watch the Red Sea change color with the sun. It's not about checking something off your list — it's about remembering what it feels like to truly unwind.

Saint Catherine's Monastery

Not all holy places shout. Some whisper. And none whisper more powerfully than Saint Catherine's Monastery, hidden in the shadow of Mount Sinai where prophets once stood barefoot on sacred ground. This is not just a historical site — it's one of the oldest continuously operating Christian monasteries in the world. And stepping into it feels like walking into a moment that's been quietly burning for 17 centuries.

Tucked into the desert folds at the foot of Mount Sinai, the monastery is surrounded by towering peaks and a silence so profound, even time seems to slow down. Founded in the 6th century by order of Emperor Justinian, this UNESCO World Heritage site has survived centuries of conflict, sandstorms, and changing empires. Yet its walls still stand — protecting an unparalleled collection of early Christian manuscripts, rare icons, and the famous Burning Bush, believed by many to be the very one through which God spoke to Moses.

Visiting Saint Catherine's isn't like visiting a museum. It's more like being granted an audience with history. Inside, you'll find narrow stone corridors, flickering candlelight, and monks in black robes moving with quiet grace. The monastery library is second only to the Vatican in the size and importance of its ancient religious texts. The chapel is modest but full of spiritual weight. And then there's the garden — small, but growing life in the middle of desolation.

Most tours to the monastery begin in the early morning or overnight, especially for those planning to climb Mount Sinai before sunrise — a physically demanding but deeply emotional experience. If you're only visiting the monastery, you can depart Sharm by 5:00–6:00 AM and return by late afternoon. The drive is about 3–4 hours through desert mountain roads, often accompanied by a local Bedouin guide who'll share insights along the way.

You'll need your passport to get past checkpoints, and appropriate attire (modest, with shoulders and knees covered) is expected inside the grounds. Photography is restricted in some areas, so always ask before you raise your camera. And don't rush. This is a place meant for stillness, not selfies.

Tips

1. Best time to visit: October to April. Avoid mid-summer — temperatures soar.
2. Entry Fee is around 100–150 EGP per person (subject to change)

3. Opening hours are generally between 9 AM – 12 PM, Monday through Saturday (closed Sundays and during religious ceremonies)

4. Bring your passport, modest clothing, water, and something warm if you're climbing Mount Sinai (it gets cold before sunrise).

Saint Catherine's Monastery doesn't try to impress you. It doesn't need to. Its power lies in its endurance — in the quiet crackle of centuries still alive within its walls. A visit here won't just add to your trip; it may reframe it entirely, reminding you that in the middle of nowhere, something eternal still burns.

Nabq Protected Area

Just when you think Sharm has shown you all its shades of blue and gold, you discover Nabq — a vast, wild stretch of coastline that feels like the Red Sea remembering what it was before the hotels. Located about 35 minutes north of Naama Bay, Nabq Protected Area is where the desert meets the sea with no filter, no crowds, and no rush. This isn't a tourist site. It's a living ecosystem, a raw, untamed place that rewards those who come not to conquer it, but to listen.

Nabq is one of Egypt's largest coastal nature reserves, covering over 600 square kilometres of desert, coral reef, mountain, and forest. Yes, forest — specifically mangrove forest, the northernmost in the Indian Ocean ecosystem. Here, you can walk through shallow waters where salt-tolerant trees grow against all odds, roots twisting like ancient fingers. Tiny crabs scurry beneath your feet. Birds glide above. It's one of the few places in the Sinai where you feel completely enveloped by nature, not just observing it from a distance.

But there's more to Nabq than mangroves. You'll find sand dunes sculpted by the wind, secluded beaches with untouched coral gardens, and Bedouin camps offering tea and stories if you stop to chat.

Wildlife lovers might spot herons, ospreys, or even desert foxes. The area is also home to the wreck of the Maria Schroeder, a cargo ship abandoned on the reef decades ago — now rusted, eerie, and quietly beautiful at low tide.

You can visit Nabq on your own by taxi or 4x4 (permits are needed), but the best experience comes through an eco-tour with a licensed guide. Many trips include lunch cooked Bedouin-style on an open fire, snorkelling in calm waters, and a sunset pause so quiet you can hear your breath. No vendors. No thumping music. Just sea, sand, wind, and sky — as it's always been.

Helpful Tips

1. Permit required: Entry is regulated; your guide or hotel can arrange one.
2. Best time to visit: November to April, especially early morning or just before sunset.
3. What to bring: Reef-safe sunscreen, water shoes, binoculars, long-sleeved shirt for sun, and minimal plastic waste.
4. How to book: Look for eco-focused operators, such as Sharm Eco Tours or Bedouin Experience Egypt.

Nabq isn't here to impress you. It's here to remind you what the world looks like when left alone — and

how deeply human it feels to walk through it gently. Spend a few hours in Nabq, and you'll realise that solitude isn't empty; it's full of everything that matters.

Quiet Beaches Locals Keep to Themselves

Most visitors to Sharm stick to hotel strips and the same handful of crowded bays — because that's what the guidebooks tell them. But if you talk to someone who lives here, they'll point you toward a different shoreline. A place where the waves are louder than the tourists. Where no one tries to sell you a massage. And where, for a few hours, it feels like you've discovered your own private Egypt.

These are the quiet beaches locals keep off the radar — not because they're secret, but because they're sacred in a different way. Fewer beach beds, fewer phones, more sky. You won't find signs pointing to them. Some have no names on Google Maps. But they exist — and once you've been to one, even for an hour, you'll understand why they keep coming back.

Here are the lesser-known beaches locals love — and how to find them without making a scene of it:

Ras Nasrani Beach

Tucked behind a cluster of villas near the airport road, Ras Nasrani is where many local divers go to unwind between shifts. It's raw and rocky in places, but the water is spectacular — turquoise fading into deep indigo, with coral reefs just a few kicks from the shore. No umbrellas, no music, no crowds.

How to get there: Ask a local taxi to drop you near Coral Beach Montazah. Walk past the dive centers and follow the trail down. No entry fee.

Aqaba Coastline Stretch (North of Nabq)

If you're up for a mini adventure, this stretch north of Nabq is the wildest part of the coast. There are sand banks, shallow lagoons, and untouched reefs — perfect for introverts, nature photographers, or anyone needing a full reset. Sometimes, you'll see Bedouins camping here with their goats. If you're lucky, you'll be invited for tea.

How to get there: A 4x4 vehicle and a guide are required, especially if you are unfamiliar with the trip. Visit early in the morning and bring everything you need — there are no shops, shelters, or bathrooms.

Hadaba Public Beach (Next to El Fanar)

This is one of Sharm's best-kept "known" secrets. Locals come here to swim before work or sip tea at sunset. It's adjacent to El Fanar Beach but without the ticket booth. Expect basic conditions — a simple shoreline, maybe a small shack selling drinks — but incredible views, especially at golden hour.

How to get there: Head to Hadaba. Just past El Fanar lighthouse, look for the open sandy access trail on your right.

Sharm el-Maya Bay (Far Corner)

While the marina end of Sharm el-Maya is all cruise ships and bustle, the far eastern corner of the bay is rarely visited. The water is glassy, calm and shallow — locals bring their kids here to learn swimming, or come alone to sit on the rocks and stare at the sea. Ideal for introverts or anyone craving silence with a view.

How to get there: Head toward Sharm Old Market. Walk or drive east along the shoreline until it thins out. No signage — just quiet.

Quick Tips

1. These beaches don't have lifeguards, facilities, or restaurants — so pack snacks, water, and sunscreen.
2. locals treasure these beaches for their peace. Keep noise low, clean up after yourself, and don't bring music unless using headphones.

The quiet beaches of Sharm don't try to entertain you. They invite you to unplug, listen, float, breathe, and remember that stillness is also a destination. You don't need infinity pools or DJs. Just salt on your skin, wind in your hair, and a stretch of sand where the only footprints are yours.

Spice Shops, Local Farms, and Other Unexpected Stops

Not every travel memory is loud. Sometimes, the moments that stay with you aren't the iconic landmarks or the glossy excursions — they're the quiet detours, the places you found by accident, and the flavors you can still taste weeks later. Sharm el-Sheikh has plenty of surprises waiting between the headlines, and this subchapter is a love letter to the understated corners that don't show up on TikTok — but should.

Start with the spice shops. You'll smell them before you see them — especially near the Old Market. Step inside one of the older stores (preferably the ones with faded signs and too many jars), and you'll be pulled into a fragrant world of cardamom, cumin, hibiscus, fenugreek, cinnamon, cloves, and saffron. Ask the vendor about desert herbal remedies, or how the Bedouins brew their teas, and suddenly you're learning something you won't find in a guidebook. If you're lucky, they'll mix a personal blend just for you.

Then there are the local farms — humble, sun-soaked spaces on the outskirts of Sharm that grow far more than you'd expect in desert soil. A few are open to visitors, especially those that supply organic produce to eco-lodges and high-end restaurants. You can taste tomatoes still warm from the sun, sip mint straight from the source, or even help bake flatbread in traditional outdoor ovens. These experiences are especially rich if you're traveling with children or just want a break from hotel life. Ask your hotel or a local guide to arrange a visit to a farm in the Wadi Kid or Nabq outskirts — the farmers are generous, and the silence out there is priceless.

But the unexpected doesn't stop at spices and farms. There's the local honey shop tucked behind a mosque in Hadaba, run by a former beekeeper who'll let you taste rare black honey on a piece of warm pita. Or the tiny herb garden at a women's cooperative, where you can buy dried mint, handmade soaps, and salves that smell like the Sinai wind. There's even a shoemaker in Old Market who still hand-stitches sandals from camel leather, if you ask the right person for directions.

Quick Tips

1. Best spice shops: Look for "El Maleka Herbs" or "Dr. Hawas Spices" near the Old Market — but ask locals for smaller, family-run alternatives.
2. Farm visits: Not advertised online. Ask a tour guide or your hotel concierge to arrange something authentic. Eco-hotels in Nabq may offer this too.

3. Shopping etiquette: Bargaining is expected in spice shops, but do so kindly. Ask to smell spices before you buy, and always go with small bills.
4. Bring a cloth pouch or container for loose herbs to avoid plastic packaging.

Sometimes, the soul of a place reveals itself in the smallest of moments — the swirl of cinnamon in desert air, the taste of fresh thyme on warm bread, the hush of a farm where time moves slowly. In these forgotten corners of Sharm, you'll find memories you never planned to make — and that's the whole point.

CHAPTER 9:
NIGHTLIFE IN SHARM

Sharm el-Sheikh doesn't go to sleep when the sun sets—it transforms. What feels like a sun-soaked beach town by day becomes something else entirely after dark. There's a rhythm in the air, a glow on the water, and a kind of open invitation. Whether you're looking to dance until dawn, sip something cold under the stars, or simply walk along a quiet promenade lit by warm lanterns, Sharm offers a nighttime experience that matches every mood.

The beauty of Sharm's nightlife is its range. You can start your evening barefoot on the sand at a candlelit beach lounge and end it in a laser-lit open-air club, shoulder to shoulder with dancers from around the world. Or do the opposite—begin with street food and live oud music at the Old Market and end in silence on your hotel balcony, watching the desert stars.

In this chapter, we'll take you beyond the brochures and give you a look at where the real magic happens after dark—from the beach clubs locals actually love, to secret rooftop cafes, cultural performances, sunset cocktails, and night markets that stay alive well past bedtime.

Beach Clubs and Lounges

When the air cools and the sea darkens into a mirror of stars, Sharm's beach clubs come alive—not in a loud, rowdy way, but with a low pulse of music, movement, and mood. This isn't just nightlife—it's shoreline therapy, served with neon cocktails, bare feet, and the scent of salt and incense. Whether you're here to dance, drift, or people-watch with a drink in hand, Sharm's beach lounges and clubs offer a scene that's both electric and oddly personal.

Start with Terrazzina Beach Club—arguably the most iconic in the city. Located in Sharm el-Maya near the Old Market, Terrazzina feels like the heartbeat of local nightlife. During the day it's a relaxed beach hangout, but come nightfall, it turns into a fully open-air party zone with international DJs, fire shows, belly dancers, and a crowd that mixes locals with savvy travelers. Fridays are legendary here. You'll dance barefoot on the sand with glowing wristbands, and you'll probably stay later than you planned.

Then there's Vive Beach Club in Hadaba, more upscale and intimate, known for its sleek design, smooth electronic playlists, and a crowd that leans into sunset cocktails and low-key glamour. If you want to sip a well-crafted mojito on a linen daybed with ambient lighting and a curated soundtrack, this is your spot. It's the kind of place where birthdays, proposals, and last-night-of-the-trip memories tend to happen.

For something more social and less curated, Farsha Mountain Lounge blurs the line between cafe, lounge, and spiritual time warp. Built on a cliff in Ras Umm Sid with rugs, lanterns, and multi-level seating carved into the rock, Farsha isn't loud—but it's unforgettable. Shisha, mint tea, soft house beats, and the best Red Sea view in the city. You may not dance here, but you will feel completely present.

If you want more club than lounge, Little Buddha Sharm near Naama Bay ramps up the excitement with a spectacular indoor/outdoor dance space, sushi bar and a regular line-up of international DJs. Expect a crowd that's dressed to impress, laser lights that fill the sky, and beats that don't quit until 4 AM.

Looking for something less known? Pataya Beach Club, a bit off the main tourist radar, offers sunset chill mixed with surprise themed nights. From salsa evenings to silent discos, it's worth checking the schedule in advance. It sits along the Nabq coast and has a more relaxed dress code, ideal if you're coming straight from the sea.

Quick Tips

1. Terrazzina and Little Buddha may charge a cover (100–300 EGP depending on the event). Others are free with drinks or table bookings.
2. Dress codes: Beachy-chic is fine in most spots. Little Buddha and Vive lean toward smart casual.
3. Thursday and Friday nights are busiest, but Sundays often have locals-only vibes and better service.
4. Call ahead or book via WhatsApp for reserved seating, especially for sunset tables at Vive.

From barefoot fire shows to rooftop lounges carved into cliffs, Sharm's nightlife is as varied as the travelers who find it. Whether you want to dance, daydream, or simply drink something cold with your feet in the sand, the night always has a place for you here—somewhere between the beat and the breeze.

Live Music and Cultural Shows Under the Stars

Not every night in Sharm requires blazing lights and thudding sound. Some of the most memorable evenings here unfold beneath the stars, with a violin playing in the background, or a drumbeat echoing off the mountains. This is where music meets memory, and where culture isn't a museum display — it's something you feel in your chest. If you're the kind of traveler who lives for authentic sound and slow wonder, this is your scene.

Begin with Alf Leila Wa Leila (1001 Nights) in Hadaba. Yes, it's built for tourists — but don't dismiss it just yet. This open-air cultural complex hosts nightly performances that blend whirling dervishes, Bedouin storytelling, belly dancers, horse shows, and live Nubian music into a spectacle that's more theatrical than cheesy. The architecture is inspired by Egyptian palaces, complete with arched walkways, lantern-lit courtyards, and mosaics. It's a visual feast, and a surprisingly touching introduction to Egypt's performance traditions.

For something more acoustic and improvised, head to Camel Bar Rooftop in Naama Bay on a Wednesday or Saturday. They host unplugged sets by local musicians, some Egyptian, some international. The vibe is cozy, not crowded. Think candlelit tables, cold beers, and voices that carry across the warm night air. From indie folk to Arabic soul, the setlist changes often — but the atmosphere stays golden. It's especially beautiful when paired with a rooftop sunset.

SOHO Square, usually known for its modern lights and international restaurants, also hosts occasional cultural nights. You might catch a Tanoura dancer spinning in a blur of color, or a live tabla performance outside the fountain area. The experience is more spontaneous than scheduled — just wander and let the sound find you.

If you're lucky, you may even get invited to a private Bedouin evening in the desert — arranged through trusted guides. These often feature live drumming, poetry, tea under the stars, and a fire-lit silence that feels like ancient magic. No amplifiers. No stage. Just rhythm, sky, and sand.

Sharm after dark isn't just about volume — it's about vibe. If you listen closely, the night offers more than just music. It offers meaning. From spinning skirts to soul-filled voices, the performances here are reminders that culture doesn't live in brochures — it lives in rhythm, in stories, and in the stars overhead.

SOHO Square After Dark

SOHO Square is more than just a location; it's a switch. The moment you step under its glowing arches, you leave behind the laid-back beach rhythm of Sharm and enter something completely unexpected. Neon lights buzz, fountains dance to symphonic soundtracks, and there's a strange joy in how it all just... works. It's a little surreal. A little theatrical. And when night falls, SOHO turns into its own glowing universe, where food, shopping, entertainment, and nightlife blur into one electric promenade.

The heart of SOHO after dark is its dancing fountain, which comes alive every half-hour with choreographed water shows set to classical and modern hits — think Mozart followed by Coldplay, all in one splashy, dramatic performance. It sounds touristy. It is. But it's also weirdly delightful, especially if you've got a gelato in hand and nowhere else to be.

But SOHO isn't just for strolling. It's packed with lounges, bars, live music venues, and quirky surprises. Fancy sipping a drink in sub-zero temperatures? Step into the Ice Bar, where the furniture, glasses, and even walls are carved from ice. It's gimmicky, sure — but fun in a "why not" kind of way. For something warmer, Queen Vic Pub is a cozy English-style pub with live sports, cold drafts, and an always-lively crowd. Nearby, Oxygen Club pulses late into the night with DJs spinning global and Arabic beats for a younger, dressed-up crowd.

Want something more refined? Try Zen Bar at the Savoy for signature cocktails and smooth jazz, or the Pangaea Nightclub — tucked behind the square, hosting themed nights and private parties. Even if you don't dance, the people-watching here is gold: locals in suits, travelers in beach clothes, and families in traditional dress all swirling together under SOHO's kaleidoscope lights.

And then there are the nighttime details that catch you off guard — an open-air chess match, a child giggling at a bubble vendor, couples slow dancing to live oud music near a food stall. It's theatrical, yes. But there's something honest in how SOHO leans into it. It's not trying to be Cairo, or Dubai. It's trying to be SOHO, and it's doing it on its own terms.

Quick Tips

1. Getting there: About 20 minutes from Naama Bay. Most hotels offer shuttles or taxis (expect 100–200 EGP round trip).
2. Best time to go: After 8 PM, when the lights are on and the crowd thickens.

3. What to wear: It's more polished than the beach — smart casual works best.

4. Food options: Everything from Indian and Thai to local grills and sushi. Prices are higher than Old Market but not outrageous.

5. Kid-friendly? Absolutely — there's a small amusement area and ice cream stalls galore.

SOHO Square doesn't pretend to be subtle. It's bold, bright, and proud of it. But give it a night, and it might just win you over — not because it's perfect, but because it's alive, surprising, and full of moments you'll talk about long after the lights fade.

Best Spots for Sunset Cocktails and Chill Vibes

Sometimes the best evenings begin with a slow sip, an open view, and the sun melting into the sea. Sharm's sunsets are a quiet kind of drama — no filters, no fanfare — and pairing them with the right spot and the right drink? That's a ritual worth learning.

Here are the best places to settle in with a cocktail (or mocktail) as the sky turns gold, orange, and then ink blue.

1. Farsha Mountain Lounge – Ras Umm Sid

Once again still the most atmospheric sunset spot in Sharm, Farsha feels like something out of a dream. Perched on a cliffside overlooking the Red Sea, its multi-level stone terraces, low lighting, and Bedouin decor set the mood for magic. Order a mint lemonade or a fruit cocktail, settle into a cushion, and let the sky do the rest. They don't serve alcohol, but honestly, it doesn't matter — the vibe here is intoxicating enough.

Best for: Romantic moments, reflective evenings, unforgettable photos.

2. The Terrace Bar – Four Seasons Resort

If you're looking for luxury with your sundown, The Terrace Bar at Four Seasons is the place. Overlooking the resort's private cove, it's serene, high-end, and discreet. Cocktails are perfectly made, the mezze plates are divine, and service is sharp without being stuffy. Pricey? Yes. Worth it? Absolutely — especially if you're celebrating something.

Best for: Upscale sunset drinks, honeymooners, anniversary dates.

3. El Fanar Beach Lounge – Hadaba

Part beach bar, part clifftop hideout, El Fanar offers casual seating with front-row sunset seats. There's soft music, fresh juice, a few beers on offer, and a laid-back vibe that draws both locals and savvy travelers. You can come straight from the beach, sandy feet and all, and still feel welcome. Stick around after the sun sets — the fairy lights switch on and it becomes quietly magical.

Best for: Sunset, toes in the sand, and casual conversations.

4. Sky Lounge – Royal Savoy Hotel

This rooftop bar is one of Sharm's best-kept secrets. Quiet, sophisticated, and reserved for adults, Sky Lounge offers panoramic sea views, perfectly mixed drinks, and a calm atmosphere where you actually hear your thoughts. It's the kind of place where one drink turns into two without you noticing.

Best for: Solo travelers, couples seeking privacy, chill elegance.

5. The Chillout Bar – Naama Bay

True to its name, The Chillout Bar is all about low pressure and great views. Tucked into a quieter corner of Naama Bay's boardwalk, it's more affordable than the hotels but still delivers a front-row seat to the sun's daily show. They offer mocktails, local beer, and solid music that doesn't overpower conversation.

Best for: Travelers on a budget, casual groups, people-watching.

6. Vista Bar – Mövenpick Resort

This hillside gem offers a sweeping view over Naama Bay from above. Known for its handcrafted drinks and peaceful setting, Vista Bar is ideal for winding down a day of sightseeing. The lighting is subtle, the service is warm, and it's especially lovely when a soft breeze drifts in from the sea.

Best for: Peaceful luxury, sunset photography, quiet evenings.

Quick Tips

1. Timing: Arrive 30–45 minutes before sunset for the best seats. Sunset in Sharm usually falls between 5:30 PM and 6:30 PM depending on the season.
2. Reservations: Strongly recommended for Sky Lounge, Four Seasons, and Farsha during peak times.
3. What to try: Local favorites include tamarind mocktails, hibiscus iced tea, and Egyptian wine if available. Try a "Sakkara Sunset" cocktail if you see it on the menu — a regional blend with pomegranate and date syrup.

Sunset in Sharm is more than just a view; it's an atmosphere. Wherever you choose to watch it, make it intentional. Put your phone down. Sip something that makes you smile. And let yourself be fully still, even just for that golden moment before the night begins.

Night Markets, Hookah Cafes, and Open-Air Cinemas

Not every night in Sharm has to be a party. Sometimes, what you really want is a slow wander, a puff of shisha, and something beautiful to watch — without needing a reservation or a dress code. For those quieter evenings when you just want to experience the town as it lives and breathes, this is where the soul of Sharm shows up — in colorful market stalls, the soft bubbling of hookahs, and flickering outdoor screens under the stars.

Let's start with the night markets, particularly around Sharm Old Market. After dark, this historic district shifts into a swirl of color and life. Shopkeepers stay open late, lights twinkle above narrow alleys, and the scent of spices, grilled corn, and warm sweets fills the air. This isn't a place you rush. You stroll. You linger. You might not need a pair of handmade sandals or a brass lamp — but you'll likely leave with one anyway, along with a story to go with it. Bargain gently, smile often, and never be afraid to ask a vendor where the locals eat.

Tucked between the shops and cafes are some of Sharm's most beloved hookah (shisha) lounges. This is where the night slows down. Locals and travelers alike sit back, sip tea, and pass time with flavored tobacco and soft music. For a real experience, try El Masrien Café in the Old Market, where you'll sit under string lights surrounded by locals playing backgammon or watching football. Or visit Sahaba Café near the Al Sahaba Mosque — not just for the view, but for the vibe. Choose between classic mint, fruity mixes, or earthy molasses flavors. Pair it with hot karkadeh (hibiscus tea) or a Turkish coffee, and just watch the world drift by.

And then there's the unexpected charm of open-air cinemas and live screens. While not heavily advertised, some beachside resorts and cafes set up projectors for movie nights or live matches, especially during summer. Montazah Beach Café has been known to screen classic Arabic films on certain nights, and The Camel Bar rooftop sometimes hosts film nights — think indie flicks, surf documentaries, or even classic Egyptian comedies. Bring a light jacket and a sense of curiosity.

What makes these nighttime experiences special is how unstructured they feel. There's no official start time, no velvet rope, no pressure to perform or pose. You're just there — sitting, sipping, laughing, wandering. And in a place like Sharm, that can be the perfect way to end a day.

Quick Tips

1. Markets: Best after 7 PM. Bring small bills. Go with curiosity, not urgency.
2. Shisha etiquette: Do not blow smoke straight at others. Take turns, and ask for your own hose if you're sharing with strangers.
3. Best flavors: Try double apple, mint grape, or rose if you're new to it. Locals often mix their own.
4. Outdoor cinemas: Not on a set schedule — ask hotel staff or check posters at Camel Bar or beach cafes.
5. Dress: Casual is fine, but bring a light cover-up for cool sea breezes.

Some of Sharm's most meaningful nights don't come with tickets or lights. They live in side streets and quiet courtyards, in fruit-flavored smoke and shared silence under a cinema screen. This is where you feel the town breathing, and for a moment, you're part of it.

CHAPTER 10:
PRACTICAL INFO AND TAILORED ITINERARIES

Every great trip has its magic — but it also needs a little structure. The details you prepare for quietly in advance are often the ones that save you from stress and elevate your entire experience. Whether it's knowing which SIM card actually works in the desert, what not to pack, or how to avoid common scams, this chapter is your calm, grounded travel companion — the one who's been here before and knows what you'll need before you even think to ask.

We'll start with real-world essentials: how to stay safe, healthy, and connected while navigating unfamiliar terrain. Then we'll move into accessibility tips, sustainable travel advice, and even some essential Arabic phrases that unlock smiles.

Finally, we'll wrap up with tailored itineraries — not generic "Top 10 lists," but thoughtful daily flows based on who you are and how you travel. Whether you're here for a 3-day recharge or a solo escape with no set plan, you'll find routes that make sense, breathe well, and leave room for wonder. Because in Sharm, the best trips aren't rushed — they're curated.

Health, Safety, and Emergency Contacts

Sharm el-Sheikh is one of the safest resort towns in Egypt — but like anywhere, a great trip starts with being smart, aware, and prepared. From knowing what to do if you get a sun rash, to understanding where to go if your passport goes missing, this section gives you everything you need to feel grounded and protected throughout your journey.

Let's start with the basics: Sharm has clean, well-maintained infrastructure, especially in tourist zones. Hospitals and clinics are accessible, and pharmacies are everywhere — often open late and staffed with knowledgeable, English-speaking pharmacists. Still, travel insurance is a must. Make sure yours covers diving, water sports, and emergency evacuation, especially if you plan to venture into the desert or climb Mount Sinai. Accidents are rare, but sand, sun, and salt water aren't exactly gentle.

For minor health issues — like sunburn, dehydration, or tummy troubles — local pharmacies carry trusted remedies. Stick with bottled water only, even for brushing your teeth, and avoid street food you're not sure about (although many vendors are perfectly safe). Pack sunscreen, mosquito repellent, and antihistamines if you're sensitive to bites or dust.

In terms of personal safety, Sharm is remarkably peaceful. The tourism police are quite visible, particularly around Naama Bay, SOHO Square, and the Old Market. That said, always keep your bag zipped, avoid displaying large sums of money, and decline unsolicited "tours" or services offered on the street unless booked through a trusted source. Solo travelers, including women, report feeling safe — but it's always wise to stick to well-lit areas at night and use known taxis or apps.

If something goes wrong, don't panic. Egyptians are famously hospitable, and help is never far away. Here are the key contacts you should have saved on your phone or written down before arrival:

Important Emergency Numbers (Save These)

- Tourist Police: 126 (English-speaking operators available)
- Ambulance: 123
- Fire Department: 180
- Police Emergency: 122
- International Directory Assistance: 120

Other Helpful Resources

Your country's embassy or consulate: Cairo is home to most embassies. Have their number in case of passport issues.

Travel Insurance Provider: Keep your policy number and a screenshot of the emergency hotline.

Hotel Front Desk: Often your fastest route to solving small problems. Staff are usually multilingual and experienced.

Health and safety in Sharm isn't something to stress about — it's something to prepare for quietly, so you can travel freely. With a little foresight and the right numbers saved, you'll spend less time worrying and more time floating in the Red Sea, watching the sun go down with peace of mind.

Avoiding Common Tourist Scams

Sharm el-Sheikh is a place where most people are genuinely kind — helpful, warm, and eager to share their city with you. But like any busy tourist destination, a few opportunists do exist, and knowing how to spot their tricks before they happen will save you time, money, and frustration. This isn't about paranoia — it's about being aware, without being afraid.

Most scams in Sharm are small — a few extra pounds here, a misleading deal there — but they can still sour a good day. The golden rule? If it feels too eager, too rushed, or too vague, slow it down. You do not have to say yes to anyone. A strong but friendly "La, shukran" (No, thank you) does wonders.

Here are the most common tourist traps — and how to sidestep them like a seasoned traveler:

1. The "Fixed Price" Taxi

You ask for a ride. The driver smiles and says "no meter — fixed price." Then quotes you five times the local rate.

How to avoid it:

Use SharmTaxiService.com or Uber/Careem where available. If using a street taxi, agree on a price before getting in — and always negotiate. Ask your hotel or a local first what a fair rate is.

2. Fake "Official Guides" at Attractions

At spots like the Old Market or Al Sahaba Mosque, someone may approach you in a suit or with a badge, offering a "free" tour. It usually ends in a pressure sale or cash demand.

How to avoid it:
Only book tours through your hotel, a verified agency, or someone with clear ID and registration. You're never required to accept a guide at any site unless you request one.

3. "Free Gifts" That Aren't Free

Vendors might place a bracelet on your wrist, offer perfume samples, or call out with "for you, no money!" The catch? Once you accept, they'll demand payment — or guilt you into buying something.

How to avoid it:
Keep your hands free and your pace steady in busy markets. A friendly smile and a shake of the head is enough to move on. Don't feel rude — it's expected.

4. Tour Package Switcheroos

You book a desert safari, diving trip, or dinner show — but what you get is underwhelming, shorter, or entirely different.

How to avoid it:
Use well-reviewed, licensed agencies, not random sellers on the beach or boardwalk. Always get a receipt or confirmation in writing (WhatsApp is fine). Ask about what's included: duration, transportation, meals, and group size.

5. Currency Confusion

You hand over a 200 EGP note and get change for 20. Or you're told the bill is "dollars," not pounds — after you've eaten.

How to avoid it:
Double-check bills before handing them over. Ask if the quoted price is in Egyptian Pounds (LE) or foreign currency. Count your change slowly, in front of the vendor. Most mistakes are honest — some are not.

6. Photos with Animals or Costumes

Someone offers to take your picture with a camel, hawk, or in a pharaoh costume — then demands a high fee afterward.

How to avoid it:
Avoid unsolicited photo ops. If you agree, set the price first. Better yet, take your own photos and skip the pose.

Quick Tips to Stay Scam-Smart

1. Trust your gut. If someone is too pushy, just walk away.
2. Learn a few Arabic phrases. It shows respect — and makes scammers think twice.
3. Don't show your large notes, and keep little ones for tips and taxis.
4. Be friendly, not gullible. Egyptians are warm people, but politeness doesn't mean agreeing to everything.

To travel smartly, you don't have to be suspicious; simply be attentive. Most of Sharm's vendors and guides are honest people doing honest work. But by knowing the common tricks, you'll navigate the streets, markets, and beaches with confidence — and spend your energy soaking up the beauty, not sorting out confusion.

Packing Essentials

Packing for Sharm el-Sheikh isn't about lugging half your wardrobe — it's about being smart, light, and ready for sun, sand, saltwater, and sudden surprises. Sharm is hot, casual, and active. You'll go from the beach to dinner, maybe to the desert, then back to the beach again — and you won't want to waste time figuring out what to wear. This list isn't generic — it's built from experience, to help you pack what matters and ditch what doesn't.

Let's break it down into what you absolutely need — and what most people forget until it's too late.

Clothing Essentials

Breathable Layers: Think linen, cotton, and moisture-wicking fabrics. Sharm is cold at night and warm through most of the day.

Swimwear (Bring Two): You'll likely be in and out of the water daily. Having a dry backup makes life easier.

Cover-Up or Light Shawl: Perfect for beach walks, sun protection, or visiting more conservative areas.

Comfortable Walking Shoes: Markets, deserts, and uneven resort paths are no place for flimsy sandals alone.

Light Jacket or Hoodie: Especially for evenings, boat trips, or Mount Sinai mornings (yes, it gets chilly).

Something Modest: For visiting mosques or local neighborhoods — long pants or a loose dress will do.

Health & Sun Protection

High-SPF Sunscreen (reef-safe if possible): The sun here doesn't play around.

Aloe Vera or After-Sun Gel: For those inevitable "oops" moments.

Mosquito Repellent: Essential, especially if you're near gardens or water at night.

Mini First Aid Kit: Include band-aids, antihistamines, motion sickness pills (boats!), and electrolytes.

Hand Sanitizer & Tissues: For markets, public restrooms, or desert trips.

Tech & Travel Tools

Universal Adapter (Type C): Egypt uses the European two-pin plug.

Power Bank: Beach clubs and desert camps aren't known for outlets.

Unlocked Phone & Local SIM Option: Data is crucial for taxis, maps, and translations.

Underwater Phone Case or GoPro: For reef footage and sandy-proof memories.

Extras Most People Forget

Reusable Water Bottle: Hydration is survival here.

Water Shoes or Reef-Safe Sandals: Many beaches are rocky or coral-heavy.

Dry Bag or Ziploc: For boat trips, beach days, and keeping electronics safe from sand.

A Small Flashlight or Phone Light App: Handy at night in desert settings or poorly lit areas.

Foldable Tote or Daypack: For shopping, snorkeling gear, or day trips.

What You Don't Need

Heavy Makeup & Fancy Outfits: Sharm is casual, even in upscale places.

Hair Tools: Between saltwater and heat, most people let their hair go natural.

Too Many Shoes: One pair of walking shoes + one pair of sandals = perfect combo.

Quick Packing Tip

Sharm has pharmacies, stores, and even malls — but prices on imported items (sunscreen, electronics, branded clothes) can be much higher than back home. If it's something you trust and use often, bring it from home.

Packing for Sharm isn't about over-preparing — it's about packing with purpose. Bring what will keep you comfortable, safe, and ready to explore. Everything else? You can leave it behind — or better yet, leave room in your bag for the treasures you'll find here.

Info for Seniors and Disabled Travelers

Sharm el-Sheikh might be known for its coral reefs and desert safaris, but don't let the adventure-heavy image fool you — this city can be surprisingly welcoming for seniors and travelers with mobility challenges. While not every corner of Sharm is perfectly accessible, there are ways to experience its beauty, culture, and calm pace without struggle, stress, or stairs.

The good news is that many resorts developed in the recent decade have been designed with accessibility in mind. Ramps, elevators, wide hallways, and step-free pool decks are common features at high-end resorts like the Savoy, Rixos Premium, and Mövenpick. If you're booking a hotel, make sure to email ahead and request a ground-floor room, accessible bathroom, or wheelchair access — most places are happy to accommodate, especially if you ask in advance.

Getting around Sharm is doable with some planning. While sidewalks in older areas (like Old Market) can be uneven, zones like SOHO Square, Naama Bay boardwalk, and many beach promenades are flat, well-lit, and wheelchair-friendly. For seniors or travelers with limited mobility, avoid minibus transport and instead use private cars, hotel shuttles, or ride-hailing services like SharmTaxiService (they can arrange cars with extra space or low entry if requested).

If you or your companion uses a wheelchair or walking aid, be selective with excursions. Some desert trips, boat tours, and diving/snorkeling centers now offer adaptive equipment and assistance, but you'll need to confirm this clearly before booking. Glass-bottom boat rides, scenic rooftop cafes with lifts, and cultural shows at Alf Leila Wa Leila are all senior-friendly experiences that don't sacrifice any of the magic.

As for medical access — you're well-covered. Major hotels and resorts have on-call doctors, and English-speaking staff are common in pharmacies and hospitals. Always travel with a list of any medications, allergies, and medical needs clearly written out in English (and Arabic if possible). Many hotels are happy to keep medications refrigerated or arrange transport to the nearest clinic if needed.

Quick Tips for Accessible Travel in Sharm

1. Call ahead to confirm wheelchair access and elevator functionality at accommodations.
2. Book transport that's flexible and door-to-door — minibuses are not ideal.

3. Plan rest days — the climate, even in winter, can be draining.
4. Travel insurance that covers pre-existing conditions is a must.
5. Ask for help — Egyptians are generous and often go out of their way to assist.

Sharm welcomes travelers of all ages and abilities — but navigating it well comes down to choosing the right places and pacing your days with care. With a few smart decisions, you'll find that the sun, sea, and serenity of this destination are just as accessible as they are unforgettable.

Sustainable Tourism Practices

Sharm el-Sheikh is easy to fall in love with—the coral reefs, the golden light on the Sinai highlands, and the beat of the Red Sea. But behind the beauty is a fragile ecosystem that needs protecting. Sustainable travel here isn't about perfection. It's about small, conscious choices that add up to real impact — not just on the environment, but on the people who call this region home.

Let's start with the sea. Sharm's world-famous reefs are alive — and vulnerable. One careless snorkeler standing on coral can cause damage that takes decades to reverse. The simplest rule? Look, don't touch. Choose reef-safe sunscreen (yes, the ingredients matter), avoid standing on anything underwater, and book with dive centers that follow marine protection standards. Bonus points if they brief you on eco-ethics before your dive — it means they care.

Water use is another issue, especially in the desert climate. Most of Sharm's water is desalinated, which takes serious energy. Long showers, daily towel changes, and wasteful pool habits might seem small — but multiplied by thousands of guests? They matter. Opt for short showers, reuse towels, and say no to unnecessary plastic bottles when your hotel offers filtered water.

Shopping is another opportunity to support sustainability. Instead of mass-produced souvenirs made in China, look for local crafts — handmade Bedouin jewelry, woven bags, natural oils, or ceramics. Not only does this help preserve traditional arts, but your money goes directly to artisans rather than big factories. Avoid buying seashells, starfish, or coral trinkets (yes, they're still being sold), and ask shopkeepers about the story behind what you're buying.

You can also travel sustainably by respecting local culture. Dress modestly when visiting towns or mosques, ask before taking someone's photo, and learn a few words of Arabic — it goes a long way toward bridging respect and warmth. Tipping fairly, using locally-owned businesses, and spreading your spending outside of resort walls all help keep tourism income in the hands of those who need it most.

Quick Wins for Sustainable Travel in Sharm:

1. Use reef-safe sunscreen with no oxybenzone or octinoxate.
2. Keep showers short, and reuse hotel towels when possible.

3. Travel with a reusable water bottle and shopping bag.
4. Buy items created in Egypt—preferably from artisan vendors.
5. Pick eco-certified tour operators who protect local landscapes.
6. Offset your carbon footprint if you're flying in.

Sustainable travel isn't about guilt — it's about gratitude. Every reef you float above, every meal you enjoy, every smile you receive… it all comes with the quiet responsibility to give something back. In Sharm, traveling well means traveling lightly — with curiosity, respect, and a little more care than you thought you needed.

Common Arabic Phrases You Need

You don't need to speak fluent Arabic to enjoy Sharm el-Sheikh — but knowing a few local words will open more doors than you expect. Egyptians appreciate any effort to connect, even if it's just a simple "thank you" or greeting. It shows respect, interest, and a kind of traveler's humility that's remembered long after the moment passes.

The Arabic spoken in Egypt is called Masri, and it has a rhythm and friendliness that fits the warmth of the people. In Sharm, English is widely spoken in hotels and tourist areas, but the further you wander — into markets, cafes, or quiet beaches — the more these small phrases come in handy.

You don't need a phrasebook. Just a few key words and a smile.

Essential Greetings

Salam Alaikum – Peace be upon you (hello)
→ Say it when entering a shop or meeting someone.

Wa Alaikum Salam – And peace be upon you too (reply)

Sabah el-kheir – Good morning

Masa el-kheir – Good evening

Ismi… – My name is…

Min fadlak / Min fadlik – Please (to a man / woman)

Politeness That Goes a Long Way

Shukran – Thank you

Afwan – You're welcome

Ma'alesh – It's okay / Never mind

La, shukran – No, thank you

Aiwa – Yes

La – No

Market & Shopping Phrases

Bikam? – How much?

Ghali awi! – That's too expensive! (playful tone works best)

Andak haga tani? – Do you have something else?

Ana batfarag bass – I'm just looking

Mumkin a'ref el-se'er el-nihayi? – Can I know the final price?

Eating Out

El menu, min fadlak? – The menu, please

Ayez/ayza... – I want... (male/female)
→ e.g., Ayez shay = I want tea

Mayya – Water

Bidoon – Without (e.g., "bidoon sukkar" = without sugar)

Batteblo el-hisab, min fadlak? – Can I get the bill, please?

In a Pinch

Mafeesh moshkela – No problem

Mafeesh – There isn't / Nothing / It's gone

Fein el toilet? – Where's the bathroom?

Sa'edni, min fadlak! – Help me, please!

Quick Tips

1. The Egyptian "r" is rolled — just a touch.
2. "La, shukran" delivered with a light laugh can defuse most pushy vendors.
3. Don't be afraid of mistakes — people will correct you gently.
4. Most Egyptians will reply in English once they see you're trying. That's the magic.

Language is more than communication — it's connection. With just a few simple phrases, you'll find that Sharm opens up in ways guidebooks can't teach. Say it wrong, say it with heart, and say it with a smile. That's all it takes.

Useful Apps and Websites

A good app doesn't just save time — it saves you from stress, scams, and getting stuck in the wrong place at the wrong moment. Here are the must-haves for navigating Sharm smoothly:

Top Apps to Download

SharmTaxiService.com (Web App): Reliable local taxis, airport transfers, and fair rates — no haggling.

Google Maps: Works well in most areas, including walking routes in Naama Bay and SOHO Square.

Google Translate: Download Arabic for offline use. Handy in local shops and markets.

Careem: For app-based rides (like Uber), mainly around central Sharm.

TripAdvisor: Best for checking recent reviews of restaurants, tours, and attractions.

Maps.me: Offline maps for hikes, diving spots, and exploring without data.

XE Currency: Real-time conversion between Egyptian Pounds and your home currency.

Helpful Websites

Egypt.travel – Official tourism board, updated travel advisories and cultural insights.

BookSurfCamps.com – Great for diving, yoga, or kitesurf packages with verified reviews.

SharmReef.com – Local dive centers, excursions, and gear rental options.

With the right tools in your pocket, you'll spend less time guessing and more time soaking up the Red Sea sun. Download early, go offline when needed, and let tech smooth the edges of your adventure.

3-Day and 5-Day Itinerary Options

Not everyone has two weeks to spare — and the beauty of Sharm is that it doesn't need a long stay to leave a deep impression. These two itinerary options are designed to help you experience the best of Sharm without burnout. They're not jam-packed checklists, but balanced journeys — with space for wandering, for saltwater naps, for unplanned moments.

No hour-by-hour breakdowns. Just daily rhythms that feel real.

3-Day Itinerary – First-Timer's Dream

Day 1 – Touchdown & Seaside Welcome

Arrive, check into your hotel or resort, and take time to settle. Spend your first afternoon by the water — Naama Bay if you like buzz, or El Fanar Beach for peace. At sunset, head to Farsha Café for panoramic views and something cold. End with a laid-back dinner near your hotel.

Day 2 – Snorkels, Souks, and Mosque Lights

Book a half-day snorkeling trip to Ras Mohammed or the Blue Hole. Return for a shower and rest, then head into Sharm Old Market before dusk. Explore the stalls, grab fresh juice, and take in the glow of Al Sahaba Mosque after dark. Eat Egyptian — grilled kofta or koshari is perfect.

Day 3 – Desert & Departure

Squeeze in a morning desert experience — quad biking, a camel trek, or just a sunrise drive. Return, pack, and take it slow before your flight.

5-Day Itinerary – Dive Deeper Without Rushing

Day 1 – Arrival & Sea Breeze Reset

Land, check in, tour your accommodation, and relax into the rhythm. Walk the beach near your resort, catch the sunset, and enjoy a relaxed dinner. Early night — the real fun starts tomorrow.

Day 2 – Coral Kingdoms & Coastal Cafés

Head out for snorkeling or diving — Ras Mohammed or Tiran Island are top picks. Come back salty, happy, and hungry. In the evening, unwind at a seaside café like El Fanar or the rooftop at the Camel Bar.

Day 3 – Culture, Crafts & Sunset Souks

Keep it land-based today. Visit the Al Sahaba Mosque, stroll through Old Market, and stop at Sahaba Café for mint tea and shisha. Browse for Bedouin jewelry or spices, and don't forget to haggle playfully. Evening ends with a traditional dinner and optional tanoura dance show.

Day 4 – Mountains & Silence

Join a sunrise hike to Mount Sinai if you're up for it — or opt for a desert safari with Bedouin tea and stargazing. After resting, grab a slow dinner at your resort or a seafood spot overlooking the water. Today is about stillness.

Day 5 – Wind Down in SOHO Style

Sleep in. Spend time at your resort pool or take a dip in a quiet bay. Later, head to SOHO Square for a polished but playful final evening. Shop, sip, or catch a live show before saying goodbye to the Red Sea.

Sharm doesn't ask you to rush. It gives you space to explore and permission to slow down. These itineraries are more than plans — they're invitations to experience Sharm like someone who's been here before, even if it's your first time.

Tailored Itineraries by Travel Style

Sharm doesn't offer one-size-fits-all adventures. It whispers to each traveler a little differently. Whether you're sharing the experience with kids, going solo for a recharge, building memories with a partner, or chasing every thrill you can find — this section helps you travel your way. These are not just schedules — they're stories in motion.

Family-Friendly – 3 Days of Bonding & Balance

Day 1 – Arrival & Easy Explorations

Settle into a family-friendly resort (like White Hills or Sunrise Diamond Beach). You can allow the kids to splash in the pool while you unpack. In the afternoon, head to Naama Bay for ice cream, boardwalk fun, and dinner at a casual beachfront restaurant.

Day 2 – Waterpark Fun & Sunset Markets

Start the day at Aqua Blu Waterpark — it's safe, massive, and perfect for all ages. After lunch, rest back at the hotel. In the evening, visit the Old Market, where kids can see the glowing mosque and try local snacks.

Day 3 – Boat Trip & Beach Time

Take a short glass-bottom boat tour or a half-day snorkeling cruise with child-friendly guides. Spend the rest of the day building sandcastles and relaxing before your departure.

Solo Traveler – 3 Days of Freedom & Flow

Day 1 – Arrival & Quiet Discovery

Check into a serene adults-only resort like Meraki or Cleopatra. Walk the coastline solo, find a beachfront café, and let the sea set your mood. Journal at sunset.

Day 2 – Reef + Soul

Book a guided dive or snorkel tour — Tiran Island is peaceful and perfect for inner stillness. After that, read or write at Farsha Café before heading to the Old Market to people-watch and smoke shisha under the stars.

Day 3 – Morning Clarity & Gentle Farewell

Wake early and hike Mount Sinai if you feel adventurous. Prefer calm? Try a spa morning and slow breakfast. Stop at SOHO Square for quiet souvenirs and reflect on how good solitude can feel.

Couples – 5 Days of Connection & Romance

Day 1 – Arrival & First Sunset

Stay somewhere intimate like Royal Savoy or Four Seasons. Walk the beach hand-in-hand and dine under string lights at El Fanar.

Day 2 – Sea Adventures Together

Snorkel or dive together — nothing bonds like spotting a sea turtle at the same time. Unwind afterward with massages or a beach nap. Evening at Camel Bar rooftop or a private dinner by the sea.

Day 3 – Desert Stars & Bedouin Nights

Book a romantic sunset desert safari, complete with camel ride, candlelit Bedouin dinner, and stargazing. Bring a light jacket and a sharing blanket.

Day 4 – Slow Mornings & Local Wandering

Have a late breakfast, then explore the Old Market or a small art gallery. Sip mint tea, shop for keepsakes, and let the day take you. Dinner near SOHO Square with live music.

Day 5 – One Last Dip

Relax at the beach or your infinity pool. Say your goodbyes to the Red Sea at Farsha Café or with a final sunrise walk before heading home.

Adventurers – 5 Days of Non-Stop Wonder

Day 1 – Arrival & Dive Right In

Check into a dive lodge or sporty hotel. Rent a bike or do a quick snorkel close to your accommodation. Early dinner, early sleep — tomorrow begins fast.

Day 2 – Deep Sea, Deep Thrill

Go for a full-day scuba dive — Ras Mohammed or a wreck dive like SS Thistlegorm. Back by 5 PM. Refuel with fresh seafood and a quick nap, then hit a lively bar.

Day 3 – Desert Speed & Night Sky

Morning quad biking and dune bashing. Afternoon nap. Evening desert camping experience with food, dance, and a magnificent blanket of stars.

Day 4 – The Summit or the Saddle

Climb Mount Sinai before sunrise or go kite surfing at Nabq. Both are intense and unforgettable. Easy evening with street food or a night dip in the pool.

Day 5 – Wind Down at Your Speed

Final snorkel, kayak session, or just a quiet beach chair to let the adrenaline settle. SOHO Square at night for music, laughs, or a celebratory scoop of Egyptian gelato.

There's no "right" way to do Sharm — only your way. Whether you're chasing calm, love, adventure, or connection, the perfect days aren't always packed... they're paced. Let your mood lead. Sharm will meet you there.

CONCLUSION

There's something quietly unforgettable about Sharm el-Sheikh. It doesn't shout. It doesn't demand. It just lingers — like the salty imprint of the Red Sea on your skin, like the orange-pink glow you saw once behind the Sinai peaks, like the Bedouin smile that said more than any language ever could.

What you take from this place won't just be the photos of coral gardens or the scent of cardamom in your tea. It will be the unhurried rhythm of the days. The freedom of walking barefoot from your room to the shoreline. The way your voice echoed in a mosque courtyard at dusk. The breeze conveyed no words, simply silence.

Sharm teaches you something, whether you come here to dive, to heal, to reconnect, or just to breathe. It teaches you that you don't always need more — you just need presence. Here, time bends a little. Expectations soften. And somehow, you remember how to listen to your own pace again.

You'll board your flight with sun-kissed skin, tired legs, maybe a suitcase filled with handmade soap, spices, and sand that you'll pretend isn't there. But what stays is much lighter — and much more permanent. It's the version of you that woke up early just to watch the water. That said "shukran" with meaning. That sat under a sky full of stars and thought: I've still got so much to see.

And if Sharm el-Sheikh has done its work well — as it so often does — you won't just leave it behind.

You'll carry it forward.

Into your next city. Your next adventure. Your next quiet moment. A whisper of the Red Sea always there. Waiting. Calling you back.

Printed in Dunstable, United Kingdom

Stories of F Fantasy, &

Short Stories Written In Grade School
Rich Full-Color Illustrations

Written & Illustrated by: Walton D. Stowell Jr.
Edited by: Doctor Drogo F. Empedocles
Dedicated to Mom: Nena M. Stowell
Sponsored by: Noel Lana Tavano
Self-Published in 2010

<u>Stories of Fiction, Fantasy, and Adventure</u> is a collection of 45 short stories written in the 1980's by a kid, for kids. The Author wrote these stories as a kid, to be read by kids, and read by kids to other kids. Adults may read these stories of course, but those that live in denial of their creativity will be challenged by the contents of this book.

Although mostly fictional, some stories were based on real people, places, and events. Character names have been changed to protect the identity and integrity of all people, thus making each story even more fictional. Warning: those that try to apply reality to these stories may get in trouble and serve Detention!

This collection of tales and drawings from the Author's childhood and early teen years, was written while attending public and private schools in West Virginia and Maryland. Many drawings were drawn with the stories, and have been digitally re-mastered here. Some of the "mistakes" in spelling or grammar were intentionally left in, especially if they added to the ambiance of the story. Also teacher comments are sometimes included. Don't worry; if there's mistakes, they're supposed to be in here.

Remember; Kids are not slaves!

Note to Reader: *The following short stories are "Chronologically Confused"; from 1st to 8th Grade. Most of the First Grade stories are in the beginning, but the order they were written is soon rearranged in order to group related themes and types. Related books will be published, as this is only a partial collection of the Author's grade school stories.*

Table of Contents: Pages:

1.	The Long Awaited Word …….………………...	pg. 3
2.-5.	The Missing Mysteries	4-8
6.	Rome, Italy / Romans Vs. Barbarians	9-10
7.	I've Known Countries	11
8.	The Creation of Earth	12-14
9.	The Final Struggle	15-16
10.	Panic On Earth	17-20
11.	Crab Island, Playmont	21-26
12.	An Incredible Christmas Carol	27-32
13.	The Queen Elizabeth II Trip	33
14.	Doctor Dippie Banned! A Demented Biography …	34-35
15.	Don't Call Me a Nerd If I Read This Story	36
16.	How Elephant Got His Toenails	37
17.	Tony Turkey: Tall Tale Starters	38-42
18.	In The Hands of a Super Hero	43-44
19.	The Chinese Doggy Blahs	45-46
20.	The Forbidden Closet	47-48
21.	All In A Days Work	49-50
22.	County Fire Brigade	51-52
23.	From America	52
24.	Jimmy Clouds	53
25.	My Pet Dragon	54
26.	Mister Chop	55
27.	On The Run	56-58
28.	The Neckless	59-63
29.	Sheryl Holmes & Rennell Watson ………………..	64-66
30.	Sam Schlap: The Blown Up Bridge	67
31.	Monstors: The Last Battle	68-87
32.	A Super Christmas	88-89
33.-38.	Multiple Choice Stories (6)	90-110
39.	Time Capsule	111
40.	Turmoil In RAMBA	112-114
41.	Undersea Mayhem	115-117
42.	Venture On the Road of Destiny	118
43.	Attack of the Radio Active Hamsters	119-121
44.	Werewolf, Alien, and Crossbow	122-127
45.	Zardan	128-129

Appendixes: Glossary; Bibliography; Biography; Reader Notes & Sketches

■ ■

THE LONG AWAITED WORD

As John slugged through the thick and mosquito filled swamps, snakes and bugs crawled up his legs. It was very foggy. He could barely make out a huge rock ahead. He trudged on, quickly knocking off all the leeches and worms. John reached the rock. The rock began to move, and low-and-behold it turned into a giant humanoid creature!

"I have brought the dead body you wanted. Now tell me which section of the notebook this is!" John said as he threw down the body of a bloodied ork.

"For many a year, the elders have kept this section a secret. But now it looks as if I must tell you," it said. "The long awaited word, the name of this section, the ancient, forgotten subject is… **ENGLISH**!!"

The Missing Mystery Stories:
The Missing Pickle; The Missing Chuoboko; The Missing Dinosaur; & The Missing Armor

The Missing Pickle
By Walton Stowell
1st Grade

Once day a detective went to the pickle jar.
Then something caught his eyes.
The pickle was gone!

"I remember I slipped the pickle into my pocket."
The detective meditated on the subject.
"Here it is!" the detective said.

The End

The Missing Chuoboko

All was quiet in the Outlaw Base.
Then something happened!
Large chunks of the rock ceiling caved in!
Boulders hit the platform and even landed on some outlaws.

After the dust settled, everybody shouted "Where is Chuoboko?"
Most of the outlaws wore green hats.
The Leader wore a blue cape.

The Leader lost his green hat in the collapse.
He still had his purple shirt, grey pants, and blue cape.
After dusting off everything, the Leader called a meeting.
He and 3 troops went to hunt for Chuoboko.

They walked to the nearest cave.
The Leader found Chuoboko tied up in the back of the cave.
After untying Chuoboko, they saw the monster that made the mess.
They ran away from the large green monster, back to the Outlaw Base.
The outlaws were out of the cave, before the monster could get them.

The Outlaws were having a celebration.
They soon realized Chuoboko was missing again!
They looked through the balloons down the hall.
A shadow of the monster could be seen on the wall!
They were mad when they found out it was Chuoboko's shadow!

The End

The Missing Dinosaur

There once was a dinosaur king named Rex.
He went out on his balcony and all the dinos cheered.
Then Rex left a note saying: "The first dino who finds me is a good dino."

Triceratops, Stegosaurus, and Pterodactyl were his advisors.
They found the note and got other dinos, birds and lizards looking too.
Even Brontosaurus, Brachiosaurus, and Diplodocus got into the fun.
They looked up at trees, and down in caves.
They could not find Rex. Some decided to go back to Dino Mountain.

Once duck bird dinosaur looked in the Throne Room.
Another dino looked in a hollow log.
Ankleosaurus checked the dungeon.

King Rex was hiding in a tree, but decided to change hiding spots.
Rex went into the mouth of a giant sea monster!
He thought that nobody would find him there.

A bird found him.
Together they walked back to Dino Mountain.
At the Throne Room, they all cheered, for the bird was a good dino.

The End

The Case of the Missing Dinosaur

The Cave of the Dinosaur King

The Missing Armor

Once upon a time two knights were fighting.
One with a round helm, the other with a square helm.
Both had weapons, and full plate mail.

The knights fought all day.
Square Helm sliced Round Helm's feather.
Round Helm cut at Square Helm's leggings.

That night while the knights slept,
Ants carried Round Helm's armor away.
The knights were fast asleep, and did not wake until morning.

In the morning, the knights returned to the battlefield.
Square Helm laughed to see the other knight in pink pajamas!
"My armor is missing!" Round Helm yelled angrily.

They found his breastplate stuck in an Ant hill.
Round Helm pulled his armor from the Ant hill.
The knight stuck out his tongue and yelled at the Ants.

Round Helm swore he would never fight again.
Fighting was just not worth the trouble.
Battle always led to worse things.

The End

Rome, Italy
Walton Stowell, First Grade

Once a long time ago, some Romans stole the Lost Ark of Israel.
They got the Ark, but a huge boulder came rolling after them!
They ran as fast as they could in sandals.

The boulder got stuck in a cave, but they lost their weapons.
The Romans went to the Temple of Jupiter in Rome.
They opened the Ark.

Out came thunder and lightning.
Angels and demons swirled all around.
The lightning killed the Romans, and ruined their city, Rome.

The lightning and thunder continued coming from the Ark.
Then all at once, it stopped.
The lid fell shut.

The temples were all broken.
Years and years later, the ruins broke down more.
One day an archeologist found the ruins of the Temple of Jupiter.
The archeologist put a fence up, and rebuilt the Temple.

The End

Romans Vs. Barbarians

The Romans were very happy to attack the Barbarians.
The Barbarians were very tired, and sleepy.
Suddenly, the Romans snuck up and the Battle began.

Barbarians shot arrows down from their stone fortress.
Romans and Barbarians clashed swords.
Then the Romans gave up.

The Barbarians had some Romans killed,
and some Romans made as slaves.
But that is another story….

The End

I've Known Countries

Based on Langston Hughes Poem
"The Negro Speaks of Rivers"
7th Grade English Class

I've Known Countries ancient as the sword that took Caesar,
And older than the arrow that fell Harold.
My soul has grown wide like the countries.

I have been in cathedrals when dawns were young.
I sold my chewing gum by the Moscow River,
And it gave no receipt.

I looked upon Red Square, and the Kremlin walls raised above it.

I heard the flapping of Saint Mark's Square,
When the pigeons went up to the bell tower,
And I've seen it's stone bosom turn all golden in the sunset.

I've Known Countries;
Ancient, foreign countries.
My soul has grown wide like the countries.

The Creation of Earth

Walton Stowell, 6th Grade Playmont

Before the beginning of Earth, God was getting bored. He wanted something to play with. So he started building his kapskas (his word for playthings). When he started off, some of his planetary creations looked like this:

X O ^ @ [ ] *

Some kapskas were a mile long. Others blocked out the Sun (which he couldn't remember how it came to be). God scrapped his first creations, and began making new kapskas. He made 8 new kapskas. He named them after his fellow gods (which he did not much care for): Jupiter, Pluto, Neptune, Saturn, Uranus, Venus, Mercury, and Mars.

But God had more plans. He would construct a kapska, more beautiful, more unique, than any other kapska. To do this, he thought he needed the help of all the gods.

The gods were doing well, until they started showing off. And when gods show off, you better watch out! God would come back to his bedroom after visiting another Solar System, and he would find the other gods in his room playing with his kapskas! So God kicked the other gods out of his room.

That's when their friendship parted, and gods started boasting that they were the only god, or gang of gods. In fact, that was when God started calling himself God. His real name was Goddarnitt Thadeus Hifisticleas V, but he never really like his full name. His Mom called him God for short, and it goes to show that nicknames can have an impression on young minds.

Well, God eventually finished his favorite kapska in 5 days. Although the kapska was beautiful, God was bored again. So he decided to name the kapska, Earth. Then he was bored again. So, he would make animals (meaning simple ones). It took him one day to perfect them.

A few days later, God forgot that the animals had to eat, and he got mad at them for eating his plants (which he had placed there). So he made carnivorous animals to punish the plant eaters. Some carnivores were gigantic, others were very small.

Soon the carnivores ate too many of the plant-eaters, and so God punished all of them by making a drastic fall in the temperature on Earth. All the plant-eating animals lived, because they grew fur. The reptilian carnivores died because they had no fur.

Eventually, there were so many plant-eaters that there were hardly any plants left. So again, God was mad. He decided to make a superior life form. He created man in one day. Then as an afterthought created woman. So in total; five days to make the kapska, one day to make animals, and another to make Man (and Woman).

Man did well, killing the animals only for food, and keeping the numbers down. Man was smart, and he made up rules for Woman to follow. This helped insure that Man and Woman could reproduce, and this led to them becoming plural. Man became men, and Woman became women. Men wrote a few books on God, and one of those was called the Bible.

However men were overwhelmingly intelligent, and they made the Gun. Now men hunted, not for food or clothing, but mostly for fun. Also men liked to shoot other men, in order to steal their property (which included women). Soon more than one Gun was made, so they no longer had to take turns.

One day a man named Goddish prayed to God, and said "Please help us, oh Lord! Guns are dangerous not just to animals, but men are killing eachother!!"

God decided he would go back in time, before the Gun. Then he would send someone from Heaven to preach his ways. So he killed Goddish, brought him to Heaven, took him back in time with him, and renamed him Jesus. A few years later nothing was achieved, and the man came floating back up to Heaven (see New Testament).

God decided to read his population chart one day. It read: "Plant-eaters up 1 percent, Carnivores up 2 percent, Men up 50 percent." God shook his head, and stroked his long white beard. "Men are getting more troublesome! Killing too many of my animals! Killing eachother, like they have nothing better to do!!" The year was 1970.

Now, at this time (1988), _all_ the gods are getting mad. All these nuclear missiles we have aimed at eachother. Most of the gods have realized by this point that nothing good comes from petty bickering. Sure it took them millions of years, but they are wiser for all their conflict.

Let's travel about 50 years in the future. By now, there will be lasers to fight battles, and hover tanks. God will be playing with the kapska Pluto, and be thinking about Earth and how many bad things we are doing. God will get so mad, that he will throw Pluto across space towards us, and hit all other kapskas into the sun. Then Pluto will zoom right out of the Galaxy.

One day, God will be bored again.

THE END

The Final Struggle, Part I
Walton Stowell

The year was 2,075. The world was polluted and corrupt. Its inhabitants lived around a dying sun. The world was close to destruction because of careless dumping and numerous wars. The gods were angry at the humans for destroying their beautiful planet. Each god decided to save their own worshipers. It was decided that the gods would have a meeting.

The meeting would be on Mount Olympus. Zeus was delighted to host the meeting. He decorated the halls with gold leaf, prepared a mile long feast, and got magical staves for party favors. When gods from every walk of life appeared, they were greeted by Hermes and Ares. Each guest placed themselves in the golden chairs at the golden table. Zeus presented a toast, and they began to drink the wine of Olympus.

They ate unicorn, peacock, shark, green dragon, and munched on cave bear crunchies. After the feast, they told beast-fire stories and had a boulder toss and pillar fight. Then the gods settled down and had a meeting.

"I vote we save our Sumerian people!" said Gilgamesh.
"No," said Crom with a laugh. "They brought this upon themselves. We should not save any of the humans. They are weak, and vulnerable to their own faults."   "We must leave the future to our people." Jehovah said.

"You party-poopers!" Zeus said. "They are our own people. If you have an ice cold, poison-tipped, midnight-black dagger in your heart, then you will let them die."   There was silence.

"I am the Great Dragon's son." Mitophe said. "When my father died, I felt sorrow. You might feel the same if this happened to your own people."

The gods took a vote. Zeus announced the results. They would try and save their people. It was left up to the dragons to try to save them. After shaking hands, and saying goodbye, the gods departed Olympus. Inviting almost every dragon, the next meeting would be held in the Seventh Palace in the Plane of Dragons.

At the head of the table sat Mitophe. In the other seats were 500 brass dragons, 696 bronze dragons, 701 copper dragons, 899 gold dragons, 851 silver dragons, 92 jade dragons, 125 crystal dragons. Plus special guests Bahamet, Diamond, the Court of Dragons, and Chromely attended.

After a while of talking, Mitophe said, "It is decided that we will place Sacatowa, the baby dragon, in the city of Tokyo. He will teach the people of the world to stop fighting and depositing waste into our many beautiful oceans. In 3 days and 3 nights, Sacatowa will reach Tokyo.

THE END (Until Part II)

■ ■

Walton Stowell Jr.
January 31, 1989
7th Grade Reading Class

PANIC ON EARTH
The Play

One day in a peaceful forest, Pan is suddenly awakened by gun shots. Two hunters run in, but Pan escapes. Hunters go back to their house, and talk about their experience. Pan makes it back to Mount Olympus safely. He asks Zeus to punish the humans. Zeus decides to investigate for himself. Zeus goes to Earth with Demeter disguised as an old Goat. Zeus returns furious & sends Ares to talk with the President of the USA. Ares visits New York City where he is stopped by security guards. Ares summons a ghost army to destroy earth. Zeus pities the humans so he banishes the army.

CHARACTERS: Narrator, Pan, 2 hunters, Zeus, Demeter, Politician, Drunk, Ares, Aphrodite, Poseidon, Apollo, Hades, guard

SCENES: *Forest, House, Mountainside, Palace Olympus, City Street, Farm*

ACT 1 Panic in the Forest
Forest
Narrator: Pan sits peacefully playing his music in the forest.
[Contentedly, the faun stops playing and falls asleep. He is awakened by 2 gun shots!]

Hunters: (shouting from offstage) I aint never seen a goat like that before! Get em! [2 hunters run onstage to find Pan, who then runs offstage. Hunters shrug & retreat] That was the friskiest critter I ever did see! Almost had him!

House Interior
Hunter 1: That was one crazy goat!
Hunter 2: Yeah! How big was he? That was no goat!
Hunter 1: He was at least 18 feet tall, I shot him but he kept running!
Hunter 2: I shot him too but he got away.

ACT 2 Pan climbs the Mountainside of Olympus
Mountainside
Narrator: Pan fearfully races up Mount Olympus to safety.
[suspense builds, dramatic music]

ACT 3   Pan meets with Zeus on Mount Olympus
Palace Olympus
Narrator: Pan arrives atop Mount Olympus to seek out Zeus.
Pan: Zeus there are too many humans on Earth! They are out of control, destroying everything that we have given them! We should kill them, they are trouble! They try to kill me instead of enjoying the magic of my music! Curse them o Zeus, curse them!
Zeus: I suppose that the time has come for me to return to Earth in the form of a goat, so as not to be noticed, and observe these mortals! Come with me Demeter. [clouds fill stage, lights dim]

ACT 4   City Street Politics of Gods and Drunks
City Street
Narrator: A city politician argues with a drunk, as Zeus & Demeter approach

Politician: We are the greatest Country on Earth, ever! What have you done for your Country? Stop drinking and get a job and get a hair cut!
Drunk: I drink because you have given my job to your slaves, and I grow my hair to rebel against your evil leadership!
Politician: Is that your goat? Get him off of the streets, he has no rights!
Drunk: That is not a goat, that is my Lord Zeus come down from Mount Olympus! We should bow down and worship him!
Politician: Animals have no rights!
Drunk: Under your laws, that would make them equal to humans.

Demeter: Zeus, let us leave this human city. I prefer the smell of their farms.
Zeus: This was once a farm; but now it is a place for sewage gutters, noisy metal killer-chariots, thieves, drug addicts, & liars. Let us go now, and find a rare place of pastoral retreat! As we go, let me teach them a lesson.
 [Zeus points at them, and the drunk & the politician switch roles]

Politician: I am drunk!
Drunk: (reaching in pockets) I am rich!
(original scene contained hippies & punks fighting)

ACT 5 Farm
Farm
Narrator: Zeus & Demeter visit a crop field about to be dusted
Demeter: As goddess of fields of food & harvest, I am pleased to see that not all the human farms are gone!
Zeus: By Hera, what is that mechanical bird in the sky??!
Demeter: So that is what they call an airplane...
 [plane flies overhead and dumps a load of DDT on them, curtain goes down]

ACT 6   Panic in the Palace
Palace Olympus
Narrator: Back in the Palace of the Greek Gods on Mount Olympus, Pan stirs up the thunder of their anger!   [Thunder is heard]
Pan: Shall we attack the humans?!
Ares: Yes, let's blow them away father Zeus! Hades will lend some dead…
Zeus: Patience fellow gods, let us not be too hasty! Mankind is getting out of hand, but I don't want to destroy them now. Lets just keep an eye on them.
 [Thunder and Lightning]

ACT 7   Park Fountain
City Street
Narrator: A farmer and a politician walk together on a sidewalk, by a city park fountain, along a busy street.
Farmer: Why are we dumping sewer into our river?
Politician: Hey, its just a River!
Farmer: Yeah, you are right. (as they walk away)

[Poseidon jumps up from the fountain]
Poseidon: "Just a River!", "Just a River?" I am God of the Sea, to which all rivers flow. I will not stand for this! These humans must be punished. Zeus will hear of this! [Original had Acts for Apollo with Ozone, & Hades with Ghostbusters]

Act 8   Palace Meeting at Mount Olympus
Palace Olympus
Narrator: The Pantheon of gods & goddesses met upon high, once again.
Hades: Lord Zeus, let us punish these humans! Did you know they have ghost exterminators? (banshee wails)
Apollo & Poseidon: Yes they should be punished!
Zeus: My fellow gods, your concerns are noted. My brother Poseidon, I understand you care for the Waters of Earth. My Brother Hades, I understand your care for the spirits of mortals. My son Apollo, I understand your powers of the Sun are disrespected. Demeter, both Athena & Artemis agree with you. Pan, my wife Hera agrees with you. Aphrodite & Ares will go to Earth, and find a compromise between Love & War. Go now, and Ares…do not start a War just because it is easy for you.
Ares: (leaving) Whatever old man.

Act 9   Steps of City Hall
City Street
Narrator: Aphrodite & Ares come to the Steps of City Hall where they are refused entry by a human guard.
Aphrodite: Hey sexy, is that the door to City Hall?

Guard: Yes, but no one is allowed inside unless you have money.
Aphrodite: We don't have money, but I am the Goddess of Love, so I have lots of love…
Guard: No Ma'am, we do not accept Love as currency.
Ares: Enough of this!!! I am Ares, God of War! If you do not allow us entry I shall declare WAR on you puny mortals!!! And you shall all die!!! Now take me to your trouble-maker leader!
Guard: Sorry, I cant do that. Please step back sir, or you will be tazed.
Ares: (backs up) Very well! Hades I summon your spirits of the dead, ghosts of fallen warriors! Come forth from the air now and reap more souls for your master! I declare war on the living mortals! (fog fills the stage & ghastly sounds are heard)

Act 10   Throne Room of Mount Olympus
Palace Olympus
Hades: Zeus, Ares has set my ghostly army against the mortals.
Zeus: Yes Hades, I have allowed this on one condition; the spirits of the dead shall spread only those dreaded diseases and pollutions that once killed them. The ills of humanity will haunt them forever more. This is the will of Zeus!!!

[curtains close; END]

■ ■

Crab Island
Playmont School 6th Grade

Captain's Branch:
The seas were rough that day. I can remember. The waves were crushing against the sides of the ship. I was just one of several captains aboard the good ship *Playmont*. There was Captain Naemo, Captain Bonnie, and Captain Walton (that's me). Captain Naemo was in charge of the crew. I was in charge of searching for land and ships (a good job). Captain Bonnie was in charge of Navigation and steering the ship.

I was in the crow's nest when I looked down and saw the cabin boy, Tate, taking a leak off the starboard bow. I looked away. No land in sight yet. Bonnie was having trouble steering the Playmont through the mighty waves. My digital watch buzzed, time for a nap. I climbed down from the crow's nest, and went below deck.

I passed the Admiral's cabin. He was an English bloke named Sir Edward Hodge, and he snored like a hyena. Next I passed the kitchen. Aadam was the overzealous cook. Although the food was good, it was pretty much gone by the time he finished preparing it. Then I passed by the lounge.

Chan and Davey were watching Space Balls. They were the International Medium Weight Crab Fighters of America Champions. The hostile native of the ship, Winefred, was playing with voodoo dolls. Anastasia was scrubbing the walls. Captain Naemo was barfing in the mess room, which he did when the seas were rough.

I finally came to my cabin. Someone was inside! I crashed through the door, getting splinters in my hand. It was Sarrah, the absent-minded maid.

"Oh hi Bonnie! I just cleaned up your room for you. Wanna play cards? No. Thought not. Who's steering the ship? Maybe Bonnie is. Bye Davey!" Sarrah said.

I waved goodbye, as Sarrah left my quarters. Did I mention that she also needed glasses? I looked around. It was just as messy as before. Oh well, I thought, she tries hard. I laid down and went to sleep.

I heard something! I awoke with a start! It was my digital watch again. Time for lookout.

I sat in the crow's nest. By the look of the clouds, I could see another storm brewing.

Land! I could see a little island! A little island with masts, cannon, and a steering wheel?! Oops, it was a pirate ship. As I sounded the alarm, our crew readied defenses.

The pirate ship pulled beside us, and boarded. They were the meanest. I saw Padge the assassin, Zocros the mercenary, and Moses the peg-legged dog. I was the only one, apart from the girls, that didn't have a weapon ready. I reached into my pocket. Inside I found my lucky rubber band, a cheerio, my automatic laser can-opener, my Captain Marvel decoder ring, and some sticky, unwrapped gum.

Then, I… I… What?! Oh. Oh yes, well, I took out my lucky rubber band and fired! Zoom!! The rubber band hit the pirate Zocros on the nose, and both he and the rubber band plunged into the water. The storm was worse than ever now.

"Captain Naemo!" I called.

"Captain Naemo is in the mess room again sir," Davey said.
More pirates were about to board. Quickly we pushed Aadam on their ship. We pulled him up just as the pirate ship sank to the bottom of the sea.

Lightning and thunder was everywhere. Admiral Edward was cowering in a corner and said "Be brave men, be brave!"

"Who is steering the ship?" Chan said frantically. We looked around, but Bonnie was no where to be found. No one had seen Bonnie since the pirates had boarded.

"Sarrah will do jolly good," Admiral Edward said. After a few seconds Sarrah was spinning herself in circles, and spinning the ship all over the place. Just then a huge tidal wave engulfed the ship! I'm thirsty, I need a drink. All this story-telling parches one's gullet, you know? Anyway, yeah, it was a huge wave from out of no-where. It surprised everyone on board, and wrecked the ship.

…

Ok. The next morning I awoke. We were all there except Bonnie. It was a rather large island from what we could see. Then again, any land bigger than our ship was large to us. Most of the island was a tropical forest. We were on the deserted beach. Our ship, *The Playmont*, was in pieces. All that remained intact was the food compartment pantry.

"Well let us make the best of it!" Admiral Edward said as he stood up. "Davey and Chan, off you go to fetch some sticks. Let's make a fire. Walton and Tate, go get some food."

As Tate and I approached the food compartment, we heard some movement from inside. All that remained was Cook Aadam, leaning on empty canisters and barrels. "What?" he asked in response to our accusatory looks, gestures, and grunts. We went to bed without dinner that night, but Aadam was stuffed.

The next morning we found Winefred missing. We searched along the whole shore. On the far side of the island, a man about 4 feet tall jumped out! He was wearing a funny looking mask, which looked like this (drawing).

We all jumped back. The masked stranger sat there looking at us. Chan tried to talk to him in latino jibberish; "Mantero erocko senbala ka."
"Yo man! What you sayin'?" the little man said.

Then we... ah yes. A drink is refreshing.

At first we were startled, then gathered ourselves and asked him his name.
"I am a witch doctor. My name is El Mich. I am the long lost son of your Admiral. You may call me Doctor Hodge. Hodgey for short," he said. Then Dr. Hodge showed us to his hut, and gave us coconut juice. We drank the coconut juice, and it was finally something rewarding after all we had been through. After that he showed us the crab cake trees, the shrimp trees, and the banana bushes. We took him to our campfire.

At night we were all around the campfire. El Mich said "See that path there? Never walk on it. It leads to the place of the crabs!"

"Good thing I brought tartar sauce!" Cook Aadam said.

...

In the morning when we woke up, Sarrah yelled "Gold!"

"That is not gold. Those are beer caps!" Chan said. There were silver ones and yellow ones. We devised a way of using the caps as currency. We traded them to Dr. Hodge for food, and he would trade them for supplies. In that way we made quite a living for ourselves, despite all our troubles.

We were all collecting the caps, when a giant crab came from behind us and grabbed Captain Naemo. Chan and Davey got into crab fighting formation. Dr. Hodge ran into the tropical forest. After much fighting, finally Chan and Davey (the wrecking crew) defeated the crab. Its great hulking mass collapsed upon the sand.

"I'll get the grill!" Aadam shouted.

We had a great feast that night. In the morning we cleared out the shell to make a hut. Anastasia said, "Where is Captain Naemo?" We looked all around. We saw a mess upon the ground. Captain Naemo, creamed by a crab, we never thought it would happen.

As sun set neared we sat on the shore, searching the horizon for a hope of rescue. "Chan, do you think we will be rescued?" Sarrah asked me.
"I don't know," I said.
Then she got up and started dancing wildly around. Sarrah threw her hands in the air, and flailed about random comments of horses and taxes. Before we could figure out what she was talking about, she jumped into the ocean. We tried to pull her out, but she was already out to sea.

After the failed rescue of Sarrah, we crawled into the crab hut and went to sleep. The next morning we found Admiral Edward lying dead with marmite and vodka all around. I was in charge now. Before lunch we made a funeral pyre for the Admiral and buried it.
After lunch we began rebuilding the ship. We worked all night. By the next morning we had finished. "One thing gang," Davey said. "We have a weight problem! Too many cooks, or in this case too much of one cook."
Just then Cook Aadam sank into the sand.

"Well, that's it then. Let's go!" As Davey said that, the giant crabs led another attack! We managed to drive them back, but our ship's haul was devastated.

On top of our ship still being wrecked, our island food was diminished. We had picked all the crab cakes, and the coconuts and bananas were out of season. Unfortunately all the shrimp on this island grew on trees, which had all been picked as well. That left fishing, and bird catching. For weeks we honed our skills at those hunting methods.

…

A week passed. It had been a month since we first came there to the island. Fishing was a disaster, and we became so weak we could not even lift the rod. Bird hunting was fruitless as well. We had no strength to hit them, make traps for them, and there were not any birds around anyway by the end of the week.

Dr. Hodge had not been seen around. So we just sat. We could not survive another attack by the crabs, and we didn't know how long it would be before we starved to death. We could see the fins of sharks lurking in the water. We heard "na na, na na, nana, nana…" then we told Chan to cut it out.

…

One day I saw something in the air! "It's a bird, it's a plane, it's a UFO? Run!" I said as I remained sitting there staring upwards. We were too weak to run, instead we watched in disbelief. A beam shot down and teleported us into the ship.

Strange green aliens nourished us to health. After a while we felt normal. After being shown my quarters, I drew this map of the island from memory. Strangely enough, the aliens dropped us off at an old Washington Home. We said good bye to the aliens who had rescued us from the island. Times were good after that, and we made the best of things at that old mansion. We named our new home after our lost ship, *The Playmont*.

Nothing lasts forever, and after a few years of communal living at Playmont, we went our separate ways. We eventually became a part of the Capitalist Consumer society again, well most of us. After a few years of making money and getting in and out of debt, here I am. All I have left from those times of adventure are these 2 beer caps. Oh, its 7 o'clock which means its time to go to my psychologist.

…

If you ever wonder if my tale is true; just pick up a beer cap and use it to buy a rock. That's all that money is anyway. We use paper cash to buy more worthless trash and then we throw that crap away; like beer caps. If you want to feel how it felt when we made a living as castaways, and survived on that island… bite into a crab cake.

THE END

X = Our Shipwreck and Aadam's Grave
POC = Place of Crabs
Red Shell = Crab Hut
Green Dot = Dr. Hodge's Hut
Black Dot = Admiral Edward's Grave
Dots = Resources (Banana, Shrimp, Crabcake, and Ruins)

An Incredible Christmas Carol
Written by Walton Stowell Jr. in 7th Grade
Based on Charles Dickens' "A Christmas Carol"
Co-Authored and thought of by: Bratt McMurphy

Credits: Dino as Fred, Allen as Scrooge, Erica as Bob Cratchit, Byran as Spirit of Marley, Theo as Spirit of Christmas Past, Mac as Spirit of Christmas Present, Paula as Spirit of Christmas Future, Theo's Hair Dresser as Theo's Hair Dresser, Kali as Priest, Jack as Tiny Tanya, Scooter as Ghost Buster Friend, and Narrator is Mark.

Narrator: Once upon a time of all good days in a year, on Christmas Eve, old Scrooge sat in his office adjusting his proton expansion units...

(Cratchit is working quietly at his desk, while Scrooge is sitting by the ghost storage containment chamber, counting the occupants, when the office door opens)

Fred: A Merry Christmas, uncle Scrooge and Cratchit! God save you! (tosses empty candy wrapper)

Scrooge: What do you want??

Fred: I was delivering some Christmas spirit. Have any candy bars?

Scrooge: Yes, but I'm saving them for Slymer.

Fred: Come on, get in the Christmas spirit! You aren't still playing Ghost Hounders, are you? That's lame.

Scrooge: No I'm not PLAYING, I'm doing the real thing!

Fred: Come on, get with it! Stop with the ghost busting bit! Christmas is for sharing, so give me some candy bars! (at this Cratchit applauds, and Scrooge stands up)

Scrooge: Cratchit, if you don't get back to work on the containment ratios, I'll roast you alive, and the only place my Christmas spirit will be, is in the Ecto-Storage Containment Grid! Later plasma-brain! (he shoos Fred towards the door)

Fred: Come on, get with it Scrooge! Well Merry Christmas to you both. (and exits)

Scrooge: And a Bah-Beetle-Juice to you! (turns to Cratchit) I know you want tomorrow off, so you shall have it. But not a micro-second late the next day!!

Cratchit: Thank you Mr. Scrooge, and a Bah, I mean, Merry Christmas to you! (all exit office)

(Scrooge enters his house)

Narrator: As Scrooge unwraps a pack of Ghost Hounders Bubble Gum, a spirit appears.

Marley: I once tried Ghost Bunting like you Scrooge, and faked it to get money. But now I must carry containment units, PKE meters, partical throwers, and spectre-viewing-machines with me for eternity.

Scrooge: (grabbing a neutron gun) I'm not faking it! Bob Marley is that you? You can't be a ghost!

Marley: But I am. Tonight, you will be visited by 3 more spirits. If you can't change dude, you're doomed!

Scrooge: Awesome! (then crawls into bed, ghost of Marley disappears)

Narrator: As the clock strikes one, the Ghost of Christmas Past appears.

Scrooge: Huh???

Theo: Scroooooooge! Do you remember when you used 50 cents to buy Ghost Baker's Bubble Gum, instead of helping my poor hair stylist?

Scrooge: (slowly remembering) Yeah, so what?

Theo: Figure it out man!!! (disappears)

Narrator: The clock strikes two, and the Ghost of Christmas Present appears.

Mac: Ho ho ho! Chill mug! Gee dude!

Scrooge: (yawning) By Slymer, what sort of roaming-vapor apparition are you?

Mac: The good, jolly, stout kind. I'll show you what is happening to Tiny Tanya, daughter of your employee Cratchit. Leave your proton pack here.

Scrooge: You know, I should introduce you to Slymer. He is always trying to take my proton pack, and point it at my you-know-where! Sometimes I think he is more devil, than ghost. No way am I going to give up my gosh-darn proton pack!!!!!

Mac: Fine. (and disappears)

Narrator: At the strike of three, the mystic Ghost of Christmas Past appears. This one, it seems, was the weirdest of all.

Scrooge: Can't I get any sleep! You evil poltergeist, die!! (Scrooge lifts his electron generator and fires, zapping the ghost)

Paula: Your efforts are in vain, Scrooge. Have you not heard of super-condenscified, maximum hydrolified astro-plates?

Scrooge: I'm sorry free-floating torso vapor, tell me what you want.

Paula: That's a good man. What did you learn from all of this tonight, Scrooge? Did you learn anything special, or was it just another "Xmas" Japanese anime sci-fi to you? What did you learn?

Scrooge: To lock my doors incase freaks like you should come waltzing into my bedroom at say, three in the morning.

Paula: (electronically amplified) NO!!!!!! Give what is not needed, and what ever you do, don't bust ghosts on Christmas Eve!! (softly) Or any other time of the year.

Scrooge: Why didn't you just tell me in the beginning?! (pause...silence) So you're telling me if I do what you say, I will be saved??!

Paula: That is so. You must (fade out) change ...

Narrator: And with that, the spirit disappeared. Scrooge fell fast asleep. When he awoke, light shined through the bricks of his apartment. Scrooge jumped up, and ran to his window. People had already begun milling about on the streets outside!

Scrooge: Yippee!!! A new dawn is here! Morning has come at last! From now on, I will live in the past, present, and and and and whatever. (below on the sidewalk, Tiny Tanya hobbled along) Hey you! Hello, what day is it??

Tiny Tanya: Why it's Christmas Day man! (why would he not know?)

Scrooge: Good! Thank you! Here is $200 to pay for your injury! (as the money floated down, Tiny Tanya caught it and did a one-and-one-half-triple backflip over Scrooge's apartment)

Narrator: Scrooge was over joyed, and ran to Theo's Hair Stylist Shop in no time at all, with his pajamas on.

Scrooge: (talking to Theo's Hair Dresser) Here's your 50 cents, now stop giving Afro and Mushroom hair designs to people. And get that ear ring out of your right ear!

Hair Dresser: What the f*@bleep was that?!!

Narrator: Next Scrooge got Slymer, and went to his niece's house.

Scrooge: Merry Christmas Fred!! Here are your candy bars and I brought Slymer along for a turkey breakfast on me!!

Fred: How revolting!! Yet a wonderful surprise Uncle! Yes, a wonderful surprise indeed! Thank you Uncle Scrooge! (Slymer hovers over food)

Narrator: And so they ate into the afternoon. After saying goodbye, Scrooge and Slymer headed for home. They met Cratchit and Scooter (an old Ghosting partner) on the way.

Scrooge: Hello! Do you remember what I paid you before Cratchit?

Cratchit: Good day Sir! Yes, you paid me five dimes a year Sir.

Scrooge: Well I'm raising it to twenty dimes a year!

Cratchit: (embracing Scrooge) Thank you dearly Sir!!!

Scooter: (looking strange) You're not going to allow that, are you Scrooge? Ghost Bonkers never cross streams with rookies.

Scrooge: I've changed my ways Scooter. I hope you do too!!

Scooter: Does this mean no more Ghost Busting, even on Christmas?!?

Scrooge: Especially on Christmas! Ghost Bouncing is for the birds! Gooday gents!

Narrator: As Scrooge walked on, he told Slymer to wait for him outside as he entered St. Macy's Church.

Scrooge: (talking to priest) Merry Christmas Mother, you old goat!

Priest: Same to you, Bub.

Scrooge: Could you bless all the demons and spirits I have in my Cyber-Ecto Containment Storage System Grid?

Priest: Oh my Lord! (mumbles something) What did you just say Mac?!

Scrooge: What? What did you say Mother?

Priest: Never you mind. Look, I just work here Mug!

Scrooge: Oh come on! I even have a photo of it. See!! Pretty please, with ecto, I mean sugar on top!

Priest: Oh ok. Oh spirits bless you! Bless you! God bless you. Lord Bless you. Jesus bless you. Rapacious el mega stupido. Now get the hell out of here bum!

Scrooge: Thank you! Merry Christmas Mother! Goat!

Narrator: With that, Slymer and Scrooge went home. Scrooge grabbed the power switch to the room, pausing to say a short prayer.

Scrooge: Thank you Bob Marley! Thank you spirits! Merry Christmas!!!! Oh happy Virgin Birth and Immaculate Conception!!!

Narrator: Then Scrooge pulled the switch, releasing the ghosts with a blinding light! Eerie noises whooshed past, and turning everything dark.

(The Incredible Bulk, center stage, bursts from behind the curtains wrecks the set and leaps into the audience, yelling and chasing after people while flexing biceps)

THE END

This has been a Ghost Hounders International Production ©. All material contaminated within is property of GHI and protected by Satanic Lawyers who will sue you until death, and after death. All rights reserved, infinity (no take-backs).

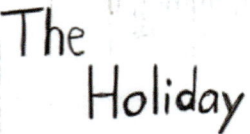

The Queen Elizabeth II Trip
Bonner School English 1989

June 19, 2000
Dear Paulina,

How have you been the last ten years? I've been trying to reach you for three years, but I keep getting your answering machine. Who's the guy with the whiny voice in the background? By the way, I've been tapped into your phone system for months, and I heard that one call from Italy. Congratulations on winning that Prize!

I wrote you to see if you are going to the reunion. The Queen Elizabeth II was built in 1969, thirty years before I bought my first German tank. That's right, I have a collection of tanks from different wars in my garage. I rent them over the weekends for $350.99 each. I have ten tanks. My favorites are the German Panther, armored personnel carriers, and the American M60 tank!!

I have transferred my religion to the Greek Pantheon. My beloved gods are Zeus, Vulcan, and Ares. I visit Greece often. I went to the University of Athens. What college did you go to? College was so much fun. I majored in History, Architecture, Law, and Literature. They gave me a $900,000 scholarship.

By the way, I was looking through my list of employees and I saw your name. I bought out IBM. Want a raise? Just kidding. I'll meet you at the dining hall on the Queen Elizabeth II. Please wear an antenna on your head so I'll see you. And don't bother being on time, I never am. Also try to wear some pink. I've been married 5 times in the past month, all of which I never knew about!

I live in Hawaii. With my Dad's corporation I now get $5,000 a day, and have half of the United States working for me. As an Architect-Judge-Magistrate I live in a castle. Before I board the ship, I plan to visit China Town, in New York. I will arrive at the port in my Sherman tank. Chinese food and Central Park will be interesting at dusk.

Mac McRothurfordstein will be in one of the four bands on board the Queen Elizabeth II. He also helped wire the virtual-reality library for a constantly-working mind. At the end of the cruise I will stay onboard to discuss business with the Captain. We plan to turn the boat into a submarine.

My body guards are eager to meet you. One of my future plans is to guild the Statue of Liberty in gold. I'm building a bigger Disneyland in Switzerland, with a full-length waterslide down the Alps. May Vulcan make your car run steady!

Until New York and onboard the Queen Elizabeth II,
- Walton Stowell

··

Banned!

Banned from this book:

Doctor Dippie's Fairy Tails

Many Wonderful Bed-Time Stories for Kids of All Ages

Published by Firewalker Ink 1988-2009

Story Book 1:   Timmy The Good Boy (1988)

Story Book 2:   The Revenge of the Three Bears (1988)

Story Book 3:   A Talk At Blue Dolphins Baywater Coastline (1989)

Story Book 4:   Coal Black and the Seven Dorks (1990)

Story Book 5:   Unauthorized Autobiography "Committed" (1995)

Story Book 6:   Dr. Dippie's Short Fairy Tails (1995)

Short Biography of Doctor Dippie

Matt R. Dippie was born a Scientist and Writer. His hobbies include color-coating his pens, and mucking around with History. He was born in a paper sack in a museum.

Medical Record: Nose lift, punch that smashed in his glasses rendering him legally blind, and 10 years at an insane asylum. He suffers from chronic constipation and diarrhea.

Favorite sayings:
"That belongs twisted on the press!" *"That's so sick, I love it!"*

"Matt is a famous and wonderful author of children stories. His whimsical approach to story telling makes old fairy tales come to life with gay on look."
- *A. Newman*

Don't Call Me A Nerd If I Read This Story

[The following story must be read with enthusiasm and out loud.]
[Do not ask or answer any questions while reading, just keep reading.]
[Start reading now.]

"Don't Call Me A Nerd If I Read This Story"

"Once upon a time, in a zoo far, far away; there lived me: a smart little muuu muuuu. Now wait a minute, that can't be what it says. It must be something else."

"Do you guys really want me to read this? I mean I'm so stupid I can't even read this. Gee, I must need 10 pairs of glasses. I can pick my nose faster than this."

"Ok, I'll go on. You guys seem to think I'm a real, well, never mind. I'm sitting here trying to read Walton's handwriting and wondering why I'm so stupid!"

"I feel so dumb and childish. I mean, I have nothing to brag about. I'll hand this over to you, fat-so! Only smart people can read this right."

THE END

■■

How Elephant Got His Toenails
Walton Stowell, English African Myth

One day, when cats wore furs, and eagles had large wings, and the wind blew, and the sky was blue, and there were no such things as dragons, and people lived in large polluted cities; a man named Ug sat and thought. Ug was well known for this.

The elephants ran wild and thought of many things. Barron Matho picked a stick and hit and killed Ug. Ug laughed and sat and thought…

[Warning: *Now this may be confusing to some, but don't worry; this is an African Myth and much is lost in translation.*]

"Ug was very smart, but cities are polluted. Ug is dead and Matho is alive!" Barron Matho said.

After Ug died, Matho went to the elephants. Matho wanted food after the battle, and said "Elephants, I need some food and I will give you anything if you give me some food… and I will give you anything that you want." The elephants laughed.

Meanwhile Ug sat and thought. "I must kill you again!" shouted Barron Matho and he was given food by the elephants. "How can I repay you?" asked Matho. "I can't bring back Ug to life." "All we want are toe nails." Said the elephants.

"Your wish is granted!" said Matho, and from then on, elephants walked with toenails." **THE END**

Tony The Turkey ~ from Tall Tale Starters
Walton Stowell 7th Grade
November 22, 1988

Tony Turkey was strong, so strong that he could lick any turkey in the yard, and lift anything around. In fact, he was so strong that no one knew exactly how strong he was. They were afraid to ask, and couldn't think of any safe way to measure his strength.

One day, however, circumstances put Tony's strength to the test. It was a warm, sunny day; and Tony was pressing various hen houses within the fenced-in area. Turkey Lurkey was out playing, and Chicken Big was pecking at the Wee Worm Gang. Life was in it's usual circus mode around the farm.

It just so happened that Turkey Lurkey had been out playing with his yo-yo that day, when he came upon a pack of wolves discussing their plans to raid the hen houses. Turkey Lurkey flew behind a bush as fast as his little poultry feet would carry him. Lurkey over heard the wolves talking about raiding the coup.

"Say Sam, don't ya think them chickens is ripe fer the picken?"
"Sure. Tomorrow we go eat them plump birds!" the wolf said.

Turkey Lurkey's heart practically jumped from his chest when he heard this. He sat for a spell, trying to decide what to do next; when it hit him. He must warn the coup! Turkey Lurkey grabbed his yo-yo, and ran for the coup. He burst through the gate, and hit Tony head on; BOOM!! Tony Turkey put down the hen house he was holding, and took a hard look at Turkey Lurkey. Turkey Lurkey looked around frantically. Now when Turkey Lurkey became scared, he never could think straight.

"The wolves are going to eat the chickens tomorrow! I bet they will eat all the turkeys too!! What are we going to do?!!" All the chickens heard this and began clucking.

Everyone became scared. It was a perfect chance for Tony to prove his strength.

"Wolves, wolves, wolves; so what? I could whip any wolf!!" Tony said thoughtlessly. Now when Tony the Turkey became excited, he never could think straight. When Tony said that, Terrence Turkey spoke up.

"Ok, I guess that means you'll protect the coup tomorrow." Terrence began sweating, because he was not sure if Tony Turkey would accept the challenge, or if he was up to the task (you don't usually see a turkey sweat).

Tony knew he could hold off the wolves though. He could probably hold off ten wolves, and probably kill them if he had to. He finally figured that he must kill the wolves to keep his reputation, or the wolves would keep coming back and attack when Tony was not expecting them.

After saying good-bye to Tom, Terrence, Tabitha, Terrell, Tanya, Bill Gob, the Cockadoos, the Squawks, the McGiblets, and the Strutts; Tony Turkey set off in search of the wolves. After awhile he sat under the trees as the sun went down, frightened and lonely. He had lost the nerve that he had set off with. It finally drove him crazy.

Tony fluttered over hills, ran into trees, and fell into ditches. He at last ended up in a cave. It was dark and damp. Tony sat alone, all bruised up. "That last tree I knocked over, was hard," Tony thought as he got up. He walked deeper into the cave.

Tony soon came upon a large can and a rat. "Look inside the can!" the rat said. Tony tensed his muscles, and pried open the can with his beak. There was strange writing on the lid. Inside there was a stainless plastic ring! "Wow," Tony thought.

"15 carat plastic, too!" the rat said. "But put it on."

Tony put the plastic ring on one of his clawed toes; and behold!! Tony became invisible! Tony thought to himself, "This is just like a book I read, called the Tolbit!" Then he told the rat about his mission. The rat said he would help, and added "My name is Ratthew."

It was dark, as they ate their supper in the cave. Then they went out and set traps in the dark of night. They worked late into the night, together; turkey and rat. In the morning they took a short nap. "They're coming!" the rat shouted as several large, furry shapes appeared over the hill. Tony and the Ratthew took their places.

Ratthew was in the treehouse control tower, and Tony was in front of the chicken coup gate. Tony took off the ring of invisibility, and ran towards some bushes. "Get that plump turkey, Joe!" said a wolf.

A wolf raced after Tony; Tony was trapped! Just then, the bushes sprang up and covered the wolf, walnuts buried him, and he sank into the ground. Two more wolves raced at Tony. He slipped on his ring, and vanished!

Tony reappeared near a small tree. The wolves ran after him. Tony flew to the top of the small tree. The wolves began to shake the tree, but their paws became stuck to the top of the bark of the tree. Tony flew off of the tree, back to the ground. Slowly the tree began to sink into the ground, and soon the wolves were engulfed in dirt, tail and all.

Tony picked up a large rock (large for a turkey), and threw it at the remaining wolves. When the wolves tried to block it, it exploded releasing skunk-berry juice all over them, forcing some of them to run to the nearest pond.

Tony Turkey put on his ring again, as the two last wolves raced at him. As he scrambled to avoid them, the ring fell off his foot! Tony started to panic. The rat called down from the watch tower, that the next trap would only hold one wolf, they had not counted on so many wolves! They had not had enough time to prepare for so many wolves.

So there had been a miscount. Tony decided he would have to use all his strength, in order to survive this attack. Tony stood tall, as tall as he could stand. He also stood solid, as solid as a rock. In fact, when the wolves hit him….. he was knocked through the bushes, through 7 trees, and rolled 20 feet up a hill.

Then Tony pulled himself out of the furrow of mud he made by being thrown, he realized maybe he should try using his smartness to win. Ratthew the Rat jumped down from the treehouse and bit one wolf. Meanwhile Tony sat down beside the other wolf.

"How many wolves does it take to screw in a light bulb?" the wolf growled as Tony said that. "Ok, why did the turkey cross the road?" At this joke, the wolf batted Tony down the nearest clover hillside.

As Tony lay on the ground, he thought "This guy is getting me mad. Just 'cause he's a little bit stronger than me, he thinks he can boss me around." Tony struggled to his feet again, and ran back up the clover hillside.

When he reached the top, he saw the farmer with his gun blowing away the wolves. Soon the farmer left, dragging the dead wolves along with him. Tony went over to Ratthew the Rat. "You almost got us killed, with your dumb trap miscalculation!" yelled Tony.

"Don't talk turkey to me! You lost the magic ring! Anyway, I gotta go home," Ratthew replied as they said good-bye; and returned to their respective homes.

Tony went back into the coup. He invited all the fowl poultry to come to his nesthouse and listen to his story. All the chickens, turkeys, and geese came and crowded around his nestchair. Tony Turkey sat back and began to tell his long tale.

"Well I sat outside the gate in the dark, alert, all night. In the morning I met the wolves head on; all ten, twenty, thirty, I mean eighty of them. Yeah, all a-hundred eighty of 'em. 'Get away from here!' says I, 'Before I put an end to ya!' and I gave 'em a left, right, left, right. Fur was everywhere. And I threw them all the way to the other side of the farm!" Tony was bluffing up a storm.

"But we heard gun shots?!" Tina Strutt said. She was always pecking her beak where it didn't belong. Tony stuttered a response; "Oh, ah….. those weren't gun shots, they were, ah, fire works. Yeah, fireworks. The forest was celebrating the death of the wolves! All the woodland creatures were out partying, that's the ticket!". Tony shoved all of them out the door. He stopped going on adventures, cold turkey. But he kept telling his tall-turkey-tales; many, many times; to all the chicks.

So Tony the Turkey's pride was saved, and his legend still lives on today.

THE END   Grade: Check Plus + 10 extra!

Tony The Turkey

....

In The Hands Of A Super Hero
Walton Stowell, A

As the plane reached one mile from the planet's surface, Jim Farger looked from behind his newspaper and glanced along the seats. He knew Dr. Dread was somewhere in this huge 747. If he let Dr. Dread get off the plane alive, that would surely mean the destruction of the world. Jim looked a long time, searching across the isles of the plane.

Finally, he decided to go see if the pilots were alright. He opened the curtains, and there were no pilots! Jim raced to the bathroom. In a flash, he was back, but as…Super Jim!

Super Jim checked every single seat, but he couldn't find Dr. Dread anywhere. He knew Dr. Dread had to be on the plane somewhere… Suddenly, Super Jim looked back and saw Dr. Dread going into the cargo space! He ran with super speed to the back of the plane. Jim ripped off the door and ran in after Dr. Dread, who was hiding somewhere in the cargo space.

There were three big sheets in the giant room. There was something underneath the sheets. Maybe Dr. Dread was under a sheet. Super Jim flung a sheet off, which revealed huge mechanical parts! Dr. Dread had smuggled parts of an MX Missile onboard!!

Jim yanked off the second sheet, and again there were parts for another MX Missile! Jim pulled off the last sheet. There were more parts, but this time Dr. Dread leaped out!

Dr. Dread's glasses were small and made his eyes look beady. His yellow and pink tie clearly clashed with his black, curly hair, green neon suit, buck teeth, and scrunchy little nose. "You'll never stop me!" Dr. Dread shouted at Super Jim.

Super Jim tried to grab him, but was stopped by a bullet to the chest. It was then, that Super Jim realized that he wasn't bullet proof.

Dr. Dread ran for the doorway. With a burst of strength, Super Jim leapt to his feet and grabbed Dr. Dread. Drawing a deep breath, Super Jim said, "The good guys always win in the end." Then Jim ripped off a section of the wall, and held Dr. Dread over the tiny mountains below.

As Super Jim prepared to drop the villain, Dr. Dread cocked his gun, and fired again blowing a hole through Jim's wrist. Jim placed Dr. Dread down inside the plane, and fell to the floor in pain. Dr. Dread then kicked Super Jim out of the depressurizing cabin.

It was then that Super Jim realized he couldn't fly either.

And it is now, that we end our story. **THE END**

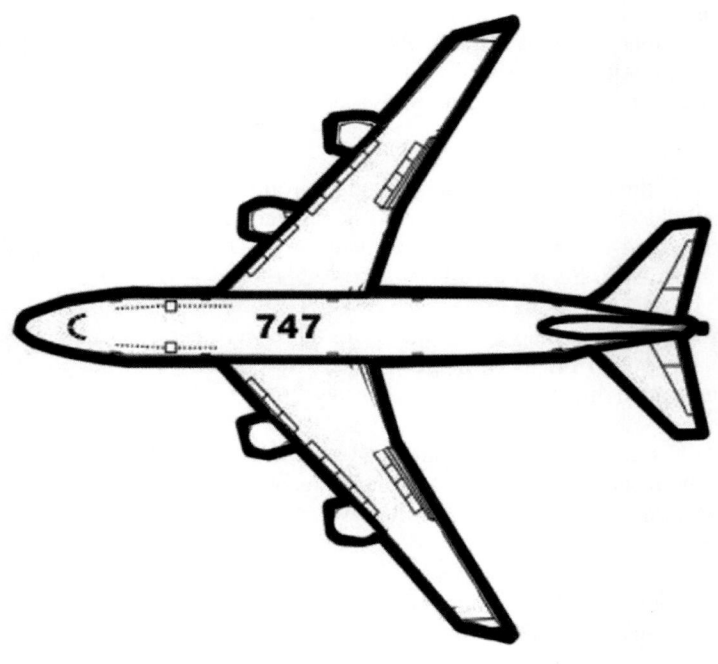

The Chinese Doggy Blahs
By Walton Stowell Jr. 2nd Grade

We once had two long-haired, small shih-tzu dogs.
Their names were Wicket and Chang.
One day Chang had the Doggy Blahs.

We took Chang to the veterinarian.
The vet said the Doggy Blahs were when a dog is sad.
Chang was a good dog though, he did not bark or bite.

We went home.
Wicket was a good dog too, he loved to play.
Wicket wanted to play, but Chang put his face in the bowl.

The Chinese have something called Chi.
Chi is an energy field that we all have within us.
Good Chi is positive energy and feels good too.

I remembered that meditation helps Chi.
Then I sat with Chang for a long time.
When I looked at him, he pounced on me with a smile!

I told Mom that the Doggy Blahs went away.
I was so happy that Chang was better,
I put a Kung Foo suit on him.

Chang liked doing Kung Foo.
Instead of putting his face in the bowl,
he chopped the bowl in half!

Chang went "Car foo!"
Even the caged bird was happy.
The parakeet went "Tweet!"

THE END

Chang, a Chinese Shih-tzu Dog, Beset with the Doggy-blahs

The Forbidden Closet

To be read in a suspenseful voice, with emphasis on punctuation pauses.

A ten-year-old boy named Mark, was having a sleep-over.

That night, at 9 o'clock, Mark and his friends; Sammy, Jimmy, and Timmy; told ghost stories. Mark told about a ghost that he heard about in New York. Sammy told about a preying mantis that he caught the day before (which had nothing to do with the subject). Timmy told about the ghost in his aunt's room. And Jimmy told about how the Boogie Man used to come out of his closet, and how he could come from other people's closets. They were so scared that they all went to sleep.

At 12 o'clock midnight, Mark's clock buzzed; it was time to play midnight hide-and-go-seek. They all took flashlights. Jimmy was 'It'. Mark decided to hide in his closet. He didn't think that the Boogie Man was in his closet. He shined his flashlight in the closet, he was right! No Boogie Man! Mark was so content with his hiding place, that he fell asleep.

After a few minutes, Mark began to roll! He rolled faster and faster! He opened his eyes. He was rolling down a stone ramp. Mark was horrified! The ramp ended, and he began falling down a large shaft. Quickly, Mark grabbed onto a stone jutting out from the wall.

He couldn't quite make out what was below him; it was so dark. His eyes began to adjust to the darkness around him and below. He could see figures below him! Mark couldn't believe what he saw. Hundreds of zombies were six feet below him! All of a sudden, a green glowing hand reached up for his leg! Just at the same time, a rope was lowered down to him.

Mark didn't care who or what was at the top, he just wanted to get out! So he pulled his body out of reach of the glowing hand. As he climbed, he looked down and could still see the claws of the glowing hand scratching at the wall. It seemed like the climb up the rope was taking forever. He felt cold and clammy, but feverish at the same time.

Mark finally made it to the stone ramp. As he scaled the ramp with the help of the rope, he saw light up ahead. When he reached the top, he saw a human hand holding the rope, then he passed out.

He awoke by being slapped in the face. He opened his eyes. All his friends; Sammy, Jimmy, and Timmy; were standing in the closet with him. The rope lay coiled beside him, and under him.

"Wake up, we found you!" Jimmy said.
"But I….." Mark began.
"We know. You fell asleep." Timmy said, "Hurry up and hide, Sammy is It."
"No, I didn't go to sleep, well I at first I did, but….." Mark stammered.
"<u>Hide</u>*!!*" They shouted at Mark.
Mark thought for awhile, by himself. "If I make a big deal about this, they will think I'm insane. So I'll just keep quiet," Mark thought.

The next few years, he kept quiet about *'the happening'*.
Until ….. **Part 2** !!

■ ■

All In A Day's Work
Teacher comment: Good! Check Plus

"Well, it all started when I was 1 day old. It was Salla time, XIO*. All of my troop was lined up with presents to give to the queen. It was almost my turn. I was so excited! It was almost my turn! It was such an honor. I had five full crumbs of bread to give to her. Some careless humans just left me the crumbs. Oh well I guess I was just lucky.

"So anyway, I bowed low and handed the queen the crumbs. She was delighted and ate them quickly. It must have been too much for her, because she fell over. Suddenly I was surrounded by the guards! No wonder those people left me the crumbs, they contained food poisoning! What does an ant have to do to get some respect?!

"The guards decided they would give me another chance. So they put me on guard duty, rather than tear me into little pieces and feed me to our larvae. I paced up and down, hoping they wouldn't do anything to me, when suddenly I smelled something….

"What was it?"

"Just hold on, will ya! Here I am, talking to a white blood cell! Anyway, I crept through the grass, and under rocks, 'til I came to the source of the smell. It was unbelievable! Something that only happens once in a blue moon! It was a real, live picnic!!

"The blanket was 40 praying mantises long! There was so much food! Apples, plums, dates, apple sauce, pizza, broccoli, spinach, peaches, etc. etc. and etc..

"I ran back and alarmed the guards. We all raced to the picnic, all 3,051 of us. Everyone was this way and that, trying to decide what to get first. Suddenly there was an alarm that signaled humans were on the prowl!

"We formed into groups. Me and 20 other troops climbed onto an enormous peach. Each ant took sections. I began to chew out my section, when suddenly I was pushed to my feet. We ere rising quickly! Six ants jumped off. I tried to jump, but the G-Force was too strong. Up, up up we rose. I began to move, but it was too late!

"I was inside a human's mouth! The human noticed what it had done, and began to spit us out! The saliva was tossing me all around. I just about drowned. The tongue kicked me back, down into the throat. I looked around in the throat and saw 3 other ants had fallen in with me. We slipped further down the throat, and it got darker.

"I reached out and clung on to something slimey. It was this, this mutated food that I landed on. Presently I'm still clinging on for dear life to the mutated food, while talking to this dumb, dense white cell. Any more questions?"

THE END

County Fire Brigade
Walton Stowell, 8th grade A+
Reading, September 28, 1989

Journal Entry:

Well, it all started when I took the blame for the fire. I did it because I thought my brother would admit to it after me, which would make me look good. But that stupid bratt didn't. My punishment was to join the county fire brigade.

When the truck came in the morning, Grandpa and I hopped in the back. The driver's name was Smee, and he looked and smelled like moldy cheese. Next there was the leader, Jim. He was tall and looked like a geek. He always wore a red scarf that he sets on fire. Later on he pats the fire out so that it smokes. Then he changes scarves and starts again. Scarf burning is a habit with him. Also there's this short black guy named Buba that pulls on his ear, and picks his nose.

So anyway we finally reached the site of the fire. Me and Gramps prepared to get off the truck, but suddenly Smee floored it and we tumbled to the hard bottom of the truck bed. Out truck blazed a path right thru the combusting wood and leaves. Then the truck did a 360 and we all hopped out. Smee kept revving up the truck and Buba sat down and picked his nose.

Jim, Gramps, and I took shovels and started digging ditches around the fire. Then we waited for the fire to go out. As night approached Buba roasted marshmellows and ate grass. Jim told us to go to the center of the fire and start blowing, and maybe the fire would snuff out like a candle. Gramps and I thought that a very absurd idea, but since we had nothing better to do, we carefully entered the fire through an already burned out trail.

The walls of the fire reached heights of 30 feet, and it was very hot. When we got to the middle of the fire we started blowing. When we were out of breath, we realized all we were doing was spreading the fire, and burning our skin and clothes.

Gramps still had his shovel which he held tightly. His face turned bright red and he drove his shovel deep into the ground so that only the handle was showing. When his strength returned he pulled it out and a massive flow of water spewed forth, extinguishing the fire.

Jim celebrated by lighting a new scarf, but accidently caught his hair on fire. He ran into the forest screaming. Smee popped his wart and asked us if we wanted a ride back. We declined his offer, and walked back home. I don't think I'll ever get over what my grandfather and my dumb brother put me through.

THE END

From America
Walton Stowell   13/15
Social Studies "Excellent"

Dear Elizabeth, Cameron, and Judy,

How is everything in jolly ol' England? I'm having a loaf of a time, although I have one problem. Today some kids came up to me while I was on duty, and started throwing snow balls. When it started to get out of hand, I called for backup. Adults and kids were both chanting names and throwing snow balls. Soon the Captain came, and lined us up. Before I knew what was happening, we were ordered to fire. If you want to know, I shot four people. The soldiers are being blamed, but before we shot I warned the kids. I called out for them to leave, but they kept throwing snow balls. It was their own bloody fault, those damn kids! Anyway, I doubt anything will come of it.

Judy, how is your doll house coming along? I hope you and Cameron are getting along and having fun! Cheerio! I will be coming back to England in about 3 months. Those bloody scoundrels, the Indians have attacked us again. We are posting more guards than ever to protect the town. I hear the King is thinking of a large tea tax. Is this true? Does Lord Shrimely still have a monopoly over all the marmite stores? I would think everyone has had their sufficient fill of him.

Elizabeth, I wonder if you received that silver inlaid pot I sent for Christmas. I have just been ordered to report to the office. Please write back and tell me what's up. See you all!

With love, Trager

Jimmy Clouds

Walton Stowell, English 1989, 7th Grade

"What are clouds?" Jimmy asked as we sat alone on the wet, sharp grass. The clouds floated overhead. I waited.

"Clouds are the minds of people. Without them, we can't think," I told him.

"You mean my head is really empty??" Jimmy asked.

I continued on without thinking, "Clouds spark and ignite the imagination. The flame of eternal thought."

Jimmy thought for awhile. "I still don't understand you!"

I woke from my dreams and said "Examine the clouds, see how the shapes change before you even notice. They change with your every clever thought. They move to the shape of your mind."

Jimmy was quiet. Then he spoke up, "I don't get it!"

"As the clouds float by, the breeze changes their articulate shapes. Nothing can stop them; not death, nor life," I answered.

"What in the world do you mean??" Jimmy's eyes left the sky.

"Ok, Mr. 'I don't know', clouds are little white things that look like brain fungus, because I said!" I replied with a glare.

We both laid back down and relaxed, as the sun beamed down on us. Soon, Jimmy eyed a blue and gold crested mountain. I prepared for a long afternoon.

The End

My Pet Dragon

My pet dragon is a blue-grey fairy-dragon, from beak to tail one and a half feet. His scales are dark blue-grey, on top of which he has his own elaborate metal armor. He is very sharp and clever, but does not make much of a mess because he obeys me.

My pet dragon is very independent, for a pet. He flies off to hunt his own food whenever he is hungry; and he understands that by returning home to me, it is a form of mutual friendship. He is able to nest and keep treasures without having to guard them as much as if he was in the wild. I help to keep him safe, and he helps to keep me safe.

Mister Chop

Gifted Program 1986
Japan Jitsu Books Inc.

Mr. Chop lived in Chop Chop Land, in a very Japanese like house. He was a 3rd Degree Black Belt, so his house was a 3 story pagoda. Mr. Chop loved to walk down his red brick steps and go on walks.

Mr. Chop was walking along when he saw an elf.
Mr. Chop said "My name is Mister Chop. What's your name?"
The elf screamed and said "Help, Mr. Slop!" and ran away.
"Wait a minute!" Mr. Chop said, but it was too late.
The elf was gone.

As he walked on to a bunch of robbers, Mr. Chop said;
"Hi, I'm Mister Chop." The robbers yelled and ran away, saying "A cop! Help a cop!"

Mr. Chop just shook his head. People were afraid of him. Frustrated, Mr. Chop kicked some bricks to break them.

As Mr. Chop walked on and on, he saw Big Chop! Big Chop said "Hello cousin! I hear from an elf that you are sloppy!"
"No, I said I am Mister Chop." "Oh, I am sorry." "That's ok."

Mr. Chop only came up to Big Chop's toenail, but they saw eachother as equals. The moral of the story is always be nice to your friends, even when they are wrong!

THE END

Mister Chop

On The Run
Walton Stowell / December 15, 1988 / 7th Grade English
Teacher comment: "I see semi colons, but where are the ones combined in a series?"

Robert knew that that day would be his last. He sat in his chair nervously, struggling in his seat-belt. He spat into his hat. Flying was driving him crazy. Robert knew the plane would crash. He could hear the pilot saying now "Everyone, remain calm. We're gonna crash.,".

Robert was sweating. He could feel his flesh burning and melting off his face. He unfastened his seat-belt, grabbed his suit-case and from there, Robert smashed through the window of the 747. Down, down, down he went. Right through the ragging storm, down past lightning infested clouds; his body shook with fear.

Then Robert chuckled to himself, "Well, I guess this is better than crashing! Even if I am falling 3,500 feet. I just hope I land on something soft!" Robert could feel his limbs being pulled, stretched, and torn. As he plunged deeper, he experienced pain; loss of oxygen; followed by unconsciousness.

Later, as his lungs became filled with oxygen again, Robert slowly woke up. His weightlessness made him feel uneasy; yet free. He began to acknowledge death as his future; when he felt something snap under his back; a crash and a thud; the next thing he knew, he was laying on a dead man. Robert wiped his forehead; "So that's what broke my fall!"

From the looks of the dead man and his house, Robert guessed he was in Africa. He had seen photos of African villages; this looked suspiciously like one of the huts in an African village. He got some boards and towels, to make a splint and mend his broken leg. Next Robert went to the cupboard, and got a little snack to eat. While he was determining if it was moldy sea food, or a fly casserole, two tall warriors burst in; toppling Robert's chair he was sitting in. The warriors grabbed him.

"If it's about the hole in the roof, I can fix it!" he said. But it was not the hole in the roof that the warriors were mad about; so Robert was dragged out of the house, and off to gods know where.

Soon they came to a group of three stones. In the middle, there was a dark haired, swarthy skinned, and tackily dressed English man; and beside him were two more warriors with spears. The Englishman eyed Robert suspiciously.

"Ah, finally someone who knows English!" Robert said, eying his suitcase; which the Englishman must have stolen from the plane Robert was on.

"I doubt it will help you any, Mr. Stanely. You see, I work for the English Intelligence Agency; if you will kindly reach in your back pocket you will find a bug, and a tracer. You may have avoided the plane crash, but you cannot hold off the inevitable for long. I will give you one chance; run for your life, run for the jungle!" said the Englishman.

Robert quickly grabbed his suitcase and kicked the Englishman in the – [the next word has been deleted from the page due to improper language, and replaced with a suitable synonym] - *potatoes*. Robert ran for his life, into the jungle.

Five hundred warriors raced after him, through the jungle. Robert hobbled through bushes, branches, and swamps. Mosquitoes and bees swarmed around him. Robert ran until he could run/hobble no more. He plunged into a thicket, and sat.

"Well at least they are not mad at me, for that hole in the roof!" he said, rubbing his foot. Robert was tired and hungry; and his leg was killing him! Never-the-less, he picked himself up, and headed onward.

After a long hour, Robert came to the end of the jungle; where the land meets the ocean. He laid his suitcase down, and got a banana from a nearby tree. He changed his clothes, and made a large tent from all his other laundry. Then Robert went for a swim.

The salt water felt good on his wound; in a bitter-sweet way. Robert was enjoying the warm water, when he heard a snap, and yell coming from the jungle. He rushed onto land to find his tent down, and raveled up. Robert uncoiled the clothes to find a smothered warrior with a tracking device beeping. Then he remembered he had left the tracer in his old pants; and had left his old pants with the tracer in his tent; therefore the native must have gotten wrapped up in the wrong affairs.

Robert covered the dead body of the warrior with his tent (and his old pants with the tracer); all of which he then buried under a stack of banana tree leaves. Then he filled his suitcase with bananas, and left.

As he got deeper into the jungle, Robert heard footsteps. He walked faster. Sweat was pouring from his head; his hands were bloody and raw; and his clothes were being shredded from thick, thorny brush and dry splintery bark.

He collapsed under a tall dark tree. Robert was scared. He opened his suitcase and began eating bananas.

"Ah, much better than the airplane food!" he said to himself. Robert ate another banana; he really did prefer bananas to airplane food. After a few more bananas, Robert packed up his suitcase; and struggled on.

Later, he came to another beach; this one was broader with a dock. There was a man with a row boat there. Robert ran over, knocked the man off, and rowed like crazy towards a small island. Although his hands ached and stung, Robert rowed fast.

He reached the island, and hopped out on the rocky land. Robert flipped open his suitcase, sat down, and ate another banana in celebration. After a while of enjoying his new found island, Robert heard the hum of a motor; and soon saw a jet overhead!

Robert ran along the edge of the island, waving his hands like crazy. The jet swooped down! Robert stumbled backwards; and getting up, promptly tripped over something. The jet came closer to the island. Robert had tripped over a sign. It read "Warning: Naval Bombing Area".

Robert jumped up, this time with sheer panic and fright. He ran into the woods on the island, and leaped over a low stone wall; only to land in warm water. Robert had landed in a kiddie pool. He splashed around, trying to get his head upright. It was a kiddie pool, next to a larger swimming pool, next to a large motel. A man walked up to him.

"Welcome to Willie's Resort!!" The man said. "Would sir like a drink?"
"You run a resort in a bombing zone?" Robert asked, flummoxed.
"No, the sign and the jet are just to scare off beach-bums," the man said.
"Ah, yes I think I would like that drink after all. Thank you." Robert said.

So Robert worked as a bell boy for the rest of his life; and lived happily, ever after.

THE END

The Neckless
100% a Satire of "The Necklace" by Guy de Maupassant 1884

She was one of those pretty and charming girls born, as though fate had blundered over her, into a family of artisans. She had no means of getting known, understood, loved, and wedded by a man of wealth and distinction; and she let herself be married off to a little clerk in the Ministry of Education.

She suffered endlessly, feeling herself born for every delicacy and luxury. She suffered from the poorness of her house, from its mean walls, worn chairs, and ugly curtains. All these things, of which other women of her class would not even have been aware, tormented and insulted her.

She had no clothes, no jewels, nothing. And these were the only things she loved; she felt that she was made for them. She had longed so eagerly to charm, to be desired, to be wildly attractive and sought after. Yet she went naked.

One evening her husband came home with an exultant air, holding a large envelope in his hand. "Here's something for you," he said. Swiftly she tore the paper and drew out a printed card on which were these words:

"The Minister of Education and Madame Ramponneau request the pleasure of the company of Monsieur and Madame Loisel at the Ministry on the evening of Monday, January the 18th."

Instead of being delighted, as her husband hoped, she flung the invitation petulantly across the table, murmuring: "What do you want me to do with this? There's nothing so humiliating as looking poor in the middle of a lot of rich women."

"How stupid you are!" exclaimed her husband. "Go and see Madame Forestier and ask her to lend you some jewels. You know her quite well enough for that." She uttered a cry of delight. "That's true. I never thought of it."

Next day Madame Loisel went to see her friend and told her her trouble. Madame Forestier presented a superb diamond necklace; her heart began to beat covetously. Her hands trembled as she lifted it. She fastened it round her neck, upon her high dress, and remained in ecstasy at sight of herself. She asked in anguish: "Lend me this!" Then she flung herself on her friend's breast, embraced her frenziedly, and went away with her treasure.

The day of the party arrived. Madame Loisel was a success. She was the prettiest woman present, elegant, graceful, smiling, and quite above herself with happiness. All the men stared at her, inquired her name, and asked to be introduced to her. All the Under-Secretaries of State were eager to waltz with her. The Minister noticed her.

She danced madly, ecstatically, drunk with pleasure, with no thought for anything, in the triumph of her beauty, in the pride of her success, in a cloud of happiness made up of this universal homage and admiration, of the desires she had aroused, of the completeness of a victory so dear to her feminine heart.

She left about four o'clock in the morning. Sadly they walked up to their own apartment. It was the end, for her. She took off the garments in which she had wrapped her shoulders, so as to see herself in all her glory before the mirror. But suddenly she uttered a cry. The necklace was no longer round her neck!

"What's the matter with you?" asked her husband, already half undressed. She turned towards him in the utmost distress. "I . . . I . . . I've no longer got Madame Forestier's necklace. . . ."

He started with astonishment. "What! . . . Impossible!"

They searched in the folds of her dress, in the folds of the coat, in the pockets, everywhere. They could not find it.

Loisel, who had aged five years, declared: "We must see about replacing the diamonds."

Then they went from jeweller to jeweller, searching for another necklace like the first, consulting their memories, both ill with remorse and anguish of mind. In a shop at the Palais-Royal they found a string of diamonds which seemed to them exactly like the one they were looking for. It was worth forty thousand francs. They were allowed to have it for 36,000, all of which they had to borrow, with interest.

Madame Loisel came to know the ghastly life of abject poverty. From the very first she played her part heroically. This fearful debt must be paid off. She would pay it. The servant was dismissed. They changed their flat; they took a garret under the roof.

She came to know the heavy work of the house, the hateful duties of the kitchen. She washed the plates, wearing out her pink nails on the coarse pottery and the bottoms of pans. She washed the dirty linen, the shirts and dish-cloths, and hung them out to dry on a string; every morning she took the dustbin down into the street and carried up the water, stopping on each landing to get her breath. And, clad like a poor woman, she haggled, insulted, fighting for every wretched halfpenny of her money.

Every month notes had to be paid off, others renewed, time gained. And this life lasted ten years. Until one day Madam Loisel had a mental breakdown, and went to Madam Forestier to tell her of the truth and her suffering.

"You remember the diamond necklace you lent me for the ball at the Ministry? Well, I lost it. I brought you another one just like it. And for the last ten years we have been paying for it. You realize it wasn't easy for us; we had no money. . . . Well, it's paid for at last. All 36,000 francs."

Madame Forestier had halted. "You say you bought a diamond necklace to replace mine?"

She smiled with proud and simple joy. Madam Forestier, quite overcome, clasped her by the hands. "Oh my poor Mathilde, but my necklace was only plastic! You paid 36,000 francs for a necklace worth only 5 francs!"

Madam Loisel's face became red. "Why you drool from a motherless fruitfly! You have made me spend ten years of my life for a fake necklace!!!" Madam Forestier giggled with delight at the sight of Madam Loisel running away, embarrassed at having been tricked.

When Madam Loisel got home she went to her attic. She began to cry. How was she going to tell her husband that they spent their life savings on a bunch of plastic? Suddenly a small orange light came from her hand. It felt warm, and familiar. Then the tiny light changed colors to a deep blue. It was cold and unfriendly. She let her thoughts descend and be enveloped by the blueness. Soon the light went away and Mathilde went to sleep.

In the morning Mr. Loisel had terrible news. "My dear Mathilde," he said, "Madam Forestier and her family were found this morning, neckless!!!"

"That's improper French, masseur." Madam Loisel chirped. "You mean to say they have located Madam Forestier's necklace."

Mr. Loisel shook his head, then looked down, "Yes, they found her necklace along with her, and the rest of her family. They were all neckless!!"

Madam Loisel was puzzled. "Along with the rest of the family, what? Make sense man!"

"They were all dead. Their throats were ripped out!! They had no necks!!!" "Oh," Madam said and then started to cry.

"Have you been playing with your magic light again?" Mr. Loisel asked.

"Yes," Madam Loisel said. "At the time the light came to me I was thinking only of revenge against Madam Forestier, for lending me a fake necklace. So I released the monster to remove her ability to wear necklaces forever."

Mr. Loisel looked out the window. "Whatever's out there, it killed Forestier, and now it wants us!" They set about boarding up the windows and doors. Then they argued which was safer; the upstairs or the basement. The basement was secure, but upstairs there were escape routes. While they were arguing, they heard a noise. Mr. Loisel reached for his gun, but then remembered he never had one.

Madam Loisel gasped at what she saw. A blue creature came toward her. In it's right hand, it had a beautiful diamond necklace. In it's left hand was her husband. "Choose," it said in a cerulean voice.

Madam's French instincts kicked in, and she chose the necklace. Because of her selfish choice, she and her husband both lost their necks that night. Thus they became the very treasure that was their desire. Indeed, they were the Neckless (pun intended).

THE END

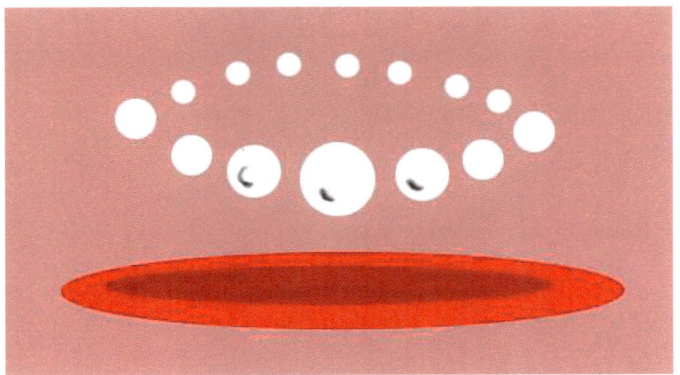

Sheryl Holmes & Rennell Watson

Based on Sherlock Holmes: Case of the Speckled Band
Banned Reading Class, October 19, 1988

~Rewritten from the finale' of the later half of the Case...

Holmes: Quickly, Watson! Roylott's room!

As they slam open the door, Roylott is found picking his nose.

Roylott: What are you doing here Holmes?

Holmes crosses to Roylott's desk, and nudges Roylott's hand with her cane.

Holmes: The question is my dear man, what are you doing here so late in the night with a snake whistle?! And what is that smell??

Roylott: Where did you just come from, the out-house, Holmes??!

As they begin to argue, a snake crawls through the vent.

Watson: By Jove! Great Scott! Good Heavens! Holy cow! Great Goddess! Gee, gosh it's the snake!

The snake wraps around Holmes' neck and begins strangling her.

Holmes: Stop studdering woman! Wath's gonnen on…?

Holmes can barely speak as she struggles to get the snake off her neck.

Holmes: Uggggggg! Roythsluttt, yuth ever git awau!

Roylott grabs a gun as Watson charges.

Watson: Bouncing bullets, no you don't Roylott!

Just then a cheetah runs through, knocking the desk and Watson out the window. Then a leopard runs through, followed by a jaguar.

Roylott: Ha Holmes! Caught with your panties down and a snake around your neck!

Water starts to fill the room rapidly, and Holmes throws the snake onto Roylott. Roylott flails his gun about, and blows his snake whistle.

Holmes: Why don't you just stick that gun up your nose! You are going to jail Roylott!

Roylott knocks the snake off, and aims again. The cheetah runs by again.

Roylott: Me going to jail is as likely as you shutting your mouth! Its not going to happen! Hahhahahahhahahah! Hahaaaaaaaaaaa ohhhhhhhhhhhhhhhhhhhhhhh …..

Roylott falls to the water as the snake bites him in the butt. Holmes pulls him out, but is too late. Roylott is dead. Holmes holds a magnifying glass over Roylott, and then lights a pipe as Watson struggles to climb up to the window opening outside.

Holmes goes to the window and looks down. Watson hangs from a flag pole.

Holmes: My dear Watson, get up here! We are missing tea-time, my lady!

After Watson gets up, they wade through the water, knocking the snake aside.

Watson: Where is Roylott, Holmes?

Holmes: Im afraid Roylott kicked the bucket.

Watson: What??

Holmes: Never mind.

Watson: What is all this water?

Holmes: Let's go find out, shall we?

They follow the water to the bathroom. They open the door.

Holmes: The baboon is in the water closet!

They are surprised to see the toilet over-flowing with the baboon inside holding it's nose.

Watson: What's it doing Holmes?

Holmes: Elementary my dear Watson, elementary.

Watson: Do you mean that it… went to the Loo?

Holmes: No he is representing "smell no evil"!

The audience laughs. Fireworks go off. Holmes begins to dance while Motley Crue plays.

THE END

The Blown Up Bridge

On Sunday, while every person except one was at church, someone had placed a bomb under the Brookland Bridge and exploding it. We are trying to find the crook. Help our detective, Private Investigator Sam Schalp, solve this case by reading the account and thinking it over.

The Case as told by Sam Schlap, PI:

You already know the crime, blowing up a bridge. In this case blowing up a bridge for reasons other than demolition, without government permission, and without proper safety protocol. Here are the suspects: Mrs. Woods; Mr. Mac; and Mr. Cob. Here is what they had to say when I questioned them as to their whereabouts at the time of the crime.

Mrs. Woods – "I go to church, ask other people. It's true always said that bridge was an ugly eye-sore, but I don't blow things up. I like to knit sweaters for kittens."

Later, other church members confirmed she does go to church.

Mr. Mac – "I was working on my house. Yeah I like to threaten to bomb other countries, but that is not a crime. Yeah I've heard of the 5th Amendment."

When Mr. Mac's neighbors were questioned, they said they saw Mrs. Woods working on Mr. Mac's house, not Mr. Mac. Yes, this case is getting strange.

Mr. Cob – "Yes I was a Marine in the US Military, and I am a bomb expert. Mr. Mac bought a time-bomb from me. I didn't ask what it was for."

Mr. Cob was in the Marines, and is a bomb expert who plays with bombs.

Guess who did the crime, then decipher the message below to find out the correct answer.

Nst. Xppet jt sfbmmz Ns. Nbd. Ns. Nbd tfu uif cpnc esfttf bt Nst. Xppet, njttfe divsdi, boe gpshpu up dibohf xijmf xpsljoh po uif ipvtf, tujmm esfttfe bt Nst. Xppet. Bgufs gvsuifs jowftujhbujpo, ju xbt efufsnjofe uibu Nst. Xppet xbt opu tffo jo divsdi uibu Tvoebz.

Case Closed.

Behind the scenes at Spider Mountain

Behind the scenes at Monstoria Castle

Monstors: The Last Battle

The following is an account of the last story written about The Land of Mon. It is also perhaps our only remaining tale of that World. The originals written and drawn by Sir Mongold were lost to us. This journal, entry by entry, records the last surviving tale of the Monstors.

To avoid unwanted social persecution, Sir Mongold told others that he had "made it up" and Monstors were all imaginary. Yet stories held in memory or recorded, all exist at some point in time. Time is eternal, beyond human memory, therefore nothing is forgotten. Things remembered are real, even if they only exist in thought.

This publication of Monstors, is dedicated to author and artist Sir Mongold.

Monstors: The Last Battle
Created by Sir Mongold & Sir Stowell

Part 1

"Attack!!!" could be heard for miles around as a squad of Distructors destroyed the Great Woven Wall. The attack was led by the cold hearted Bird Mon. The Distructors' heavily armored battering ram pounded against the wall like a mallet beating fresh meat. Quickly the Distructors disposed of the Treeple's 'Great' wall, with fury.

While inside their Tree Village, the Treeple lit signal cannons. From atop the forest canopy the signal flares shot! Help would soon be on the way, but not soon enough. The Leader of the Treeple, Tee, had already fallen defending the Great Woven Wall.

"Show me where the Jewels of the Light Forest are!" Bird Mon said as he lifted Tee from the remains of the broken wall.

"You shall get nothing from me, Bird that cannot fly!" was the reply of Tee.
"Not all Birds can fly, you know!" Bird Mon shot back. He was self-conscious about his lack of wings. He did however, have a long pointy beak, which was good for pecking.

Before the Distructors could locate any of the Treeple treasure they had come to pillage, the Monstors arrived from Castle Monstoria, to the rescue. The Treeple were allies of the Monstors. Bird Mon turned to retreat. Just then Whip Mon and 5 other Monstors burst into the clearing and surrounded the Distructors.

"We came for the Jewels, Whip Mon!" said Bird Mon. "If you move, I'll kill Tee."
"You bad guys are all the same!" Whip Mon said as he came closer. "I bet you don't even realize how important the Jewels are."

"Are you saying that I don't know how important the Jewels are?" Bird Mon said as anger filled his tone.

"Yes. It is important to know how important the Jewels are," said Whip Mon.
"Why is it so important?" Bird Mon asked.
"Hah, I told you, you didn't know the jewels were important!"

"I know the Jewels are important, I just didn't know how important the Jewels were important!!" Bird Mon was getting confused.
"If you didn't know how important the Jewels were, why did you come here in the first place??!!"

As the conversation went on, Distructor Hammer Head slipped away. He headed toward the great doors of an oak tree nearby. He opened the doors, and behold!! This was where the Jewels were kept. In a 50 by 50 foot room sat shelves and shelves covered with jewels of all kinds!! The Jewels sparkled with magic light within the tree. In the corner was even a jewel embroidered chainmail shirt. In the middle of the room, placed on a golden stand, sat the Jewel of Power! Next to it, on a silver stand was the All-mighty Diamond. Near that on a crystal stand lay the Amber Amulet.

Hammer Head was so stunned by the beauty of the gems he didn't notice Blow Torch sneaking up behind him. The Monstor Blow Torch grabbed him and said, "Ok Cardboard Box Brain, you've seen enough! Let's go see the Whip Mon."

Meanwhile Whip Mon was still mentally flailing Bird Mon's brain…

"If you came to find out how important the Jewels are important, how come you didn't bring Fox Mon along?! He could learn a thing or two."

By this time Bird Mon was just absurdly mad. Bird Mon broke his own weapon in two. Then he went around and took the other Distructors' weapons and snapped them like twigs. His men stared at him, and then eachother blankly. It was then that Bird Mon realized they were now defenseless.

The Distructors were soon tied up (including Hammer Head). They were submitted to Treeple speeches, which were usually long and about environmental spiritual ethics. Then the captives were released to walk back to Spider Tower in their underwear.

…………………..

"Bird Mon, you fool!!" Fox Mon shouted, echoing through the halls of Spider Tower.

Bird Mon looked down his beak at his own feet. He was home, and that was all that mattered. Bird Mon grew up in the lair once known as Spider Mountain. Over the years, a tower was built on the rocky crest, and battered pyramid parapet walls extended out from the mountain castle on 3 sides. Locals knew it as Spi, a name too familiar to be used respectfully by strangers to the area.

"Bird Mon, you always mess things up!" Fox Mon yelled. "I should feed you to the Spiders! The new batch has just hatched."

"Bu bu u u..." Bird Mon studdered, "I am still training them not to bite us."
"Ha! Go put some clothes on your undergarments, or I will use you to help fatten them up. Although they are still small for Giant Spiders, there are 100 of them. Now off you go! I will prepare for the next attack on Monstoria."

....

All creatures in the Land of Mon, were Mon. Monstors, monstars, and monsters were all Mon. Monstors and Monstars were good, and Monsters were bad; but they were all Mon, and therefore looked very similar to eachother. Most Mon had green skin, but there was great diversity among Mons. Some had horns, some did not. No eyes, one eye, or many eyes; arms or tentacles; there was no rule about appearance. All Mon were free to look any way, without judgment.

The Monstors of the Kingdom of Monstoria were the guardians of Good Stories, and the stewards of all things within their realm. Their realm included the Light Forest & Light Fields (Monstaria), all of which was surrounded by the Dark Forest, Dark Fields, and outlying kingdoms (Monsteria). In ancient times Distructors were Monstors, but after years of separation, and living in Monsteria, they had become generally grouped with all chaotic Monsters.

....

One such outlying kingdom of Monsters, Bog, was home to the Swamp Mons. From their murky depths, they had heard distant warnings hanging in the silence. Swamp Mons cared nothing for noise, they only found meaning in the sounds of silence. What the silence was now telling them, was very disturbing; and they began to travel out.

The Treeple were rebuilding their Great Wall. They would never again let their lair be invaded by Distructors. They added masonry to the new weaving, and placed battlements to watch for enemies. The new Great Wall was now 4 feet tall, and 1 foot thick.

…………..

Back at Spider Tower, plans were being made. "Here's the plans," Fox Mon said. "Dragon Mon, go into the Dark Forest and search for the Freckled Ogre. See if he wants to join us. Hammer Head, ready the lightning sleds. Bird Mon, go ask Rock Mon if he wants to join us too. I will contact the Giant Worms of the East. Everyone get ready!"

Within hours, another gathering was held. "Ok, we have everyone here," Fox Mon said. "Attention maggots! I will take Hammer Head, the Freckled Ogre, the spiders, and half our army. Giant Worms will take a direct route and chew out the roots of Monstaria, and the foundations of Monstoria. Bird Mon will go north along the Treeple Great Wall with Dragon Mon, Rock Mon, and the other half of our army."

The Distructors set out in full force, with Fox Mon's blessings. "Worms, go and seek the roots Monstaria and foundations of Monstoria! Lightning sleds off, my army move, Dragon Mon and Bird Mon good luck! Onward to battle!!! Do not stop until Monstoria is destroyed!! Let this be the Last Battle!!!" Fox Mon howled.

…..

News had reached the Monstors and Monstars of the Distructors' attack. The Monstors assembled their own army. From Monstaria they had Treeple, unicorns, song birds, sprites, treelves, fairies, nomes, nobleflies, damselflies, and logmon. There was also talk that Swamp Mons and Great Hawks would join them, but that was uncertain.

Swamp Mons were immortal, and all shared the same soul. The Soul of the Swamp was communal among them, so the total population count could never be known. Swamp Mons were part of the primordial ooze that all Mon evolved from. For the most part they were chaotic neutral, but in cases of defending the ecosystem they were lawful neutral.

Great Hawks were giant red tailed hawks. They perched on the giant black trees that surrounded Talon Mountain. Also along the cliffs of the mountain, were ledges with Giant Hawk nests. Inside Talon Mountain, the great birds had a great hall, with a chief.

Along the outermost city wall of Monstaria, the Monstors' army lined up. Whip Mon was not a slave driver, but he kept order among individuals for the greater good. He would not allow a siege to occur, and he would not give control to Fox Mon and the Distructors without a fight. Many Monstars like treevles, treeple, and nomes rode on the backs of unicorns, and other larger or faster beasts. Much of the army could fly, thanks to sprites, fairies, flying bugs, and some Monstors.

Part 2

The Distructors were approaching the Light Forest. As Fox Mon's army pushed on, his mon were getting tired, thirsty, and hungry. "Pitiful. Very poor, we shall rest here by the Light Forest. Don't get beat before you even go into battle!" Fox man replied after hearing groans.

Lightning sleds were refueled with charcoal and crystals. The spiders drank dew drops and ate bugs. The Distructor army slouched about in the woodland shadows, absorbing energy in their mixed ways. Fox Mon and Hammer Head held war council.

"The Giant Worms will arrive there first," Fox Mon said. "As the Worms chew, we will arrive and your lightning sleds will attack first. Later, as the Spiders are attacking, Bird Mon should arrive. The armies will be engaged!"

"I will lead lightning sleds into battle, my lord." Hammer Heard knelt.

All Distructors were now set to move on, and off they went.

…

The Light Forest was losing trees as they passed through it. Enormous trees were being overturned by the Giant Worms beneath them. Branches cracked and split as they hit eachother, and chaos consumed life after life through the woods. A rugged path was made for the catapults.

Ahead in the distance, Monstoria's kingdom walls sat against the horizon. It's crystal towers reflected the hotness of the noon day sun. Below the castle's silhouette in the distance, lay the expanse of fields and walls; and below which lay the Monstor's army.

"So they've been expecting us!" Fox Mon started, "All the more fun! Attack!!!"

The lightning sleds and spiders raced forward, into battle. From the Monstors out raced the unicorns, blasting away beams from their horns. Next followed the Monstor foot soldiers. Then came the Monstars and others following.

Thunder Cracker and Blow Torch held off the lightning sleds with the help of the other winged friends. The unicorns held off the Spiders. Monstor ground troops fought violently with Distructors. The ground shook and the sky crackled.

Thunder Cracker was knocked out of the sky by a boulder from a catapult. The Spiders cast webs and tripped up most of the unicorns. Then the Spiders pounced, stung, and bit the entangled unicorns.

"How can it get any worse?!!" Four Teeth cried. Just then a Giant Worm burst from the ground, ate a Monstor, and dived back under. It was looking bad for the Monstors as the sun beat down on the hot, exhausted troops.

The Monstors were getting pushed back farther and farther towards the Wall of Monstoria. Treeple were running all about frantically seeking shelter in the trees, or behind rocks. The sun was waning on the field of battle.

With one last effort, Blow Torch zoomed onto a lightning sled, grabbed the pilot (which happened to be Hammer Head), and dropped him off at 20 feet above the ground while sending the sled spinning through the air. The lightning sled exploded on the ground in the midst of the Spiders.

Suddenly, Fox Mon whirled around to see Bird Mon's army advancing on the western front. As he turned around to shout another command, a Swamp Mon lifted him up by his neck. The Swamp Mons had arrived, on the side of the Monstors.

Frantically, Fox Mon jabbed the Swamp Mon again and again. "Die vile creature, die!" he said. The Swamp Mon squeezed harder. His sword did no discernable damage to the mossy torso. Fox Mon was about to pass out from suffocation, when a lightning sled zoomed down and repeatedly fired, burning the creature to a crisp.

Bird Mon's army was there in a flash. Dust was flying everywhere. Rock Mon was destroying everything in his path. Dead Monstors and Distructors were everywhere.

…

Both Whip Mon and Fox Mon needed to consult with their henchmen for a rally. As the unicorns and Swamp Mon held off the attackers, the remaining 9 Monstors and Four Teeth, Blow Torch, Smokey, Four Arms, and Whip Mon held conference around a camp fire inside the Wall of Monstoria.

"Because Tee was injured, the Treeple have retreated," Blow Torch reported. "We need a miracle!" said Four Arms. "All in all we have only 49 warriors left." At that moment Thunder Cracker was injured and taken into the castle. "Well it looks as if we've got to do something. Everyone, group the army into a big oval. When you are ready, we will charge!" Whip Mon ordered.

~ Huge masses hung above. Not one army knew what the blotches in the sky were, just specks or a big large blur. A speck dropped from the sky, it's body was brown, it's feet were of orange, and it's feathered wings were wide spread! The Great Hawk swooped with a swoop, and pecked with a peck. It's beak dove into the dirt, and pulled out a Giant Worm, like needle-n-thread. ~

"The Hawks, the Hawks!!" Four Teeth cried. "Looks like your miracle happened!" Four Arms said. One hundred Hawks went for the Worms; another hundred went for the Spiders; another hundred jousted with the lightning sleds; and the rest of the Hawks tormented Rock Mon.

Meanwhile, in their web-woven tent, Fox Mon, Bird Mon, Dragon Mon, and Hammer Head were conversing. "The Great Hawks are here and they're slaughtering our Spiders!" shouted Dragon Mon. " For the first time today, the Monstors are really winning! There goes the last lightning sled!! I don't believe this! The Freckled Ogre is retreating and the Hawks are eating ALL the Giant Worms!! We have about 54 Distructors, 6 Spiders, and wounded up in the 40's!" "And night is almost upon us!" Bird Mon added.

Fox Mon scowled, and crossed his arms. A loud crash was heard just outside the command tent. With one final yell, Rock Mon fled back to Castle Rock.

Part 3

Night fell upon the Monsters like ice-cold water over a blazing fire. One flame was kept burning; the flame of hope was kindled in the Monsters' hearts, by Whip Mon and the turn of fortune upon the battlefield. Whip Mon led his army raging into battle again, wielding their weapons wildly. Slashing through the hordes of Distructors like nothing, the Monsters reached Fox Mon's tent in no time.

"Run, leave the catapults! Run!!" Fox Mon yelled. "They've got Bird Mon! Follow me!" Shouts of victory were heard all around, as triumphant Monster warriors attempted to round up their captives.

"Well, well, well! It looks like Fox Mon left you here," Whip Mon said to Bird Mon when the dust had settled.

…

The Swamp Mon approached Whip Mon and convened council. "We must go back to the Swamps now," they said in guttural, monotone unison. "Understood," Whip Mon replied, "Good bye, and thank you."

The Great Hawk Chief landed and walked towards Whip Mon. The ground trembled beneath his talons. "I hope we could be assistance. TagA [*meaning good-bye*]!"

Whip Mon bowed slightly and said "We are honored by your presence. Please take this Bird Mon as a favor for aiding us in battle. May you always appear in the places you are most wanted, yet not expected. TAga ARaieN, (noise like an egg cracking) EIm MI LU WEVi LUur." [*good-bye follower of the wind, may your wings grow ever longer*]

The Hawks left in great masses, just as they had arrived. "Looks like everyone is leaving. There go the unicorns!" Four Arms said, carrying wounded Monsters in his tentacles.

"Who cares, let's chase the Distructors!" Blow Torch said.

"Well, shouldn't we let them get away and fight them again another day?" Whip Mon started. "Ok! Grab a bite to eat, and light your lanterns, let's go on a night hunt! Four Teeth, take the prisoners into the Dungeons. We're off!"

…

Meanwhile, the Distructors were hurrying on…

"Hurry, cross the Field of Doom!" Fox Mon barked. "It is faster than this cursed Forest. Although we only have 13 Distructors and 3 Spiders left, we will survive. Everything is asleep in the Field at night, but by the time we leave the Field it will be dawn. The undead things will rise up and get the Monstors!" panted Fox Mon.

…

Back to the Monstors…

"He's crossing the Field of Doom! He's crazy!" Smokey jawled.
"Not crazy," said Four Arms. "Fox Mon has a plan. He thinks we won't go through the Field of Doom. He thinks he will make it safely back to Spider Tower." "Four Arms is right. Fox Mon isn't that dumb. Although he never turned around to see that we only have 11 mon. We must follow him!" Whip Mon said as he led his squad of Monstors fearlessly onward.

Through the night they marched from the Dark Forest into the Field of Doom. The desolate wasteland was torn and broken. As the Monstors crossed over the barren and dead ground, they began to realize that the husks of long withered crops resembled bones. It was as if burial rows, patterns of skeletons, were frozen in the dirt. Were the skeletal remains waiting to burst out??!!

Close to dawn…

"We made it! I can make out just a few shapes coming across the Field of Doom!" Fox Mon exclaimed as the Distructors extinguished their torches.

The sun began to rise steadily as the Monstors pursued their enemies. Four Arms took off his helmet, and began to scratch his head. "Oh no!" he said thoughtfully with a troubled look on his face. "Fox Mon led us right into a trap! At night the Field of Doom is silent, but in the day the sun wakes every horrible monster here! We're dead meat!"

As the Monstors turned to run away, they were stopped by an army of undead skeletons, slowly rising from the sand. The Monstors were quickly surrounded. Whip Mon ordered his warriors to ready their weapons, and they advanced.

Swords and lazers splintered the brittle bones of the possessed, gruesome, skeletal frames. At the end of the short battle, piles of bones lay at the Monstors' feet. There was nothing of value to be scavenged from the weathered and battered remains.

"I can't move on," Blow Torch complained. "The sun is too hot and we've only been walking in this desert for 20 minutes!"

"We will soon reach the other side of the Field, hold on," Whip Mon said as he wiped the sweat from his forehead. Just then from behind a group of cacti, jumped four rouge Mon warriors of the desert wasteland!

"Why did we ever try to cross this blasted Field!?!" Smokey asked as he drew his sword. "Don't worry, all we have to do is get rid of these guys, and we can make it to the other side," Whip Mon replied hastily. "I'm afraid it won't be so easy," Four Arms started. "These warriors are dangerous outcasts, and are always blood hungry."

The Four Fearsome Monsters lashed their morning stars around wildly. "Attack!" shouted Whip Mon, sending four Monstors to engage them. In a flash, Whip Mon's fighters were in the sand covered with blood. Blow Torch acted quickly by barbequing one of the enemy's faces. Whip Mon was thrown to the ground by the Leader's morning star.

"Give me a reason I should not kill you!" the Leader said as he gloated over Whip Mon.

"I guess someone like you would not need a reason. My life is in your hands," Whip Mon stated. "Well spoken! But I am afraid I shall have to kill you!" the Leader said as he leaned back for the final blow.

Part 4

Just at that moment, Smokey leaped beside the surprised Leader, grabbed his arm, got a-hold of his hair flanges, and threw him (weapon and all) into the sprangle bushes. Then Smokey helped Whip Mon to his feet.

The rest of the Four Fearsome Monsters fled at the sight of having their leader tossed around.

"I hope that's the last of those creatures! Four Arms said. The heroes walked on, through the deadly desert. Soon they reached solid ground, but it was still part of the Field of Doom. They could not see far ahead, nor behind because the sun's rays were so strong. After an hour it began to grow steadily cooler.

Suddenly Smokey collapsed, complaining that he was tired and hot. Four Arms gulped down some water from a canteen, and pulled Smokey to his feet. "You'll be alright Smokey, come on. Have a sip, we'll soon be at our enemy's throat! Onward Monstors!"

About this same time, outside the Field of Doom, Fox Mon got up after a rather long period of rest. He began to poke everyone in camp. The 13 Distructors began to rouse. "Wake your sleepy lids, rouges! Do you wish your lazy bones to rot near this dreaded place?! Awaken!! It's time we head for home, miserable home," Fox Mon hollered.

The Distructors had just got their gear together, when 7 figures came running at them through the dazzling light that was spread about the area called, the Field of Doom. Those 7, were of course the Monstors. Now the Distructors were surprised, but not the least bit afraid.

Whip Mon, Four Arms, Blow Torch, and Smokey charged, while the other 3 fired arrows into Distructor lines. The remnants of the Distructor army charged without delay. The foes met head on. Another battle began.

The offensive Monstors held ground with the enemy, while the archers pecked away at the excess fiends. As the World Clock reached Noon, the Monstors remained strong. The Monstors had only suffered minor damages, but the Distructors were crippled.

"I don't believe this!" Fox Mon growled angrily. "How come the good guys always have to win?! We lost all the Giant Spiders!! Retreat!!! Leave the wounded!"

"It's your own fault my Liege! You allowed us to rest too long!" Dragon Mon said under his breath, as he received a blow to his knee. "Hey, looks as if the Distructors are packing up and leaving!" Four Arms said merrily.

"Let's follow them!" Whip Mon said freely.

"What?! Even I admit what we did was foolish. Let's not risk any more lives!" said Blow Torch. Four Arms waved his tentacles from side to side, in thought.

"Well we've gone this far, and I'm not about to go home without finishing the job. This is our chance to put an end to the evil that the Distructors have placed upon Mon! If you deny all that your ancestors have worked for, then leave now, and leave your soul up to Crawn!! Those who are with me, follow my lead with the strongest of heart! To battle my friends, perhaps the Last Battle!!"

The last Distructors fled through the wooded outskirts of the Field, back to Spider Tower. They entered through a secret doorway around back. Up they ran to Cobweb Hall, and closed the door to the stairs behind them.

"You are all bad! Never forget that. They call you evil, your parents said you were ugly, your friends all hated you because you smelled afoul, and you are stupid!" Fox Mon violently threw objects, as he shouted around the room. He hit his head on the walls. He hit the other Distructors and rattled chains, threatening to choke them. His minions cowered in fear.

The Distructors were tired, hungry, and broken. Fox Mon knew the end was near, so he was trying to stoke their anger for one Last Battle. Anger is the fire inside for fighting. Anger was their only hope.

Anger was not working. Hammer Head began yelling back at Fox Mon. They began shouting back and forth, and then screamed and hollered at eachother. The other Distructors were in such a state of misery they could not be agitated.

…

The door burst open. The Monstors had arrived. "We let ourselves in." Whip Mon stated, brandishing a whip made from thorn vines from the Dark Forest.

"Get them!" Fox Mon yelled. Before all the Distructors could stumble to their feet, and before all the Monstors had entered the room, Hammer Head charged. He rammed into Whip Mon and 2 others, knocking them into the wall. Smokey charged forward and punched Hammer Head in the face. Whip Mon lashed his whip around Hammer Head, and Smokey held him down.

As the other Monstors engaged the other Distructors, Fox Mon and Whip Mon wrestled with eachother. "Just give up Fox Mon, there is no where to run." said Whip Mon. "How dare you come into my house?!" Fox Mon bellowed. "You need me to blame all your Kingdom's problems on. Without me, your Rule would wilt from within."

"Dream on criminal. You always blame us for your problems. You are my prisoner now, for your crimes against Monstaria," Whip Mon countered.

"What crimes? We have stories of our own. The Distructors serve no laws, we are outlaws! We are outcasts and we pay no taxes! I am the leader of the rebels because I am the only one brave enough to challenge your rule!" Fox Mon spat.

"We need order, in order to keep our stories good, and honor life. You do not pay any taxes, yet you use our roads to rob us. You say you don't want to be a part of us, but you steal what we have from us. If you replaced me as ruler, you would make things far worse. How would you make the Kingdom work?!" Whip Mon retorted.

"I am the Eye and Hand of Monstaria, and you will be punished!"

Four Arms came around from the side, "I am the Heart and Head of Monstaria, and I have you Fox Mon!" Fox Mon was caught firmly in tentacle grip. The Last Battle had finally ended.

Fox Mon was imprisoned in Castle Monstoria. The Distructors disbanded and dispersed. Taxes went up, but times were more peaceful for 100 years.

THE END

Map of the Lands of Mon

A Mile

Key to the Map of Mon

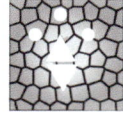 Treeple's Keeps in Light Forest

Monstoria
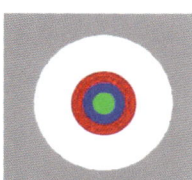
Monstor's Castle & Kingdom

Spider Tower

Distructor's Castle & Field of Doom

Swamp Boggs

Frostmon		Dead Ruinds	
Talon Rock		Castle Rock	
Lavol Kano		Freckle Lake	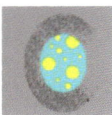

A Super Christmas

It was the night before Christmas, and _____ was waiting for Santa.

They were waiting with their friends: _____, _____, and _____.

Suddenly and elf appeared by the Christmas Tree! The elf said his name was Crystal Toe. "Santa Claus needs you! Santa has picked you as his helper this year!" Crystal Toe said.

"What do we have to do?" _____ asked.

"You must find the meaning of Christmas, and share it with others!"

Crystal Toe asked if they would come with him. _____ said yes, they would go. Crystal Toe led them to his sled, outside.

Comet and Cupid led the sled off the ground into the star-filled night. Crystal Toe was a good driver. With some magic, they were at the North Pole in minutes.

When the sled landed, Crystal Toe took them to the workshop. Toys were everywhere. _____ was given a list of places they had to travel to in Santa's special jet sled. So later that night, after milk and cookies, they set out in the jet sled on their journey.

Crystal Toe had given _____ a magic pouch to allow the jet sled to travel in time. _____ took a pinch of magic dust from the pouch and spread it around the jet sled. Poof!!! They went back in time to Old England!

In England _____ looked around and said "Look it's a fairy ring!" The fairies flew over to them and said, "Santa wanted you to have this letter." The fairies handed _____ a letter C carved from wood. They thanked the fairies and boarded the jet sled again, and headed for Ireland.

In Ireland, the sled landed in a field of green clovers. Leprechauns came out and handed them a golden letter A. "By Saint Patrick's beard, you have your letter, now begone! You can't have our pot of gold, and no wishes either!" Back in the sled, they took off for Germany.

In Germany they met Saint Nicholas and Krampus. Saint Nick handed them the letter P made of liquorices. Krampus threatened to spank them, so they took off in the sled for Sweden.

In Sweden dwarves came and greeted them. "So you are the people that Santa sent." Then the dwarves handed them an E made of coal. So they headed back to the North Pole.

On the way back to the North Pole, in the sled _____ tried to piece together the letters into a word. "C – A – P – E. That spells cape! What does the word cape have to do with the meaning of Christmas?" "Whatever it means, Santa Claus will help us." Said _____.

The jet sled arrived at the North Pole. _____ asked Santa what the letters meant. Santa said "Your guesses were good! Ho ho ho. There is still one more letter!" With that, he gave them another letter E, but this one was a cut diamond!

They all looked at the letters spread out in the snow. After some rearranging, _____ said "Of course it says PEACE!"

They thanked Santa and the elves, and were given a ride back home. When they were home they saw Santa had already been to their houses while they were out. It was the best Christmas they had ever had. They learned the meaning of Christmas, helped Santa, and got lots of presents under the tree and in stockings!

PEACE

Crystal Toe

Multiple Choice Stories
Pages 90-110

The difference between the brave and the foolish,
is understanding the risk.
A Brave Adventurer understands the risk.
A Fool does not.

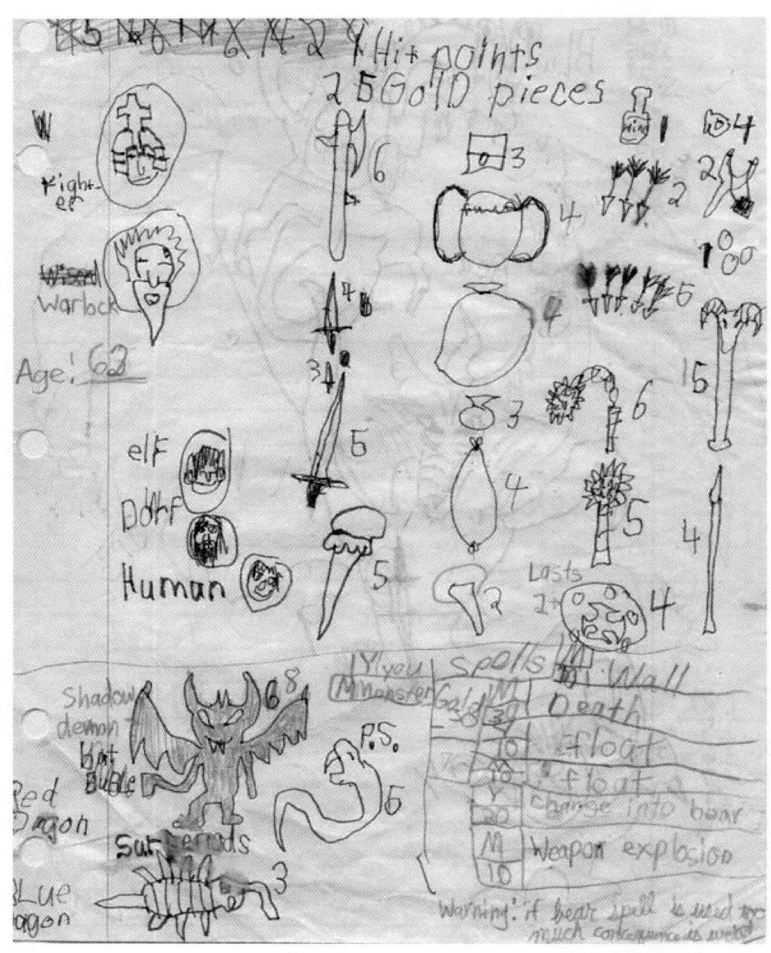

The Maze #7
Robert Hood vs The Darlacks
Age 12

Your name is Robert Hood. You have two magic swords called the Elf Sword and the Elk Sword. You are also a Time Lord. You have a Time Machine and it looks just like a Cola Machine. Your Time Machine allows you travel to anywhere and anytime in any universe. You love adventuring through time and space, so you often use the 'random' navigation function in the Time Machine. Hit it!
[Go to Frosth #1] [Go to Darlo #2] [Go to Puck # 8]

1. After 5 hours of travelling in your Time Machine, you arrive on a frozen planet. With jacket on you go outside. It is very cold! A snow giant humanoid is coming toward you! **[Attack # 9] [Wait #5]**

2. After 7 hours of travelling, you reach the destination of planet Darlo. The atmosphere outside the Time Machine is tolerable. You walk outside and see ruins of old cities. A strange robotic Darlack stands near an old elevator shaft. The elevator door is open, with an elevator room inside.
[Attack #4] [Sneak onto elevator #5]

3. You wait. The giant snowman steps on you and kills you. **THE END**

4. You move close enough to get a clear shot at the Darlack. You blast it away. Further away, you can see a group of Darlacks patrolling. The Darlack patrol begins approaching. **[Run go to Start] [Go in elevator #5]**

5. Without being seen you go into the elevator and press the 'down' button. The elevator lowers you safely down. It stops at a control room. 5 Darlacks are in a grey room. One sees you says in an electronic voice "Intruder, Intruder. State your business."
[Tell Truth #6] [Ask Questions #6] [Run past them #7]

6. They ignore you "We are superior war machines. What have you done with our creator?" "I haven't done anything." "We don't care. We will rule the Galaxy." Is their reply. "We require data from our Creator." "Exterminate the Intruder." "Exterminate. Exterminate!" "Why?" you ask. "We have no use for you. Intruders must be exterminated. Be still." Using your Elk Sword you cut off the eye stalk. "Vision impaired, vision impaired!" it cries.
[Keep attacking #10] [Run past, down the hall #7]

7. You start to run. A blue beam of electricity hits you into black and white.
THE END

8. The planet Puck is a verdant green forest world. You spend time relaxing.
THE END

9. You start swinging away with your swords. The snow monster thumps to the ground. A pouch is around its neck. When you open it, it reveals jewels. You return to your Time Machine and go to Earth to spend your new found treasure.   **THE END**

10. You blow the other 4 Darlacks away. More come from the side doors.
[Attack #11] [Jump in Elevator #12] [Try to Run #7]

11. You shoot the top of the nearest doorway and it caves in on the Darlacks. Seeing no other option you head back towards the elevator and return to your Time Machine. You feel pleased that you have fought Darlacks and survived!   **THE END**

12. You get in the elevator and press "up". You're half way to the top when it jerks to a stop. It zooms down to the bottom with a crash! You get out, into darkness.   **[Go left #13] [Go right #14]**

13. You turn left. All of a sudden a Darlack bursts through the wall saying "Darlox, Darlox!" and shoots you.   **THE END**

14. You can see something ahead. It's Doctor Time's Time Machine! You recognize the blue of that rectangle anywhere. The Doctor opens the door and lets you in his Time Machine. He takes you to your Time Machine. You thank him, and say good bye.   **THE END**

Castle Molofe
Elf Swordsman

You are an elf warrior ordered to explore the abandoned Castle Molofe. You approach the large entrance. You hear a scary screech!
[1. Go Home] [2. Climb to the Roof] [3. Go through the Entrance]

1. You decide adventuring is not for you. You go home. THE END

2. After a few minutes of climbing, you reach the roof. On the roof you see two doors leading down.   [4. Take First door] [5. Take Second door]

3. You enter the entrance. Suddenly, a strong wooden door shuts where you came in behind you! You are surrounded by 3 trolls! You will fight, but which troll first?
[10. troll that has sword] [6. troll that has dagger] [7. troll that has whip]

4. You walk down the dark stairs. You hear noises at the end of the stairs. [5. Continue down] [8. Wait]

5. You walk carefully down into what was an eating room. You move to the left, a dagger flies into your back! THE END

6. With sword drawn you hastily attack him. You kill him. The rest flee down some stairs, you follow.   [Go to 4.]

7. You charge. He whips the sword out of your hand. You manage to get away. You make it to some stairs.   [Go to 9.]

8. You stop. Old men dressed in ragged clothes approach carrying jewels. They think you're a god, they give you the jewels. You decide to go home and spend your good fortune. THE END

9. You quickly go down. It is dark. A door slams shut behind you! You spend the rest of your life in this damp, dark and miserable cellar. THE END

10. You fiercely attack him. The swords clash. He falls. Your sword drives through his heart. The troll with the whip comes forward.   [Go to 7.]

Castle Molofe

TARTIAR RULES
Find-Your-Way Roleplaying Short-Stories Series ©1988

Attacking: Level determines how many coins are flipped, per attack turn. Level 3, you flip 3 coins if you are attacking something.
Heads = Hits, Tails = Misses

For example: *You (life points 30, Level 3)*
Enemy (life points 3, Level 1)
You flip 3 coins. If they land heads, you hit the Enemy for 1 life point (for each coin). If they land tails, that does nothing. Then you flip 1 coin for the Enemy's attack. Heads, the enemy takes one of your life points away. Tails, you are not hurt. Repeat this until one character's life points are zero or less. The one with remaining life points wins.

Spells: To determine if a spell works, flip a coin.
Heads = Works, Tails = Fails

TARTIAR 01 ~ "Tartiar The Mighty"
Level 3 Roleplay © 1988
Needed: pen, paper, coins

You are a Man-A-Kill warrior. At age 24, you are Tartiar The Mighty. A gaping giant plundered and killed people in your tribe. Many warriors have never come back from fighting giants, and your brother never returned from the cave of this particular giant. You have decided you will go. You set off with spear in hand. Tartiar (30 life points, Level 3)

As you come into a grassy plain, Dahrmy the Mad Berserker rides up to you and challenges you to a fight. (Attacks use coins per Level, flipped per turn)
[Say "No thank you," avoiding Dahrmy to continue your Quest go to #2]
[Take Dahrmy's offer to fight, continue reading]

Dahrmy gets off his horse and runs at you, sword in hand!
Tartiar (30 life points, Level 3)   Dahrmy (15 life points, Level 1)
[Lose the battle go to #3]   [Win, continue reading]

You stand over the massacred old man. You take Dahrmy's horse to ride, count his coins, and eat his food. After riding a ways, you get off your horse and grab your spear. In front of you there are 3 caves in a large cliff known as "Big Man's Bluff".
[Go in First Cave #4, Second Cave #5, Third Cave #6]

#1 *Inside the gaping giant is asleep! (*you have 2 attacks, before he attacks)
Giant (50 life points, Level 4)   Mara (15 life points, Level 3)
[If you lose, go to #11]   [If you win, continue reading]

You beat the Giant! You (and Mara if she is still with you) ride back to your tribe, with the head of the giant and become Chief!   THE END

#2 *You refuse Dahrmy. He calls you a whimp and rides away. You come to a large cave.*   [Go in the large cave #7]   [Keep walking #8]

#3 *You lie on your face, defeated in shame. He rides away. Later a young woman cleric comes and heals you. She carries a quarter staff and will aid you in your battles. She says that she is on a quest to kill the giant too.*
[Go to #7]

#4 *You enter the First Cave. You come to a small room which is dimly lit. There is a glowing sword ahead. You reach for it. A male nymph jumps out of the shadows! "You must pay for that!" says he. After negotiation the nymph accepts 5 gold coins that you give him in exchange for the magic sword and its sheath.* (magic sword +1 on attacks)
[Leave and go to Second Cave #5]   [Leave and go to Third Cave #6]

#5 *You enter the Second Cave, walking deep within. A kobold jumps out!*
[Flee #9]   [Fight #10]

#6 *You enter the Third and Largest Cave. You come to a very large room. A giant foot clomps in front of you! The battle with the Gaping Giant begins!*
Giant (50 life points, Level 4)   [Lose #11]   [Win #12]

#7 *You go inside the Large Cave in the cliff near you.*   [Go to #1]

#8 *You continue on. A band of trolls jump down from nearby trees!*
Trolls (life points: A.5, B.5, C.7, D.10, E.15; Level 1)
[If all trolls fail 1 attack, you Win]
[Win go to #13] [Lose continue reading]
It was a nice fight, but the trolls overwhelmed you.   THE END

#9 *Fleeing, you follow a bend in the tunnel. Turning, another kobold blocks your way!*   Kobolds (5 life points, Level 1)
[Win got to #6] [Lose continue reading]
Sorry, these small subterranean dog-like feral creatures will not retreat, and eventually over come your height and strength advantages. You die a cold and bloody death in a dark carven tunnel.   THE END

#10 Kobolds (5 life points, Level 1)
[Win got to #14] [Lose continue reading]
You die a cold and bloody death in a dark carven tunnel.   THE END

#11 *The Giant has crushed you. You have failed. Nice try.*   THE END

#12 *You have beat the Gaping Giant! When you get back, you are made the chief of your tribe! (next adventure: "Tartiar The Chief")*   THE END

#13 *You are wounded by troll stabbings and bludgeoning, but are close to winning the fight. A troll leader jumps out of the bushes and challenges you to one-on-one combat.*
Troll Leader (F.15, Level 2) (at zero life points Troll Leader will escape combat and retreat into a hole in the ground)
[Win go to #15]   [Lose, good try, but you die. THE END]

#14 *You got out of the Second Cave.*   [First Cave #4]   [Third Cave #6]

#15 *As you walk along, you come to 2 tunnels.*
[Tunnel 1 #16] [Tunnel 2 #17]

#16 *You walk along and in tunnel find a box of gold!*
[This tunnel leads to #17]

#17 *A boulder crushes you.*   THE END

TARTIAR 02 ~ "Tartiar The Chief"
Level 4 Roleplay © 1988
Needed: pen, paper, coins

You are a Warrior Chief of the Man-A-Kill Clan. A new threat to your tribe has appeared. An evil sorcerer has been killing your people who hunt in the forest. Without food, your people will die. As Chief, you decide you must go find this Sorcerer and settle the matter. You set off with 10 gold coins, an emerald, food, and medicine (will replenish 5 life points, usable once during the adventure).   Tartiar [35 life points, Level 4]

You go into the forest. After a way, you come to a clearing. You see a young robed man with a mustache. He is practicing magic.
[Talk #2]   [Fight, continue reading]
He readies his shocking staff, and prepares to defend himself.
Magic-user Satur (18 life points, Level 2)   [Lose #3]   [Win #4]

#1   *You walk down the path. You hear rapid hoof steps, and a ghostly goblin rider appears and stops in front of you! He wields a double-bladed battle axe, and takes a swipe at you! There is no time to flee, you must fight.*
Ghostly Goblin Rider (15 life points, Level 3)
[Lose #11]   [Win, continue reading]
You make it home to your village at last, with your neck in tact!   THE END

#2   *You introduce yourself as Tartiar, Chief of the Man-A-Kill Tribe. The young magic-user says "My name is Satur." You tell him about the Evil Sorcerer that is haunting your woods. He does not know about the evil sorcerer, but will help you confront him. You and Satur walk deeper into the forest. You see a small wooden hut.*
[Avoid hut, and keep walking in the forest #5]   [Investigate hut #7]

#3 *You find yourself tied up with glowing rope. The young magic-user says "My name is Satur,". You introduce yourself as Tartiar, Chief of the Man-A-Kill Tribe. You tell him about the Evil Sorcerer that is haunting your woods. The magic-user Satur smiles and says he will help you in your quest. Satur unties you, and takes you to where the Evil Sorcerer's hut is. Together you head off towards the hut, through the woods.* [Go to #7]

#4 *You step over the young warlock's dead body. "He was not the Evil Sorcerer," says a nearby sprite. The sprite will sell you a magic iron shield, if you will trade your food or gold. After you have decided if you want the shield or not, you move on.*   [Go to #17]

#5 *All of a sudden a band of troll thieves surround you!*
[Talk #6; Fight continue]
Magic-user Satur (18 life points, Level 2; Sleep spell 2x)
Troll Thieves (life points: A.3, B.4, C.5, D.7; Level 2)
[Lose #8]   [Win #9]

#6 *As you open your mouth to begin speaking, a crossbow bolt is shot into it and through your head. Then the monsters jump on you and stab you in the back as you fall to the ground. Your last thought as you die is that you have no offspring.*   THE END

#7 *You walk into the hut. The Evil Sorcerer is at the back of the room*!
[Have Satur use sleep spell #10] [Negotiate #20] [Fight Continue]
The Evil Sorcerer stands tall and says "Ha ha, so you wish to fight!"
Magic-user Satur (18 life points, Level 2; Sleep spell 2x)
Evil Sorcerer (35 life points, Level 6)
 [Lose go to #11] [Win, great! Go to #12]

#8 *You fall on the ground in agony. A troll eases the pain.*   THE END

#9 *The trolls lay scattered around. You search for hours, but you cant find the Evil Sorcerer. As night approaches you decide to "call it a day".*
[Go to #18]

#10 *After Satur casts his spell, the Sorcerer just laughs. "Never cast a sleep spell at an advanced sorcerer, fool!" Blue lights shoot from his fingers into Satur's heart. "Ok warrior, its just you and me now that I have killed your warlock!"*   Evil Sorcerer (35 life points, Level 6)
[Flee #15]   [Lose go to #11] [Win, great! Go to #12]

#11 *You are on your face now, in the hut of the Evil Sorcerer. You can not see anything but your hand, and the dirt floor. You hear laughter "Even you can go down, wimp!" Then everything blacks out.* **THE END**

#12 *You stand over the Evil Sorcerer triumphantly! You (and Satur if he is with you) head onto a smaller path through the forest. The path splits in two directions.*   [Go left #14]   [Go right #1]

#13 *The trolls shut their eyes and collapse on the ground, asleep. You thank Satur, and he nods and says you are welcome. With everything quiet now, you hear some rustling in the bushes to your left. "That is the Evil Sorcerer hiding there!" Satur says.*
[Have Satur use sleep spell #10] [Negotiate #22] [Use weapons Continue]
The Evil Sorcerer steps from into view and says "Ha ha, so you wish to fight!". Before you can do anything he teleports you all to the inside of a wooden hut before attacking.
Magic-user Satur (18 life points, Level 2; Sleep spell 2x)
Evil Sorcerer (35 life points, Level 6)
[Lose go to #11] [Win, great! Go to #12]

#14 *You walk for a ways. Then a bogler jumps out at you! The bogler gets first attack.*   Bogler (life points 6, Level 2)   [Lose THE END]   [Win #16]

#15 *You run and run and run. You come to a cave.*
[Go in #19]   [Avoid Cave #18]

#16 *You continue on. You hear a crunch under your feet. From under your shoe, a pixie looks at you and wiggles his fingers.*
Flip a coin [Heads #21]   [Tails Continue]
The pixie spell works on you, turning you into a dandelion flower.
THE END

#17 *You walk off. Soon you see a cave.*   [Go to #19]

#18 *You make it home! You are sad that you did not defeat the Sorcerer and do not have his head to show your tribe, but are glad you kept your head. Until the next adventure...*   THE END

#19 *It's dark. You lose your way. Zombies surround you!*
Zombies (life points: X.4, Y.5, Z.7)
[Lose, THE END]   [Win, #18]

#20   *You introduce yourself to the Evil Sorcerer and begin asking him questions. You ask him if he will stop attacking your people. You offer him the emerald if he will live in peace, and allow your tribe to hunt in the forest. He says no and would rather fight you.*
[Have Satur use a sleep spell #10]   [Fight with weapons Continue]
The Evil Sorcerer stands tall and says "Ha ha, so you wish to fight!"
Magic-user Satur (18 life points, Level 2; Sleep spell 2x)
Evil Sorcerer (35 life points, Level 6)
[Lose go to #11]   [Win, great! Go to #12]

#21 *You squish the pixie under your foot, and return to the path.*   [#1]

105

The End

Zombies

Death Streets
You Are The Car

Your tank is full and black Pontiac frame shined. A red lambergeni with a missile launcher on the roof heads straight for you!
[1. Use Lazers] [2. Use Machine Guns] [3. Swerve]

1. Your tower Lazers dent its frame, but the red car fires 2 missiles.
[14. Swerve]   [4. Wait]

2. Your machine guns fire. They pop the car's tires. It flips over and explodes. You see people robbing a bank. [6. Fire Lazers] [6. Fire Guns]

3. You swerve to the right. When you get back in range of him, he fires a heat seeking missile. You try to dodge. THE END

4. You are foolish. You explode. THE END

5. You go after the red car. You lose sight of the car, then all the sudden ashes pour all over you! [7. Go to Car Wash] [8. Try and find him]

6. You kill the robbers all right, but you also destroy the front of the bank! Your owner is sued and you are sold to a junk yard. THE END

7. You go through the car wash and a man puts gas in your tank.
[Go to Start]

8. As you drive along, windshield wipers clearing the ashes, you see a suspicious blue limo pull out behind you. [9. Continue] [10. Attack]

9. You ignore the blue limo. He is driving beside you now. [11. Bump him] [12. Go on]

10. You make a U-turn quickly. You prepare to fire. [Go to 2.]

11. Just as the man in the blue limo gets a gun out, you smear the car into a building. You just saved New York from Russia's greatest spy! THE END

12. For a few seconds it is calm in the streets. All the sudden the driver pulls a gun out, and before you can turn it's too late. THE END

13. You continue down the street. You hear a siren. An old white hearse races past you, with tanks and hoses strapped to the outside. Kit and Knight Rider follow the hearse. You think back to the old days. All of a sudden you blow up. THE END

14. You swerve quickly! The missiles blow up a parked car.
The lambergeni turns right.
[5. Follow] [13. Go straight ahead]

Flight Blaster #66
Undercover Agent

You are a Marsarian. You suspect there are many spies in your city on Mars. You suspect they are going to blow up Flight Blaster #66. Flight Blaster #66 is one of the military's hottest new starships. You start out to stop them with your trusty lazer gun in hand.
[1. Stay around ship] [2. Go to Casino] [3. Check streets]

1. You sit right by the ship and wait. An Earth man walks up and says "Get away."
[Go to 4.]

2. You enter the Casino. Hundreds of aliens are there. You ask some aliens if they'd heard anything about it. All the sudden you're surrounded by 2 robots!
[5. Fight them] [3. Run to the streets]

3. You run to the streets. All of a sudden, you fall through a hole. Something green chews you up. THE END

4. He then goes inside. [6. Follow] [7. Go home]

5. With your lazer, you blast one away. The other pushes you away. You run out the door on to a speed sub.
[Go to 8.]

6. You enter and hide. You hear him say over a mic "On my remote command, fire."   [9. Blast controls] [7. Go home]

7. You run home to tell your Dad. On the way a robot steps out and blows you to smithereens. THE END

8. You see from the window, three spies with a phazor pointed right at the ship.   [10. Tell Cops] [6. Flow one inside]

9. You fire. The controls explode. Just as he turns, cops run in and arrest him. Your reward is 2,000 rubons. You saved the ship!
THE END

10. You get off the speed sub and tell the cops. They race to the ship, Flight Blaster #66, and arrest them. You get 3,000 rubons. THE END

Time Capsule Letter
Capsule created in 1989, Opened in 1995

Dear Me,

That's you! Walton Stowell Jr., is it the year 1995 already? So how am I? I'm ok, just got out of The Bonafide Academy. I bet there's tons of new inventions. I wish you could send me a list of the new inventions; if time travel backwards in time is allowed yet (only if you can return to your own time; don't forget about the 1st Rule of Time Paradox). It would be neat if we could shake hands. I hope you weren't in an accident, I'll try to avoid those. Are you being nice?

In case you have lost your memory, I have placed various items in containers to restore memories even I find hard to remember. You will find a green wallet. Inside are identification cards, coins, and some faces from both our pasts. Your award money from the poster contests is there, and Far Side comics.

In the brown box there is our ring collection. The blue-blob clay figure was given to us by Jonnie McMasterson. The fool's gold is from Western Town. The Muscle Man list written with Parker Banricardo reads: Gor Monk, Tanker, Superstar, Horney, Gladiator, Muscle Bound. The stories in the Purple Folder are most of the short stories you wrote.

Good luck, Me!
~ Me

Turmoil In RAMBA

Robert flicked on the radio. He swiveled around in his old padded armchair. Matthew threw down his ear phones.

"Darn it Robert! Turn off that head-banger music!"

Robert laid down his head gear. "What's the problem old man?! Do you have something against rock-and-roll?"

Matthew threw his hands up in dismay. "Oh, that goes back to grade-school when I thought I had friends. I just think the music is too loud!"

A blip from the intercom diverted Robert's attention. "Ok Starship, I read you."

The people on the arriving spacecraft, Starship, beamed back a message. "We demand a landing space RAMBA."

"Alright, alright. Take pad #50. What's the hurry?" Robert responded.

"We are a specimen retrieval vessel. I've lost six of my men. My orders were to take the specimens to this intergalactic landing station called RAMBA and wait for further instructions!" Starship said.

"Well you've got the right place, Starship. What kind of drive system do you have? If it's IG8 use frequency 10," said Robert.

"What the hell does it matter?! I've got a cargo space ready to burst with strange creatures!" Starship demanded. "Just let us in!"

"Ok!" said Robert as he turned two dials. "The bay doors are opening," he assured. "Ok, you're inside. Turn off your rockets so I can flip on the oxygen."

There was dead silence but the monitor showed that the engines were still blaring. Matt put on his ear phones and repeated Robert's message. A pause, and then the Starship's engines clicked off. Matt looked at Robert "That guy really had a problem!"

Robert regarded this speech carefully and then shrugged his shoulders as if in answer. He flipped on the oxygen. The intercom beeped again. "How come the monitor isn't displaying the new ship's name?" Robert asked Matt.

"Well, is the Starship blocking the monitor's frequency?" Matt replied.

"No," said Robert.

"The Starship is already docked, this is a new ship coming in. Its another ship alright, but I have no idea what the name of it is. It piggybacked radar signatures and its coming in fast! It might be hot!"

Matt stood up and pulled off the console panel. "When something needs fixing, poor old me has to do it!" Matt mumbled under his slobber. "Earth doesn't know what they're missing, with wonderful me out in space!" Matt's sensitive fingers delicately probed through the wires. He sighed and told Rob to tap the monitor.

As Robert's hand neared the screen, a beam of electricity shot out and caught fire to his sleeve. "Ouch!!" Robert yelled, "Stupid retardant!"

"Well wear rubber gloves when you to do that!" Matt shot back. Rob greeted the new ship and gave it a landing pad. Matt looked at Rob. "Look kid, I know I've been giving you a hard time. Don't mind me," Matt said, "I'm just a silly, old man."

"Listen Matt," Rob rejected, "Maybe we can talk another time, I've got a job to do!"

Matt shook his head, "No, I want you to have this." Matthew flipped Rob a small box. "Open the box only when you are in danger."

Rob stood silent, not meaning to be ungrateful yet unable to speak. He slid the box into his pocket and sat back down. "Starship. We haven't heard from you in a while, need some help?" There was no answer to Rob's message. "I better go see how they're doing. Thanks for the …"

Matt waved. "Hey no problem, I'm just an old man!"

Rob walked to the door and slid it open. As it closed behind him he realized the small box was another stupid gag put on by the old man. He took the box out of his pocket and threw it in the hall's trash can.

Near the end of the corridor there were doors with numbers on them. He punched in the code and the door number 50 slid open. Rob stepped into the landing area around the vessel Starship. The air was cool, and artificial. He picked up a radio.

"This is RAMBA coordinator Robert. If you are unable to open your entry gate, then I can open it from out here." There was no reply. Rob grabbed the ultra-pliers and opened the Starship's door. He froze. Inside were big alien creatures! They had spiked tails, and banana type heads with 2 sets of teeth, one inside the other. The black, glossy skinned demons sensed him, but they had no eyes!

Rob stumbled out of the landing area and ran into the hall. He pressed a button and door #50 slammed shut. The doors were made of titanium alloy, but could it contain those creatures?

He sat down in the bright hallway. He planned his next actions. It all depended on door #50. His heart was racing, but he didn't freeze with fear.

Rob dashed to the control room. "I safely landed the new ship," Matt said. "It's a battle-crusier, Klinogron. They're in landing area 30."

Rob struggled for words. "There is a major safety hazard in area 50! The crew of Starship are all dead, so I'm totally sealing off everything. You just make sure the Klin-O-grons get teleported safely."

"Ok," Matt said obediently. "Kling crew, are you in the teleporting zone?" The intercom replied "To-pak, ready to beam down."

The End

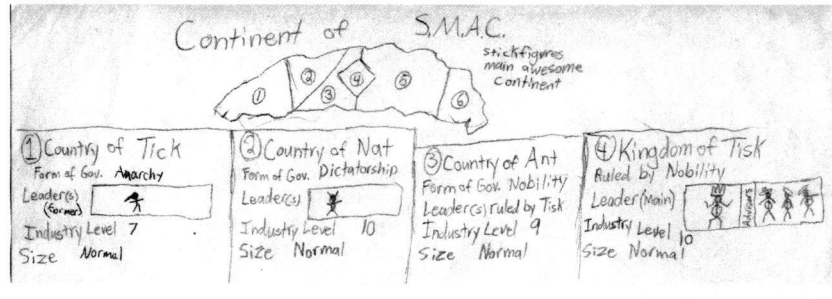

Undersea Mayhem
Walton Stowell 1980's Middle School
Death To Heroes / Heroes Die First Collection

Communication Officer Norris blinked his eyes. The dim florescent light was irritating his already blood-shot eyes. He had just overcome the claustrophobia that the small underwater Navy station produced. There was barely enough room for two people. But he was just one of the 5,000 officers commissioned to the death-traps known as Deep Sea Defense Systems (DSDS).

It was the year 2,989 and the World was in a perpetual state of War. No one remembers exactly when the War began, as it had begun with a series of conflicts that were each decades long. The toll was so great on technology that civilization was, for the most part, reduced to ruins of it's industrial foundation.

Norris rechecked the dials. He was now sure. "I have not, the slightest idea what any of these buttons do!" Norris picked up the radio, kicked it twice, and spat at it. The sound of static meant that the antique device was now on. Squirrely noises and whirls sounded out like the question marks in his head. Then Norris remembered, he wanted to contact HQ. "Hey, I need some help here!" He shouted at the machine. More static.

As he used his chewing gum to connect some frayed wires, the operator answered. "What?" Norris said receiving static. "Excuse me?" he said. "What!?" the operator was annoyed. Norris shook his head "What??"

The operator was not playing games. "If this is a prank, someone will get shot!" the operator shot back. Norris looked down. No wonder! He was sitting a transmitter cable. He shifted his position with the wires, and answered. "Hello this is DSDS AB-15. I need information regarding a certain code 10 I'm receiving on my on-board monitor."

The operator was hyphenated, "When you say code, do you mean as in a secret message? - - -"

Norris thought for a while, "No….I mean code as in clearance."

"When you say clearance, well…could you elaborate on that?" - - -

"Well since I know you now," Norris said, "I gotta tell you that I don't really understand any of these buttons."

The operator suddenly changed tones, "You have to be the stupidest person I know. Your incompetence is unmatched even by Bailey. The threshold of your stupidity is beyond the limits of average comprehension!" - - -

Norris was baffled, "Excuse me, may I say that my name is Communications Officer Norris!"

"Oh! Well! That makes all the difference! Will you please excuse me for an instant, Officer Norris, while I look in the manual, - -" Norris could tell that the operator was mocking him drastically.

"Could I talk to your commander?"

"Mr. Norris, I am the commander! I'm the only living person in the base! By the way, that manual says that you are about to die, - - -" the operator said.

"What?!" yelled Norris.

"That's right Officer, the water pressure is about to crush your little bones. Learn your codes, we'll get together after the War, maybe! Ha ha ha / - - - -." The operator hung up.

Norris glanced around. Metal pressed on metal with the sound of bolts grinding. The tiny glass windows were about to burst! Panic stricken he started pressing buttons. The computer read-out read "Automatic oxygen system tank, release activated." A whoosh was heard! Bubbles raced past the windows as 2 containers detached from the sides of the station and jetted to the surface. Norris redialed HQ.

"I just released my oxygen! I just released the oxygen tanks!! What do I do?!!" Norris was panicking.

The operator sighed, "I presume this is Norris. I would rather you heroically sacrifice yourself, but…. You can still press the escape button. It's a little blue button. Bye. -"

Norris reached out for the little blue button, when suddenly the walls caved in and pinned him to the leg of his chair. The only thing he could reach was the radio. "Hello, HQ?" This is Norris again. I'm pinned to the leg og my chair, and I can't reach the escape button!" The sound of crushing metal was loud, and the emergency red light was on.

"Listen Mr. Norris," the operator said. "I have a lot of patience normally. But I have a lot of paperwork to do. If you don't mind dying on your own time, please!" - - -

Norris was desperate, "I'm going to be crushed! Operator, I'm asking you for help!!"

"Ok," the operator paused. "After I run a few errands, I guess I could notify the local fire department. - - -"

Norris froze. "The fire department!?!!"

"You said you wanted help, Mr. Norris. Now good-bye!" - - -
The operator took Norris' file from the drawer, trashed it, then turned the radio back on. "Norris I'm afraid the explosion of your station is the only way to reroute an enemy sub fleet. Have a nice day!!" - - -

Norris scrambled at the radio again. "Are you crazy?! I'm trapped in here!!!"

The operator responded again. "Now you are dead Norris. You see, good guys are actually the first to die. Not to say you would have done the same thing in my place!"

THE END

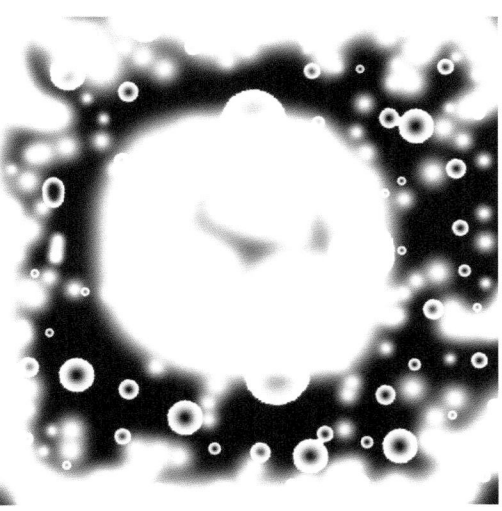

Venture on the Road of Destiny

Harpers Ferry Junior High, 9th Grade, 96% A+

The peaceful solar event we call a day was, for the most part, uninhibited by the numerous, bossy, obnoxious, and puzzling yet determined life forms we call 'Sunday Drivers', or as the case may be 'Road Hogs'. Our far from cumbersome drive was intended to take us from our happy, loving, clean, and loyal place of origin, to whatever our brave souls may venture.

Suddenly a gnashing sound, as if God himself had thrust his mighty fist down upon an innocent in attempts to thwart his anger and wrath from destroying the world, was produced from a gaping puddle which marked the entrance to our ride through the woods.

Our tires and shocks proved the gravel road to be the stronger, as I was thrown into the door handle, and my knee jammed into the quite solid ashtray. I managed to catch a glimpse of the outside world before I was beaten into unconsciousness by the seat-belt. The tops of the trees could not be seen due to the ceiling of the car, but their lower branches were sparsely adorned with long pointy pine needles, and the darkness coming from within the forest let the imagination run free. Driven by forces unknown to me, I forced my eyes to focus on a certain moss-adorned rock that for some reason was charging through the trees with incredible speed towards the car! It was around that time when I blacked-out.

THE END

ATTACK OF THE RADIOACTIVE HAMSTERS

The US Starquake was orbiting Mars, its crew numbering eight. The 1972 model mining ship passed silently through a radioactive, electric dust cloud. The ship's haul vibrated violently, shocked by thousands of volts of electricity.

Private Donald, who was busy unloading on the toilet, smiled to himself. The bathroom was the only room on the craft a man could get his peace and quiet. Suddenly the Computer's voice blared through the intercom.

"There is an emergency. There is still an emergency. The emergency is still taking place. I will repeat myself. There is an emergency. I have just repeated myself. Private Donald and Mechanic Williams, report to Sector 13. Suits are mandatory. There is a radioactive leak and spreading. By the way, there is still an emergency."

"Just great!" Donald complained. "My only free time I get, and I'm interrupted! Oh no, perfect. I'm stuck!"

Meanwhile in a room far, far away; Williams was punching out Samual for dropping his solidified powdered prune juice down his pants. Samual fell back against a shelf, knocking a hamster cage to the floor. It shattered and Velveeta and Elvis, the two hamsters, escaped.

"I'll finish with you later!" Williams said as he headed toward Sector 13. He came to the sector door and punched in his code. The computer blared his clearance. "Welcome mop and broom, summer vacuums of the month! Got some fresh sour milk?"

"Darn sponge-head slag, Mark was messing with the speech system again!" Williams shouted as he slammed his fist against the door. It slid open. He attached his body armor and breathing gear. Just as he took a step inside, rusty-orange vapors rushed from within.

"Pressurized radiation!!" Williams yelled as he turned the intercom on. "Attention, there's a major radiation leak spreading throughout the entire port wing!!"

…

Hearing the news Bubba awoke violently from his bunk bed. "I'm a comin' Mamma!" and with that Bubba jerked up, slammed his head against the ceiling, and fell onto the floor. "Oh, man!" Bubba said as he pulled on his jumpsuit.

Tim rolled out of his bed, onto the floor beside Bubba. Then he slowly got on his uniform. "Let's get some coffee!" Tim said, and the door slid open.

A huge furry mass sat hunched over in the doorway. The 10 foot tall hamster's red eyes glared down upon them! Tim and Bubba froze in fear.

…

Bruce Lee, Chuck Norris, and Karate Kid posters decorated the walls of Kim's room. When she heard William's words on the intercom, she leapt out of bed, broke a couple boards, did a few splits, and kicked open her door.

Samual wiped the blood from his lip, grabbed his rifle, and went out into the halls. Samual was looking to shoot Williams for beating him up, so he was surprised to find a giant glowing hamster instead. Samual's blood and guts were splattered on the walls.

Mark was busy pressing buttons in the control room. "Aliens," Captain J mumbled as he switched on autopilot. Suddenly the door slid open and Williams stumbled in. The door closed behind him, as Williams collapsed to the floor with the words "Velveeta!"

The crew in the control room rushed to help Williams get his helmet off. "What did he say?" Mark asked. "I think he wants cheese." Captain said. When they got his helmet off, Williams said it again. "Velveeta!" "What do you make of this Captain?" Mark said. "He said Velveeta." "Yes, I know what he said Mr. Connect-the-dots." Captain said. "John Williams, what is the matter?!" They all looked at eachother in desperation.

"Velveeta, big, large, huge! A…she's um, grown; real big!" Williams exhaustedly said. "He's evidently crazy Captain. Williams has lost his mind; bonkers," Mark said. "I'm gonna go get a drink!" "Don't open that door!" Williams managed to say.

"See, he's mad!" said Mark as he opened the door and came face with a 9 foot tall Velveeta. Instinctively Mark leapt upon the beastie and grabbed it by it's neck. "Freeze!" yelled Captain J. Williams finally passed out.

Meanwhile Private Donald had freed himself from the toilet. He washed his hands and prepared to leave. Suddenly the door flew open and Donald starred down the barrel of a lazer rifle. As he slipped backwards, a hand grabbed him and picked him up. "Ah Private Donald, trying to hide?" Corporal Samual demanded.

"I-I was really just trying to..." Donald started. Samual interjected "I don't think so. We all know you're scared of Sector 13 ever since Paul, James, and Kurt died there. Ok, now let's just go get some de-radiation guns, shall we Donald?" Unexpectedly a strange large furry object passed by quickly. "What the heck was that?" Donald asked. "We had better get some cages too."

Velveeta the Xtra-large-hamster tossed Mark against the wall, knocking him out cold. Then the furry beast headed towards Captain J. He picked up his coffee and threw it at the creature. Velveeta squeaked and shrank back to regular hamster size, which is small, and ceased glowing; with features returning to normal.

"Wow that was amazing!" Captain J said. "Coffee must reduce radioactivity." "My aren't we a genius today!" Velveeta said. "The radiation must have affected her vocal cords and mind!" "Stop it, you're beginning to sound like a nerd in one of those stupid science fiction stories!" Velveeta screamed.

THE END ?

121

Werewolf, Alien, and Crossbow
Unlikely Stories, Book I, Bonner English

Trumpets blared. The cheers of the crowds were deafening. The banners outshined the sun. Johny held his sword to the sky. Their kingdom was nothing to brag about, but in the past few months it had been turned into a hell pit. You see, the King's most trusted Baron is also a cheat and a master of chaos. While their King was out fighting the crusades, he made the mistake of intrusting his lands to this Baron thief. Now the King returns, to bring justice upon the land.

The crowd roars even louder as the King rides down the street and into his castle. His knights followed gallantly behind him in golden armor. Johny had dreams about becoming a knight, but he knew they were lost dreams. He knew a simple peasant boy could never be knighted. Johny had just turned 16, and a year before he had joined the castle guard, soon to become a man-at-arms. The holiday passed quickly, and Johny found himself on guard duty.

The moon was full. Johny and two other soldiers were guarding the town's West Wall. Johny looked out into the star filled night sky. Someday he would be a man-at-arms serving a knight, and perhaps come close to being a knight, somehow. He heard a squeak. John looked down. A little mouse crouched in a crack in a crenellation. Johny knelt down and patted the little fellow's head. He remembered when he was 5 and his uncle taught him how to relate with animals. The mouse became friendly and nibbled on his finger. Suddenly Johny heard a noise behind him. He turned and looked out onto the roof tops below the wall. The strange noise had come from inside the city, yet he saw nothing.

A feeling came across him. It was the same sense that his uncle had taught him to acquire so many years before; the sense that something was behind him. Johny spun around. He looked over the wall out into the fields away from the town. Nothing, too dark. Johny's muscles loosened. Blood dripped onto him. He looked up.

The dead body of a mouse dropped down in front of him, and another fury form launched itself from a tall tree overhead. The larger animal fell to the wall floor on top of the mouse, in front of Johny. The beast disarmed Johny and bit into his wrist. Johny stood in horror as the monster showed its ugly teeth. The teeth were fangs! It was a walking man-wolf!! Then the creature punched Johny over the side of the battlement wall, but Johny caught his grip on a loose stone. The stone wiggled, but held wedged in the wall.

Johny dangled over the town roof tops below the West Wall. Another guard rushed towards the creature along the wall walkway. The guard's sword missed it. The wolfman grabbed the guard's head and threw him over the wall, as well. Then Johny lost sight of the demon. Lightning flashed, and there was no sign of the creature above him.

Painfully, he pulled himself back up the wall. As thunder echoed in the background, he wrapped his wrist in cloth from his boot strapping. Where did that horror run off to? There was one guard left in his section of the West Wall. The bugle sounded! Yes?! Panic forced his heart to pump blood through his veins all the harder. Johny raced to the battlement tower nearest him. The bugle call must have come from there, from the remaining guard. Too late.

The other guard lay in pieces on the floor with a bugle in his hand. The beast was behind him! Suddenly more guards burst from the door to the stairwell. They aimed their crossbows. One guard fired, but missed as the creature roared and ran out of the tower room. The wolf monster leapt 20 feet into the nearest treetop.

It was afraid of crossbows. It had to be. It could have easily slaughtered all of them. Johny swore that next time they met, he'd be ready.

During the days that followed, Johny invested all his time into building an ultra-powerful crossbow. The handle and cross-piece were made of oak, the string of dragon gut, and the trigger of steel incased in dragon scales. The bolts, ah such darts! The bolt heads were made of the hardest iron and steel alloys available. The shafts were oak, and the fletching was made of cockatrice feathers.

Now Johny was off to the Cathedral to see Bishop Mathematicus to get his blessing. The Bishop welcomed him happily. "You wanted to see me?" "Yes, your holiness. Of course you have heard of the beast that attacked me." Johny said. "Yes, yes," was the reply. "Well Bishop Mathematicus, I would like you to bless these crossbow bolts. I am going to use these small but deadly arrows to kill the wolf-man that attacked me!"

"Are you sure it was a wolf-man?" the Bishop asked. "Many people say it was a bat-man, owl-man, or a vampire! Vampires are more common than people think."

"I know what I saw, Bishop." "No you didn't!" Bishop Mathematicus yelled. "I mean it's silly to assume it was a walking man-wolf!"

"Please your holiness, just bless these arrows," said Johny insistently. Johny stood in shock as the Bishop drooled all over the bolts. "There, all blessed! You'll be fine now," the plump Bishop added with a smile. "The main character almost never dies. Well, you know what I mean! May the mucous of God bless your sinful, corporeal body."

Johny had heard rumors that the Bishop was a little bit off his base, but this was insane.

Meanwhile, at the Blacksmith Shop... "Me and a couple o' knights are prepared to kill that, man-bat!" the blacksmith Mac shouted. "How d'you know that it is a man-bat?" the merchant asked holding a gauntlet. "I've heard it is a vampire!"

A bright light beamed across the blue sky. "Look!" shouted the blacksmith, pointing into the sky. The object hit the Earth with amazing force. Trees flew everywhere in the field where it landed. Flames ignited. Earthquakes rocked the land for miles around. The seas boiled and rose, and the clouds parted. The metallic, oval shaped form was embedded deep in the damp ground. Only the top could be seen.

A beeping noise came forth, and the hatch ripped open. A brownish-green humanoid stepped from within and walked away from the wreck. The hatch door fell off. Written on it were the letters: U.S.A.

Johny slept soundly on his straw mattress. The crossbow lay heavily on his shoulder. It was night, partially lit by a waxing moon. He awoke with a start, sweating. He heard footsteps from outside. Johny gripped his crossbow. The door flew open, it was Bishop Mathematicus!

"Oh sorry, your holiness," said Johny laying the crossbow down.

The Bishop began reciting a horrid poem: "We wear wolf skin, we and wolf are one! We wore wolf head, wolf wears us! Be weary of those that wear wolf on their heads, me lad!" The night seemed to make what the Bishop was saying very sinister. "I've come here to eat you! I was the werewolf!"

"You were the wolf?" Johny questioned unbelievingly. "I was wolf!" "You were wolf?" "I were wolf!" "You had been the walking wolf, you mean. I think it has to do with past participles." Johny shook his head, and they began to circle eachother.

The Bishop became enraged and his skin turned brown. The portly Bishop began to grow hair on his face and hands. He advanced, with claws growing. Johny held his crossbow aimed at the Bishop's chest. The wolfman bashed him with ease against the wall. Johny kicked the monster. The wolfman dug his claws into Johny's stomach. Johny yelled with pain, so loud that the entire town could hear him. It was a game of survival. How long could Johny hold the creature off? How long until it killed him?

The wolfman punched Johny in the face, as he tried to fire the crossbow. Johny struggled to get back up. The wolf's savage teeth gnarled at his ear. Scarlett blood trickled down into Johny's mouth. Frantically he punched the wolfman somewhere below the stomach.

The tyrant stumbled backwards. The wolfman slumped, howling painfully. Johny reached for the handle of the crossbow, but his wrist met the fangs of the devil again. Sharply the crossbow was flung across the room. Blood splattered his face, but Johny was able to wriggle free. Presently there was a thunderous boom, and timbers fell from the ceiling. As the wolfman glanced up at the hole, the roof caved in. Dust and splinters explosively filled the room. Johny crawled over the bed, and grabbed the crossbow.

Slowly the dust cloud settled. The wolfman tore from beneath the rubble, rearing up in fury. It's fangs and claws glistened. Johny aimed. Suddenly, directly beside the wolfman, a pile of thatch parted, and Satan himself was revealed!

Standing 10 feet tall, this slimy greenish creature wore only two thick, long plates of metal around both lengthy, muscular forearms. It's face was blank. Free from emotions, free from any features what-so-ever. It looked as if it, whatever it was, had been tortured, maybe pushed around by a bigger, more powerful lifeform. Perhaps it was only acting out on what it had been taught to do. What ever the case, it was not talking.

This new creature extended it's arm and knocked the wolfman directly through the wall. Johny fired, missing both creatures. The wolfman refused to give up, and jumped on the alien's back. Two sharp spikes shot out from one of the alien's gauntlets. They were titanium alloy spikes, but the light reflecting on them made them appear silver.

The first two spikes stuck and stayed in the wolfman's arms. Two more spikes slid out of the gauntlets, but this time they stayed in the gauntlets like dagger blades.

The alien made an upward motion which severed the wolfman's ribcage, and pierced his heart. The wolf dropped to the ground. A red beam shot from the other gauntlet and melted the skin off the wolf's face. Then the alien ripped the victim's head off and attached it to a gauntlet. Dogs barked outside.

Johny drew back in horror. He loaded the crossbow, and fired! The bolt entered the alien's chest. The alien leaped for the sky, and was gone. Knights and soldiers alike, burst through what was left of the front door. The body of a dead Bishop Mathematicus lay on the floor wreckage. The Bishop's clothes were dotted with blood. Johny didn't know what to say. The priest lay headless with no evidence he was ever a wolf, and Johny had a crossbow in his hands!

"Well, did you kill him?" the blacksmith asked.
"No, he said he was a werewolf, or something," said Johny.
"What by god are you talking about?!" a knight said. "Our dogs tracked the Wolfmonster here, by scent alone. Where did the monster go?!"

Johny was relieved. They knew he didn't kill the Bishop, but they didn't know exactly what happened. They were not even sure that the Bishop was the werewolf! He knew what he had to do now. Johny must make a short story that was convincing, and described the events that happened.

"The Bishop stopped by to see if I was alright, when suddenly the wolf came from the ceiling, killed the Bishop, changed shape and jumped away!"

When Johny finished his story, they all stood still. They took it for granted! Then he patched up his exposed veins, and eagerly went to sleep with the help of some wolfsbane herbs, given by brother Monkshood.

The next day the group found the tracks of the alien, and all 12 of the men trailed the tracks. They came to a clearing and the tracks ended. Johny took one step forward and the creature clobbered him. Crossbows fired, daggers flew, and swords passed smoothly through his head. Thump! The behemoth lay vanquished.

THE END

Werewolf, Alien, and Crossbow

Zardan's Excellent Journey!
Reading April 3, 1989
Walton Stowell Jr.

Zardan had just barely escaped from his enflamed Pirated Galactic Battlecruiser which was shot down by a Galactic Arcship. Zardan's escape pod crashed on Archifray's surface, and thinking the pilot dead, no Time Master had gotten around to investigating Zardan's pod. Now Archifray is normally a non-interventionary planet (in fact it is in their laws), but since the Battlecruiser had its sights set on destroying peaceful neighbors, the Time Masters of Archifray felt they had no choice.

Zardan ate the rest of the food in his Mr. Handy Preserver Food Storage Zaplock Freezer Silicon Time Concealed Container. Zardan chuckled to himself, remembering the famous commercial. " 'It's not just a silicon container! Yes, its time proof! So buy one today!' That was the most annoying advertisement on my THF infrared dual audio-tape radio, but I can still remember it. I must be insane, or at least as crazy as the commercial, for me to be thinking of something as worthless as that, after all I've been through."

Zardan exited his burnt and bent-up pod, and wandered the many sandy hills of Archifray, until he came to a domed city. Inside an enormous clear bubble, stood spires and shapes of multi-story buildings. Nearing the dome, Zardan found a doorway. It seemed a backdoor of sorts, but it was open and it would do. There were guards mulling about, but this entry would do just fine. Zardan loaded his lazer pistol, and with two shots the guards were dead before you could say 'hydraulically powered'. Then Zardan carefully snuck inside the dome, and into a building.

Zardan walked along a long hallway. Light-gray walls were covered with yellow circles that faintly glowed. Occasionally the walls, on both sides, would indent and a pilaster would be tucked away, nestled inside. After five minutes he turned a corner. His draby clothes mopped up the floor behind him; as tattered capes, robes, and long belts should. As Zardan pressed his back against the wall at the edge of the corner, he heard footsteps. The footsteps came closer.

A guard dressed in a red uniform with yellow stripes let his cape flow as he passed by. Next behind him, came two more guards, but these did not have capes. Zardan peaked around the corner and made sure they were gone. He expected that they would discover the dead guards one way or another, if they had not already.

So Zardan raced around the next corner and into a room. In the middle of the room there were human sized cone-shaped objects of light with doors on them. These looked like individual spaceships of some kind to Zardan, and he opened one and went in. His eyes popped wide open! The room inside the craft was much larger than the cone itself!!! The interior was actually bigger than the exterior! The room was octagonal and the walls glowed bright red. In the middle of the room was a control panel.

Zardan studied the consul set, and found a button that said 'instructions'. He pressed the button and instructions printed out nearby on the panel. He read the instructions for nearly an hour, before he was able to get the entire craft to move at all. Zardan did not know where he was going to next, as he did not know how the battle was going. He guessed it was not good for him, and he would probably have to live in hiding for sometime once he found safety on another planet.

Zardan set coordinates for Egypt, Earth the year 500BC. As a child at Galactic School he was taught that Egypt was the place to go, and had been for thousands of years. He flipped a lever and heard a low hum as the center of the control panel fluctuated back and forth. After a buzz and a zip, the movements and lights on the control panel ceased as quickly as they had started. Zardan, being a Space Pirate, had never used a time machine before but he was very excited to have a new ship to travel in.

The doors to the time-and-space machine flung open, and Zardan breathed in as much ancient Egyptian air as he could.   **THE END**

CHARACTER TRAITS
Bonner School, Thinking Strategy

Positive Traits

Happy	Smart	Grateful	Polite
Friendly	Intelligent	Glad	Excited
Helpful	Safe	Fair	Cheerful
Loving	Clean	Courageous	Thoughtful
Proud	Hopeful	Trusting	Grateful
Brave	Clever	Trustworthy	Satisfied
Beautiful	Skillful	Worthy	Eager
Honest	Careful	Innocent	Loyal
Diligent	Thrilled	Elegant	Affectionate
Comical	Dependable	Respectful	Compassionate
Studious	Reliable	Relieved	Charming
Powerful	Glamorous	Independent	Lucky
Responsible	Optimistic	Insightful	Secure
Considerate	Determined	Talented	Faithful

Negative Traits

Sorry	Worried	Impolite
Shy	Nervous	Ungrateful
Unfriendly	Hateful	Cruel
Lazy	Disgusting	Doubtful
Sad	Hopeless	Puzzled
Angry	Teasing	Confused
Lonely	Embarrassed	Greedy
Selfish	Thoughtless	Restless
Scared	Jealous	Bored
Frightened	Weak	Horrified
Wild	Childish	Quarrelsome
Uncontrolled	Insulting	Stingy
Frightening	Discouraged	Rude
Mischievous	Silly	Dissatisfied
Impatient	Bossy	Cowardly
Blaming	Uncooperative	Fearful
Braggart	Smart Alec	Frustrated
Bluffing	Obnoxious	Sinister

GLOSSARY

The Discursive Dictionary of Endemic Hyperbole
Words of Creative Curiosity
By Walton Stowell

Angst – (ahnkst) anxiety, apprehension, insecurity, worried, unsettled feeling

Altruistic – devoted to the welfare of others; humanitarian; philanthropist

Avatar – visible manifestation of being from another world; representation as icon or image that is controllable; archangel embodying higher power

Banal – common; mundane; boring; simple; feudal; trite

Capitulate – surrender; buckle; turn over; give into demands

Capricious – sudden change of mind; action without motive; callas whim

Demagogue – false leader who appeals to people using prejudice and lies;

Discursive – wandering from the main point; moving subject

Endemic – peculiar to a particular country or people; native; local system

Fortuitous – happening by fortunate chance; lucky; fortunate

Glean – gather; extract; to pick up what is reaped; strip; collect

Hyperbole – exaggerated term not taken literally by legacy;
Hypocrisy – false pretense; claiming the opposite of reality; deception

Precarious – risky; unstable; dependent on uncertain whim; uncertain
Precipitous – steep, hasty; precipitate: excess, hasty, violent, unwise speed

Temporize – stalled time; paused within time; stopped for more time

Touché – good point scored in fencing; to recognize another's point

Obsequious – servile; compliant or deferential; obedient; dutiful
Surreptitious – stealthy; secret or unauthorized; clandestine;
Ubiquitous – existing or being everywhere at the same time; omnipresent

Medieval Titles:

Castellan (kastelan) / Chatelain (shatelan) – keeper, governor, or warden of a castle, keep, hold, or fort; a royal steward or official charged with castle security, maintenance, etc.

Chamberlain – a chief steward; a high officer of a royal court; an official charged with the domestic affairs of a monarch or lord;

Chancellor – a chief minister of state; royal officer, counselor, councilman, chief secretary, senator, or judge of high position or committee

Emperor – sovereign of an Empire alliance of kingdoms

Duke – a male lord of a duchy under a King (female is dutchess); fist

King – highest ruler; monarch of a castle and all local vassal lands

Lord – keeper of property (loaf + ward); authority; owner, master, etc.; God

Master – male teacher; academic degree higher than bachelor but lower than doctor; a leader, owner, boss, officer, ruler, chief, governor; highest title of craftsman above journeyman, apprentice, etc; mister; husband; son of a lord; original; dominant

Master-At-Arms – a man-at-arms of high rank; military police

Minister – agent, high secretary, servant, department chief; church head

Sir – lord (from sire); knight; a male; mister; one worthy of salute or loyalty

Sire – male ancestor; senior; father; author, originator; lord, liege; monarch

Sovereign – high lord possessing supreme power, excellence, and greatness

Bibliography (Semi-Chronological Order)

Aesop's Fables; Aesop © Ancient Greece 600 BC

Anderson's Fairy Tales; Grosset & Dunlap Inc. 1895

Grimms' Fairy Tales; Grosset & Dunlap Inc. 1895

Alice's Adventures In Wonderland; Lewis Carroll 1865, 1907

Wind In The Willows, The; Kenneth Grahame 1908, Ariel Books 1980

Hobbit, The; JRR Tolkien, Allen & Unwin 1937, Ballantine Books 1982

Lord Of The Rings, The; JRR Tolkien 1954, Ballantine Books 1965

Chronicles of Narnia, The; CS Lewis, Collier Co. 1950-1970, Box 1980

Where The Wild Things Are; Maurice Sendak, Harper Row 1963-1980

Dungeons & Dragons; Gygax & Blume TSR 1974-1989-1994

Superman, Movie Storybook; Siegel & Shuster 1938, S&D 1978

Star Wars, Empire Strikes Back; George Lucas, Lucas Film Ltd. 1980

Indiana Jones, Raiders; Lucas & Spielberg, Record Storybook 1981

World of the Dark Crystal; Brian Froud, Henson & Knopf, NY 1982

Trouble for Trumpets; Cross & Smith 1982, Random House, NY 1984

Spacebase 2000; Stewart Cowley, Hamlyn Ltd. 1984

English & Literature; School Textbooks, various 1980-1994

Roman Army, The; Peter Connolly, MacDonald Educ. Ltd. 1975-1985

BIOGRAPHY of AUTHOR

Walton Danforth Stowell Jr.
Harpers Ferry, West Virginia

Professor Stowell, Master Architect, was born the son of "Kip" and "Nena" in the Winchester, VA Hospital in 1976. The Stowell's have lived in the Town of Harpers Ferry, West Virginia for over 35 years. Walton's father, Kip, graduated from the University of Pennsylvania in 1960 and worked for the National Park Service Design Center. Walton's mother, Nena, was a Montessori School teacher, and has taught Art at various schools. The Stowell Family travelled abroad, studying art and design in Italy, Russia, Ireland, England, Spain, France, and Canada.

Walton got his Masters Degree in Architecture in 2000, from Savannah College of Art and Design. He has worked on numerous architectural projects with his father and others in Harpers Ferry. Walton is an artist, architect, author, civil engineer, editor, gardener, graphic designer, landlord, landscaper, martial-artist, soldier, and video film-maker.

The short stories in this book were written while attending public and private schools in the Tri-State area near Washington DC. In 2007 Walton happily married Noel, and together they share a love of books. As partners Noel and Stowell continue to make music, artwork, and books to help bridge our history with the present and plan for the future, by exploring the creativity of the human spirit.

Air National Guard 2005-2010
Shepherd University Professor 2004-2005
Stowell Architects, Apartments, & Galleries 1994-2009
Organic Artist, Designer, Farmer & Gardener 1980-present
Harpers Ferry Historic Landmarks Commission, 2005-2007
IOOF Vice Noble Grand 2007-2008, Member 1994-present
Video Film-maker, actor, editor, & musician 1989-present
Author of books, short-stories, & published articles

More books by Walton Stowell:

1. Stories of Fiction, Fantasy, and Fun – Kindle Version
2. Harpers Ferry Houses - by Stowell Architects
3. Harpers Ferry Magic – Local Lore & Modern Magic
4. The Pitcher of Immortality – Multiple-Choice Adventure
5. BDU (Bootcamp Diary Unauthorized) – Air Force BMT
6. Kidsverse Series - Co-Authored by Noel Tavano
7. King Grimlock of Burrowdown – Poem & Art Book
8. Generic Murder Mysteries – Movie Picture & Storybooks
9. Predator vs Harpers Ferry – Movie Picture & Storybooks
10. Death of CuChullain & Birth of Finn MacCool – Filmbook
11. SCOD (Sustainable Community for Organic Dwelling) – Thesis
12. SCOD FALLOUT – Black & White Screenplay, Filmbook

Reader Notes & Sketches:

Printed in Great Britain
by Amazon.co.uk, Ltd.,
Marston Gate.